Cold Cases of Stearns County, Minnesota

Robert M. Dudley

JMS
CMVH
MRS

Cold Cases of Stearns County, Minnesota

Table of Contents

Author's Note		1
Introduction		2
Chapter One	Jackie Theel	7
Chapter Two	The Reker Sisters	22
Chapter Three	Ivend Holen	69
Chapter Four	The Huling Family	100
Chapter Five	Joanie Bierschbach	124
Chapter Six	Myrtle Cole	137
Chapter Seven	Cynthia Schmidt & Ronnie Bromenshenkel	155
Chapter Eight	Jacob Wetterling (preview only)	160
Chapter Nine	Herbert Fromelt	163
Chapter Ten	Joshua Guimond	179
Chapter Eleven	Officer Tom Decker	229
Works Cited		254

For Jackie,

wherever he is

Author's Note

When I wrote and self-published my first book, *It Can't Happen Here–The Search for Jacob Wetterling*, I had no idea that within a little more than six months of the book's release Jacob's kidnapper would be arrested. It seemed the case, which was more than a quarter-century old by that time, might never be solved. Furthermore, I had no inkling that first book would soon be followed by the release of the 2nd edition (*Answers In The Sand* is still my favorite of the three) a year later, and ultimately to a publishing deal for the McFarland book, *Finding Jacob Wetterling*.

While researching and writing about the investigation of the Wetterling case, the number of other unsolved cases in Stearns County struck me. Another aspect that stood out was the extraordinary amount of attention given to Jacob's disappearance. So many others were missing. There were so many other unsolved murders. While I certainly won't downplay the impact Jacob Wetterling's disappearance had on the world–it almost didn't seem fair. So, while my first foray into serious research and writing focused on the most well known case in the history of the state of Minnesota, I will be content researching and drawing attention to lesser-known cold cases going forward.

I would like to thank the following for their contributions to this book, directly or indirectly: Liz Collin, Rick Daniels, John Decker, Brian Guimond, Aubrey Immelman, Michael Jacobson, Patrick Marker, Jean Matua, John Michael, Michelle Pawlenty, Nick Pawlenty, Rita Reker, Fay Theel, Dave Unze, and Claude Werder. Special thanks to Betsy, Brian, Gretchen, Jennifer, Jodi, Ryan, and Sarah, and all my followers on Facebook.   Facebook.com/RobertMDudleyAuthor/

Introduction

Stearns County in central Minnesota covers just less than 1,400 square miles. Its land is made up of a blend of landscapes ranging from rolling hills, prairie grasses, pristine lakes, and wooded areas. Indigenous tribes including the Sioux, Chippewa, and Winnebago were the first to occupy the land. A wave of German Catholics settled in the area during the 1850's and was later joined by settlers from the east coast.

In 1853, Isaac Ingalls Stevens set out on an expedition from St. Paul to Puget Sound, Washington. His mission was to determine an optimal route for the Pacific Railroad to expand its tracks to the west. The area now known as Stearns County was officially founded in February 1955, as Stevens County in honor of the explorer. However, a clerical error led to the county being named Stearns County, after Charles Thomas Stearns, a politician who helped pass legislation that established the county. To compensate for the error, Minnesota lawmakers later named a county two counties to the west as Stevens County.

As of 2018, Stearns County's population was nearly 160,000. It is bordered on the east by the Mississippi River. St. Cloud, its largest city and county seat, lies on the far eastern boundary of the county, more or less centered from north to south. Stearns County boasts a number of post-secondary schools including St. Cloud State University, St. John's University in Collegeville, College of St. Benedict in St. Joseph, and St. Cloud Technical and Community College.

Stearns County is well known for it's friendly people, as well as a wide variety of outdoor activities, restaurants that specialize in hearty comfort foods, and strong winds that often blow across the county from the west and south. It is also home to a large number of unsolved or long-term murder cases, some of which are the most horrific and unimaginable crimes in the history of the state of Minnesota. This book chronicles many of those cases, beginning with the still unsolved disappearance of little Jackie Theel from the streets of Paynesville in 1944, to the seemingly solved but still open 2012 murder of Officer Tom Decker in Cold Spring, and many other cases in between.

The cases in this book span the careers of several Stearns County sheriffs including Art McIntee, Pete Lahr, Jim Ellering, Charlie Grafft, Jim Kostreba, and John Sanner. Most were generally well liked by constituents, but through the years some administrations saw their share of controversial moments. The 1978 election race between incumbent Jim Ellering and challenger Charlie Grafft was marked by accusations of prisoner abuse by deputies who supported Ellering, and by a bitter advertising campaign by both candidates. Grafft took advantage of the apparent malcontent of staff that developed under Ellering's term, and his campaign capitalized on the mishandling of a $2,200 ring that went missing from the evidence room and was later found with a prisoner.

Grafft won the 1978 election and immediately implemented improvements to the Stearns County Sheriff's Department. He moved his staff from the second floor to the first to give the public more access to his team. He wrote a manual of procedures that all deputies were required to follow, added more patrol officers to evening shifts to combat criminal activity, and sought to increase overall staff numbers to deal with the heavy load that the department continually faced. Grafft's landmark accomplishment was the 1981 implementation of the Tri-County Crime Stoppers program, a cooperative effort between Stearns, Benton, and Sherburne Counties.

Sketch courtesy of the St. Cloud Times, November 2, 1978.

The October 1989 kidnapping of Jacob Wetterling from a dead end road outside of St. Joseph proved to be a black mark on the administrations of a trio of sheriffs including Grafft, Jim Kostreba, and John Sanner. The case frustrated sheriffs, investigators, and residents alike. My books on the case raised serious questions about the investigation before the case was resolved, questions that should have been raised by the more qualified media. Unfortunately, the media seemed content to simply rehash the case over and over again, focusing more on the Wetterling family than the actual investigation.

While the murder investigations covered in this book were overseen by several Stearns County sheriffs, most of these cases have one public official in common–Stearns County Attorney Roger Van Heel. Van Heel served as the Assistant County Attorney for two years before being appointed to the top job in April 1974, at the age of 32. The beginning of Van Heel's tenure was marked by the shocking murders of sisters Mary and Susanne Reker on Labor Day, 1974. Several more unsolved or long-term murder cases occurred under Van Heel's watch as county attorney, a run that lasted nearly three decades.

Roger Van Heel's supporters point to his strong record of winning cases that he prosecuted in court. A December 1990 editorial in the *St. Cloud Times* pointed out that Van Heel's conviction rate for the first 16 years of his reign stood at a staggering 98%. By contrast, most county attorneys in central Minnesota produced conviction rates in the low-to-mid 90-percentile range. The secret to Van Heel's success in successfully prosecuting the bulk of his cases was the rock-solid cases he would build against the criminals he charged. To say that his office was busy and understaffed during much of his career would be an understatement.

Van Heel had his critics as well. His reluctance to prosecute a number of high profile cases led to public pressure from the families of victims. It was not uncommon to see families of one murder victim pressing Van Heel to take action in another victim's case. A former Minnesota Bureau of Criminal Apprehension (BCA) agent once slammed Van Heel by commenting that the prosecutor couldn't lose a

Stearns County Attorney Roger Van Heel. Photo courtesy of St. Cloud Times, April 1, 1974.

case he didn't try, a reference to his reputation for only trying cases he was all but guaranteed to win. Whether or not Van Heel's conservative approach contributed to Stearns County's reputation for having a low clearance rate in solving major crimes is unclear. What is more certain, is there has long been a general lack of confidence among residents in Stearns County's ability to solve serious cases.

When selecting cases for this book, I chose to include only cases of murdered or missing persons, and only cases that have gone unsolved for five years or more. Some of these crimes are solved; most are not.

Chapter One

The Great Mystery of Paynesville

Victim: Jackie Theel
Date: September 5, 1944
Status: Unsolved
Location: Paynesville, Minnesota

It might well be that there has never been a young lad more excited for his first day of school than 6-year-old Jackie Theel was on September 5, 1944. Dressed in shiny new black shoes and a navy blue sailor suit with long pants, Jackie walked the six blocks to the Paynesville School with his brothers, Tom and Denton. He smiled all the way, proudly toting his school supplies under one arm. He also carried with him a bag of potato chips, which he munched on between the games he and his classmates played and the songs they sung on that first day of school.

It was just a half-day for Jackie on his first day of the 1st grade, with dismissal coming at 11:30 a.m. When he walked out of the schoolhouse that morning, he left behind in his desk the small paper bag that held his tablet, pencil, and crayons. Jackie Theel had a wonderful first day of school—it was exactly the kind of day he had hoped and imagined it would be. But his first day of school would also be his last, because very soon after Jackie Theel walked away from his school in Paynesville that morning, he disappeared forever.

Jackie's mother, Bernice, had left instructions with Jackie's teacher that his older brothers, Tom and Denton, would be walking him home for lunch when school let out. However, when Mrs. Gladke, who was new to Paynesville, escorted Jackie and other students outside at 11:30, she asked Jackie if he knew which direction his home was. He pointed confidently to the west and then walked in that direction with Mrs. Gladke and a few other students. He shuffled along West Mill Street, clutching a school registration card in his little hand. When the group came to a street crossing, Mrs. Gladke again asked Jackie if he knew his way home, and he assured her that he did. Mrs. Gladke and the others split up at that point. Some of them turned north and others to the south, but Jackie went straight ahead to the west. But that was a problem, because little Jackie's home was actually six blocks northeast of school. He was going in the wrong direction. Jackie Theel was lost–he just hadn't realized it yet.

Mrs. Theel became worried when Jackie didn't arrive back home at noon as expected. She started calling neighbors and friends to ask if they had seen her son, but no one had. She called Paynesville Mayor Russell Portinga to report Jackie missing. Portinga and several other businessmen started searching for the boy immediately. Soon after, Stearns County Sheriff Art McIntee was summoned to help. McIntee, a resident of Paynesville, was an experienced law enforcement officer, having served ten years as Sherriff and six years as the chief of police in Paynesville.

Local law enforcement officials quickly launched a search for Jackie. Paynesville town constable John Deadrick, Sheriff McIntee, and agents from the Minnesota Bureau of Criminal Apprehension (BCA) combined their resources to establish a unified search effort. A missing persons bulletin was issued to area radio stations to broadcast Jackie's description and a plea for help in locating the boy. Jackie was 37 inches tall, weighed 45 lbs., and had blonde hair and blue eyes. He had a scar across his right cheek and a recently healed wound on the back of his head. Two new lower front teeth were coming in. A reward of $100 was offered for information leading to Jackie's safe return.

Volunteers searched throughout the town of Paynesville as well as the wooded areas and country farm fields surrounding the town, but searchers were unable to find any trace of Jackie. As many as 40 area Boy Scouts searched for Jackie that first day. One man searched the snakelike Crow River, which winds its way all along the northern outskirts of Paynesville. Other searchers scoured the banks on both sides of the river. It was no more than 20' at its widest points. The water was so shallow that constable Deadrick remarked that it would have been highly unlikely Jackie could have drowned in the water. Even if he had drowned, searchers would surely have found his body because the slow moving current could not have carried him away. That first day's search effort reached well into the late evening, finally wrapping up about 1:00 a.m. with no sign of the boy.

The intense search resumed a few hours later, at 6:00 a.m. A Civil Air Patrol plane was dispatched from St. Cloud. Ray Ubracken piloted the small, single-engine plane. Beryl Miller and Paynesville resident and barber, Les Spaeth, scanned the landscape from inside the plane. They saw no sign of Jackie through two exhaustive days of surveying the countryside several times from the sky.

Jackie was one of 13 children in the Theel family at the time of his disappearance. Jackie's father, Harold, was a truck driver. Without another explanation for his disappearance, many locals speculated that Jackie might have been kidnapped for ransom, but Sheriff McIntee quickly dismissed that theory on the basis that the family's modest income would preclude a would-be kidnapper from being motivated by the prospect of money. Harold Theel quickly became frustrated by the unexplained disappearance of his son. He contacted a faith healer for assistance and when he met with her she withered into a trance-like state, telling Harold about a mud hole where he would find the boy.

Hundreds of volunteers from the Paynesville community joined the intense search for Jackie. Farmers, Boy Scouts, and people from all walks of life dropped what they were doing to try to find the little boy. Paynesville High School canceled classes for all its boys on Wednesday and Thursday so they could search for Jackie. Searchers walked through city streets, plodding across farm fields and through wooded

Photo courtesy of *Paynesville Press*, September 14, 1944

Photo courtesy of *St. Cloud Times*, September 7, 1944

areas. They formed steady lines of men, women, and children spaced out at arm's length apart to cover every inch of residential yards, streets, fields, and woods. They searched buildings throughout town, even looking inside furnaces, manholes, cisterns, crawlspaces, and woodpiles. Farmers checked their barns, their haystacks, and their corncribs, but no trace of Jackie was reported.

Police checked out several tips including one about a Native American Indian who was reportedly seen hanging out in Cold Spring on Monday September 4, the day before Jackie disappeared. The man was said to be traveling to Willmar. Sheriff McIntee investigated and learned he was simply on his way to an Indian reservation. One witness reported seeing a boy fitting Jackie's description distraught and crying near the Evangelical church. The Paynesville Press reported that someone had claimed to witness an African-American woman in Paynesville offering two small boys a quarter if they would go for a ride with her. That claim later proved to be bogus.

A pair of possible sightings of Jackie on the west end of Paynesville was the strongest of possible clues to his disappearance. Between 1:00 and 1:30 p.m. on Tuesday September 5, the day of Jackie's disappearance, Mr. and Mrs. Pete Thompson were returning to Paynesville from their fishing trip out at Long Lake. Mrs. Thompson noted a small boy matching Jackie's description walking in the ditch along Highway 23 about a block out of town. The boy was clutching a piece of paper in his hand. That boy could very well have been Jackie Theel still holding onto his school registration card.

A pair of boys, 16-year-old Robert Burr and William Johnson, 14, reported seeing a boy matching Jackie's description climbing into a light brown or grey colored sedan heading west on Highway 23. That sighting was at about 4:45 p.m. on the same day and at about the same location where Mrs. Thompson believed she spotted Jackie. Investigators interviewed the boys and upon close inspection of the location they discovered footprints that seemed to corroborate the witness accounts. After getting a detailed description of the car from the boys, investigators issued a statewide bulletin for a 1940 or 1941 light-grey Plymouth sedan or coach vehicle. Three automobile service station owners in Willmar responded to the appeal and reported seeing a soldier with a boy matching Jackie's description, including wearing a sailor suit, on Tuesday, September 5. Kandiyohi County Sheriff Paul Anderson investigated and determined the man was trying to get his car starter repaired. Follow-up investigation by Willmar police, who located the mysterious car and man, found that the soldier had recently returned home from military combat and the boy with him was his little brother.

On Thursday, September 7, virtually all businesses shut down at noon. Business owners, their employees and children met at the school where Sheriff McIntee divided the volunteers into groups, fanning them out in all directions. Like the previous searches, this effort carried on until after dark. Every property and building in town was thoroughly searched, many of them for the second and third times.

Yet another organized search across the town of Paynesville was initiated on Sunday September 9, 1944. Boy Scouts from nearby Cold Spring and Richmond joined members of the Paynesville community. Once again, more than 100 volunteers searched in vain through the town that had already been torn upside down to locate the boy. Farm fields north of town were checked again, as was the Crow River. Authorities wanted to bring in bloodhounds to find Jackie's trail, but heavy rains that had fallen on Saturday temporarily compromised the ability of the dogs to detect his scent. They hoped to reconsider that possibility later, believing that Jackie's scent still clung to tree branches or to tall grasses he might have brushed up against as he wandered to his fate.

" I guess we covered every foot of ground for six square miles," said constable Deadrick. "We also went over the town very carefully, searching every business building, basement, church building, and even the woodpiles."[1]

On the weekend after Jackie disappeared, rumors were rampant that he had been found. A local radio station broadcast "very authentic" reports of the good news. Concerned individuals from across the state called the *Paynesville Press* to inquire. But a report titled "Rumor Mongers Again At Work" appeared in the next edition of the *Press*, and revealed that the rumors were just that—unfounded whispers that the boy had been located.

On Tuesday, September 12th, searchers moved their efforts to the thick wooded area that lay south of the city of Paynesville. Again, no sign of Jackie was found.

The overall search effort for Jackie Theel was very well organized and thorough, so much so that BCA agent William Conley of St. Paul complimented the effort. He said in all his years as an investigator he had never witnessed a better search for a missing person. "Paynesville can be proud of the way its citizens pitched in on this hunt," Conley said. "It was thorough and systematic."[2]

While scores of volunteers continued their exhaustive search of land, buildings, and water, Raymond Holscamp from New Ulm brought his team of bloodhounds to Paynesville to search for Jackie. Holscamp was optimistic that his three dogs would locate Jackie because they boasted a strong track record, having found missing persons in 13 of 14 attempts to date. Prior to beginning the search, Holscamp trained his dogs with articles of Jackie's clothing. The dogs made an immediate "hit" on Jackie's scent, as they were able to pick it up right outside his school, as expected.

The dogs followed Jackie's scent westward through town all the way to Schwartz's Drug Store. From there his trail turned north toward the North American Creamery before coming to a halt at the south bank of the Crow River. Small shoeprints leading down the riverbank were found at that location. Searchers then found matching shoeprints leading away from the river to the west. More of the same shoeprints that corresponded to the trail of Jackie's scent were found. The dogs tracked his scent to near the Evangelical Church in Paynesville, the very place where a witness said they saw a boy matching Jackie's description crying on the day he disappeared.

Jackie's scent continued on toward the west and south, past Bill Johnson's gasoline filling station, where it was strongest. The scent then weakened and finally vanished altogether at the very location where witnesses reported seeing Jackie getting into a car along Highway 23 on the afternoon of his disappearance. Suspecting that Jackie may have been taken away from that point, Holscamp gathered the dogs up into his truck and drove them to Hawick, six miles west of Paynesville. From there, Holscamp and BCA investigator William Conley worked the dogs in both ditches along Highway 23, all the way back to Paynesville. They hoped to pick up Jackie's scent between the two towns but they were unable to.

Following the exhaustive and fruitless series of unsuccessful searches for Jackie, Sheriff McIntee cited four possibilities for what happened to him:

1. That he was a victim of foul play.

2. He was given a ride by someone.

3. He was trapped somewhere.

4. That he was picked up by a "sexual maniac."

After a full week and a half of searching for the boy in vain, officials began to lose hope that Jackie would ever be found, dead or alive. M.E. Boerger, assistant chief of the Minnesota BCA, told reporters that his agents, along with Stearns County investigators, had fully vetted every lead to that point. He suggested that Jackie might have wandered off and died in some undetermined wooded area.

"There have been a lot of tips on the boy since he left school for home," Boerger said. "We've traced all of them, although hundreds of neighbors and friends of his parents, Mr. and Mrs. Harold Theel, have covered practically every inch of territory around Paynesville, there's still a possibility the lad strayed off beaten paths, got lost, and perished."[3]

Jackie's father, Harold, was investigated as a suspect in his own son's disappearance, even though he was working in St. Paul, more than an hour-and-a-half away, at the time Jackie went missing. Mr. Theel was a quiet man who rarely showed emotion. His apparent lack of urgency about his son's disappearance led to rumors that Mr. Theel sold Jackie for $500. Years later, Jackie's sister Annabelle joked that if their father could have fetched $500 for a child at the time, that he should have sold more of them!

About three weeks after Jackie's disappearance, officials decided to drain a 20-foot septic tank in the schoolyard to determine if the boy had fallen into the tank. Still, there was no trace of him found.

The FBI joined the case and their investigators were as baffled by Jackie's disappearance as much as Stearns County and BCA investigators had been. Sheriff McIntee speculated again at the one-year anniversary that the boy was picked up and taken away, saying "there is something in the community we haven't figured out."[4] He would not elaborate on what he meant by that remark, but his theory about Jackie's demise was strongly supported by the boy's path as suggested by the bloodhound search and witnesses who saw him along Highway 23.

1944 had already been a tragic year for several other children in Stearns County before Jackie Theel went missing. A farmhouse fire at Pleasant Lake in March claimed the lives of Mrs. Herbert Storkamp and two of her children, 6-year-old Daniel, and 3-year-old June. Herbert Storkamp and his two brothers escaped the fire, although Herbert suffered serious burns. In May 1944 a 3-year-old boy went missing between Richmond and Rockville. An overnight search failed to find the boy, but tragedy was averted when an air search was conducted the following morning and the boy was spotted wandering through a clearing. Also in May, 8-year-old Kenneth Paggen fell into the Watab Creek while fishing near Sartell. The boy was pulled under the current and drowned.

One year after Jackie's disappearance, Bernice Theel found herself wary of her youngest son, 5-year-old Fay, succumbing to the same fate of his brother as he prepared to start school. She walked Fay to school about a week prior to the start of classes, pretending to be lost along the way, encouraging Fay to find his way home.

"I hope it doesn't turn out the same way with him," she said of Fay.[5] She had developed several theories about what happened to Jackie a year earlier, but declined to discuss them publicly because she had no proof.

Two events in 1949 brought memories of Jackie's disappearance back to the front of people's minds. First, someone from Crown Point, Indiana sent a photograph of a boy resembling Jackie Theel to Sheriff McIntee. The lead was thoroughly investigated and it was determined the boy in the photo was not Jackie. Then in November 1949, the body of 3-year-old Larry Coleman was found in a swamp near Atkins, MN. Larry had been missing for three months and searchers had been unable to find any trace of the boy prior to his body being found.

The Theel family moved to Kansas in 1951. Rumors that Harold Theel was responsible for Jackie's disappearance resurfaced when bones were discovered in the well of their former home in Paynesville. Further investigation determined the bones belonged to a dog.

Hopes of answers were raised again in September 1957 when a human skull and arm bones were discovered during construction activity at a resort near Richmond. Officials initially considered that the bones might belong to Jackie, but the new sheriff downplayed the suggestion.

"The Theel case is an open case and one we would like to solve," said Stearns County Sheriff Pete Lahr. "We won't overlook any possibility."[6]

Lahr went on to say the size of the bones indicated they belonged to a small adult, and that the location where the bones were found suggested the possibility the construction at the resort had stumbled upon a Native American Indian burial ground.

Jackie's sister, Annabelle, said she received a letter from a former Paynesville school teacher in the 1960's claiming the woman had seen a young sailor who looked like Jackie get off a Navy ship in California. The teacher claimed that the man signed his name as "Jackie Theel," and another sailor told the woman that Jackie had been adopted as a child. The woman's story has never been authenticated.

In 1969, at the 25th Anniversary of the disappearance of Jackie Theel, 16-year-old Cathy Ruhland, a student from Richmond, decided to research and write about the mystery. Cathy became fascinated with the disappearance after learning about it from Fay Theel, whose family was neighbors to Cathy and her parents. Ruhland was encouraged to write about the case by ROCORI High School Principal Merel Hough. Hough previously served as the principal at Paynesville High School.

The disappearance of little Jackie Theel from Paynesville continues to be a legendary mystery in central Minnesota. His parents, Bernice and Harold, died just four months apart in October 1990 and February 1991, respectively. Jackie's siblings Fay and Judy continued to hold out hope for answers to what became of their older brother. Fay was always intrigued by the lead about the soldier seen with a boy in a sailor suit. When he returned to the Paynesville area from Kansas he inquired about the police reports, but learned that a fire at the Kandiyohi County courthouse had destroyed those records.

In about the year 2000, when Fay was 60 years old, he learned something about his brother he had never known previously. He and another relative were looking over a church directory and he saw the name Victor John Theel. "Who is that," Fay asked his relative. "Why that's Jackie—that was his real name," came the reply. When he disappeared in 1944, the family chose to use his nickname, Jackie, in the media so that his real name would be preserved to help identify him when he was found. It was a strategy the family was never given the opportunity to employ.

For sister Judy, the legend of Jackie's disappearance is particularly unique because she never actually met her brother—she wasn't born until after his 1944 disappearance. She maintains an album chock full of every newspaper article ever printed about the brother she never knew.

Whether he was a victim of abduction or foul play, got lost in the woods, or fell to some other awful fate, whatever became of Jackie Theel on September 5, 1944 came at the unfortunate intersection of youthful innocence and terrible misfortune. His disappearance is still a frequent topic of conversation and wonder in the town of Paynesville.

The disappearance of Jackie Theel remains an unsolved case. Anyone with information about Jackie is asked to call the Stearns County Sheriff's Office at 320-259-3700.

Bibliography – The Great Mystery of Paynesville

Jacobson, M. (2004, September). The Mystery of Jackie Theel - Six-Year-Old Jackie Theel Went Home for Lunch on Tuesday, Sept. 5, 1944, His First Day of School, and Disappeared. *Paynesville Press* , pp. 1-2.

Minneapolis Star Staff. (1944, September 13). Bloodhounds Trail Missing Boy, Strengthen Theory of Abduction. *Minneapolis Star* , p. 1.

Minneapolis Star Tribune Staff. (1944, September 8). City Police Join Kidnapper Search. *Minneapolis Star Tribune* , p. 13.

Minneapolis Star Tribune Staff. (1944, September 30). Tank to be Drained in Search for Boy. *Minneapolis Star Tribune* , p. 11.

Paynesville Press Editorial. (1944, September 16). A Friend in Need. *Paynesville Press* , p. 4.

Paynesville Press Staff. (1969, September). Area Girl Ponders Mystery - Paynesville Six Year Old Never Found. *Paynesville Press* .

Paynesville Press Staff. (1944, September 11). Find No Clue to Lost Boy, 6 - Searchers Baffled After Six Days. *Paynesville Press*, p. 1.

Paynesville Press Staff. (1944, September 21). Hope for Jackie Theel's Safety Wanes - Search Still Continues. *Paynesville Press*, p. 1.

Paynesville Press Staff. (1944, September 14). Mystery of Jackie Theel Unsolved. *Paynesville Press*, pp. 1, 4.

Paynesville Press Staff. (1944, September 7). Paynesville Boy Still is Missing, Search Goes On. *Paynesville Press*, p. 1.

Paynesville Press Staff. (1944, September). Rumor Mongers Again At Work. *Paynesville Press*.

Paynesville Press Staff. (1944, September 12). Search For Boy Turns to Woods - Thorough Hunt Set For Today. *Paynesville Press*, p. 7.

St. Cloud Daily Times. (1949, November 15). Body of Lost Tot is Found After 3 Months. *St. Cloud Daily Times*, p. 1.

St. Cloud Daily Times. (1944, May 24). Sartell Boy, 8, Falls in Creek, Drowns in River. *St. Cloud Daily Times*, p. 1.

St. Cloud Daily Times Staff. (1944, September 14). Bloodhounds on Paynesville Trail. *St. Cloud Daily Times*, p. 1.

St. Cloud Daily Times Staff. (1944, September 13). Paynesville Boy is Feared Dead. *St. Cloud Daily Times*, p. 1.

St. Cloud Daily Times Staff. (1944, September 8). Paynesville Lad Still Lost, Soldier 'Angle' is Solved. *St. Cloud Daily Times*, pp. 1-2.

St. Cloud Daily Times Staff. (1944, March 17). Perish in Fire - Pleasant Lake Family Trapped. *St. Cloud Daily Times*, p. 1.

St. Cloud Daily Times Staff. (1944, May 23). Tragedy Narrowly Averted. *St. Cloud Daily Times*, p. 10.

St. Cloud Daily Times Staff. (1957, September 16). 'U' Experts to Study Mystery of Richmond Skull. *St. Cloud Daily Times*, p. 1.

Thorkelson, W. (1944, September 12). Week's Hunt, 'Inch-by-Inch,' for Paynesville Boy Fails - Whole Area Assists, Draws Only Blank. *Minneapolis Star*, p. 1.

Torkelson, W. (1945, September 4). School Opening Recalls Lad's Disappearance. *Minneapolis Star*, p. 13.

Chapter Two

Two Sisters Missing

Victim: Mary and Susanne Reker
Date: September 2, 1974
Status: Main suspect is dead, case remains open
Location: St. Cloud

Author's Note: This chapter is condensed from Robert M. Dudley's book, *Two Sisters Missing—The 1974 Reker Sisters Murders*.

The Reker family lived in a residential neighborhood just west of downtown St. Cloud. There were eight family members in all living happily in their modest two-story home. Fred Reker, husband and father, worked at the Liturgical Press at St. John's Abbey in nearby Collegeville. He was the manager of the shipping room there. Wife and mother, Rita Reker, did not work outside the home but she did operate an in-home day care, caring for two little boys besides her own six children. The Rekers had four girls and two boys whose birth dates were spread out over a little more than a decade–Mary, 15; Betsy, 13; Susanne, 12; Marty, 10; Matthew, 8; and Leah, 4.

With no school classes on the Labor Day holiday on Monday, September 2, 1974, Mary, Betsy, and Susanne slept in late, rising at about 10:00 a.m. They ate a light breakfast of eggs and toast, got dressed, and discussed walking into town to do some shopping. Their mother questioned the need for Mary to go to the store again since she had just gone shopping with her friend, Anne Kinney, on Saturday. But Mary insisted, saying she needed to purchase school supplies and wanted to browse for a winter coat. Rita took note of the sense of urgency in Mary's voice as she pleaded her case. Betsy decided at the last minute to not go along on the shopping trip.

It was a relatively cool day. Although the sky was sunny and clear for much of the day, unseasonably low temperatures beckoned the onset of the fall season in central Minnesota. Fred and Rita had planned for the family's assistance in finishing up some fall yard work that afternoon, so Mary promised she and Susanne would return home in time to help. It was a promise she would be unable to keep.

Fred Reker was painting the front side of his family's home on 18th Avenue in St. Cloud shortly after 11:00 a.m. when he heard Mary and Susanne call goodbye to him. He paused from his work and peered over the green hedges, seeing Mary and Susanne waving happily at him as they walked toward the Shopko retail store. Their father smiled broadly and returned the wave. The 15-block stretch of city streets between the Reker home and Shopko was a 20-25 minute walk for the girls. The trip measured just under a mile in each direction.

Mary was a sophomore at St. Francis High School in nearby Little Falls, where she was involved in the school's band and chorus. She enjoyed playing the guitar and liked the table game foosball. Her friends noticed that Mary, like many of their other teenage girlfriends, had become a little boy-crazy over the summer, but she hadn't started to date yet. Attending school at St. Francis had been a last minute decision for Mary the year before.

Susanne was in the 7th grade at Pope John XXIII School in St. Cloud. She was a quiet, shy girl–somewhat introverted. Susanne was a devoted student of the violin, faithfully practicing the instrument for two hours each and every day. She played in the school orchestra.

The girls had dressed in typical fall fashion for their trip. Mary was wearing blue jeans, a white sweater, a green Army over shirt, and her glasses. The name R-E-K-E-R was embroidered in white just above her left pocket. Gary Reker, a 21-year-old cousin and military man from Adrian, Minnesota, had recently given the shirt to Mary. On her feet was a newer pair of tan moccasins. Susanne was wearing navy blue colored corduroy pants, gold-rimmed glasses, a white jacket and low-cut boots.

Mary and her classmates had organized a car pool schedule for the weekly 30-mile trip to and from boarding school in Little Falls. She was wearing her watch and understood she and her sister would need to return home no later than 3:00 p.m. to assist with the yard work before catching the planned 4:00 p.m. car pool ride to school. Mary was well organized. She had packed her suitcase and a science project that was due the coming week, ahead of time. Shortly after the sisters left home, that day's car pool driver called the Rekers and left a message for Mary that they would not be able to pick her up until 7:00 p.m. It was a message Mary would never receive.

Mary and Susanne arrived at the Shopko store shortly before noon. The store manager greeted the girls as they wandered their way through the store's aisles. He was familiar with the girls and their family because the Rekers were frequent shoppers at his store. The girls left Shopko early in the afternoon and then headed for the nearby Zayre Shoppers' City.

The Zayre department store was a monolith of a retail space, boasting a complete line of general merchandise, hardware, clothing, and health and beauty items. A food service counter and a grocery section rounded out the store's offerings. Mary knew two teenage boys who worked in the grocery department. One of them was a friend of a boy Mary was acquainted with. The other boy was someone she knew from nearby Luxemburg, where her grandparents lived. Mary had stayed with her grandparents and other relatives in Luxemburg quite often in August, just before the start of school.

As the girls strolled past the Zayre food counter at about 1:00 p.m., they saw one of their neighbors, Jacob Yunger. He was enjoying a lunch of a hot dog and soda. The girls spoke briefly with Jacob, an older man in his mid-70's. Mary and Susanne then walked away from the food counter toward the back of the store where the winter coats were located, just before the grocery department. The grocery section was closed for the Labor Day holiday.

As the girls were walking away from the food counter, Yunger heard Susanne say something ominous to Mary. "I don't want to go with that man. I don't like him–let's not," Susanne pleaded with her sister.

Susanne's words struck a chord in Jacob Yunger. It seemed unusual to him that she was worried about going with a man–and he was certain she had said the word "man." His worries grew when he left the store and noticed a large, nervous looking man behind the wheel of a blue car in the store parking lot. The man appeared to be waiting for someone. The car was a Chevrolet Impala with square-shaped taillights. Concerned, Yunger waited in the parking lot for a while, watching the man in the car. Yunger finally gave up and left the parking lot, with the Reker sisters apparently still inside the Zayre store.

A couple of hours later, Fred Reker was finishing his work painting the outside of the family home. He walked into the kitchen to clean the paintbrushes when he looked up at the clock and noticed it was after 3:00 p.m. Rita was in the kitchen as well. Without saying a word, Fred and Rita's eyes met and they shared the same concern–Mary and Susanne should have returned home by then.

Rita began calling neighbors and friends to ask if they had seen the girls. Some neighbors reported seeing the girls walking toward the downtown area but no one she talked to had seen or heard from them after that. She called the families of Mary's classmates in Little Falls, but again there had been no contact from her daughters. Fred and Rita took to driving around town in search of the girls

Fred Reker and his oldest son, Marty, drove to the St. Cloud Police Department at about 7:00 p.m. to report that Mary and Susanne were missing. The initial reaction from police was the girls probably had run away from home–not an uncommon occurrence in the St. Cloud area at that time. One particularly insensitive officer said, "Oh, yeah, here's another case of runaway kids." [7]

Police subsequently interviewed Fred and Rita as well as the Rekers' oldest other child, Betsy. Those interviews revealed no apparent motivation for the two girls to have run away from home. But officially, St. Cloud police treated the case as a runaway situation.

That Monday night was a long one for the Reker family. Fred and Rita slept on a foldout sofa bed in the living room while their children huddled around them in the sleeping bags. It became the family's sleeping arrangement for many nights thereafter. That first night was a particularly cold one. Outside, overnight temperatures dipped down to 30 degrees, adding another measure of concern to an already worried and anxious family.

St. Cloud police asked the Rekers to bring pictures of Mary and Susanne to the police station on Tuesday morning. The police suggested the Rekers stop by the Greyhound bus terminal on their way to the police department to see if the girls had been seen there. In a way, the parents were being tasked with conducting their own investigation. Again, that was not an unusual procedure at the time. A bus station attendant looked at the pictures and told the Rekers the girls looked familiar. He believed he might have sold them tickets along with some other girls who were riding to Little Falls. The Rekers promptly drove to Little Falls and stopped at the St. Francis School. They were able to locate the two girls who had ridden the bus from St. Cloud the day before, but the girls said neither Mary nor Susanne had been on the bus with them.

The Wednesday, September 4, 1974 edition of the *St. Cloud Daily*

Times carried a front-page story about the missing Reker girls. Photos of Mary and Susanne were featured in the short article. Descriptions of their physical appearances and the clothing they wore on Monday were published as well. Police asked that anyone who had seen the girls on Monday contact the St. Cloud police department.

The length of time the girls were missing was initially measured in hours but quickly grew to being marked by long, agonizing days of wait. The Rekers were in shock, having no idea what to do next. It seemed they were getting little support from the St. Cloud Police Department. They were frustrated at the suggestion Mary and Susanne had run away from home. They knew their daughters well, and there was no logical reason for them to have run away. Furthermore, the girls did not take a lot of money with them. Susanne had taken no money, and Mary could not have had a lot of money with her because she had left most of it in her savings account. If the sisters had been intent on running away from home, they would certainly have taken as much money as possible along with them.

The Rekers knew immediately that some awful fate had come to Mary and Susanne. As the days went by, members of law enforcement grew increasingly concerned the girls had befallen a terrible fate as well. More and more, police doubted the girls had run away. With no word from the girls, and no witnesses who reported seeing them, the likelihood of Mary and Susanne Reker being found alive was growing slimmer by the day. The Reker family spent countless hours searching for Mary and Susanne. Many relatives, friends and neighbors joined them.

The painful, dreary days of waiting and praying for answers were further darkened by the persistent rainy weather that fell upon the St. Cloud area throughout the month of September. It rained a half inch one day, then a quarter inch, and on some days the rains fell an inch or more. A record 10 inches of rain fell during the course of the damp, cold month. While the rains fell throughout much of the month of September 1974, the Reker family waited for answers about what had happened to Mary and Susanne.

Susanne was a shy, tenderhearted, and gentle girl. She and her siblings got along wonderfully, and she was fiercely loyal to her family and friends. That summer, when her sister Betsy stayed away from home with relatives for a few days, Susanne cried and told her mother how much she missed her sister. Her spare time was typically spent writing poetry about many of nature's wonders including flowers, animals, sunshine, and God. Susanne put a lot of effort into her schooling and was quietly competitive, always striving to achieve "A" grades. With an ever forward-looking perspective, Susanne spent a lot of time drawing pictures and detailed blueprints of her dream home. She was ambitious about her career goals as well, with a lofty goal of becoming a doctor one day.

Mary had always been an athletic girl and a quick learner. Every new activity she took on seemed to come naturally to her, whether it was riding her first bicycle, skating, learning musical instruments, or enrolling in challenging school classes. She taught herself to play piano and the guitar. A natural leader, she would sometimes put together impromptu classrooms in the basement, "teaching" neighborhood kids. As the eldest child of the family, her parents often counted on Mary to be in charge when they were away from home running errands. Parents in the neighborhood relied on her as well, as she was in high demand as a baby sitter. Mary always loved to take on a challenge. She ran for the Student Council as a freshman, undeterred by the fact her opponent was a well-known senior. Above all else, Mary Reker had a great excitement for life.

As the days passed without answers it became apparent to Fred and Rita Reker that whatever had become of their girls was probably not a random occurrence. Events that occurred over the prior summer seemed to add up to something unusual going on in Mary's life. Ultimately, it appeared possible Mary had intended to meet someone during that Labor Day shopping trip, and that could explain why she had been so adamant about going shopping that day.

Mary had spent much time that summer staying at her grandparents' home in nearby Luxemburg. She enjoyed the company of her grandparents, Lawrence and Hildegard, and her uncles who also lived in the area. They attended church at St. Wendelin's in Luxemburg, a very small rural community with a population of fewer than 100 residents. One Sunday, a family member noticed two young men leaving the church during the middle of the service. He knew the name of one of the two teenagers, Herb Notch, but was not familiar with the taller boy. Mary Reker left the church just minutes later. It then occurred to the man that when the boys left church, it might have been a signal for Mary to join them. She returned to church by herself a few minutes later. By the end of church service, the incident had escaped his mind and he didn't think about it again until after Mary and Susanne were reported missing.

About two weeks prior to her disappearance, Mary spent a week at the home of an aunt and uncle, babysitting their children during the day. At some point, Mary expressed a sense of urgency about going to the bank to withdraw money. She twice asked her aunt to drive her to town, telling her "You can't imagine how much trouble I will be in if I don't get that money." [8]

As surprising as this information had been to Fred and Rita Reker, it paled in comparison to a chilling, ominous entry Mary had written in her diary. It was the very last entry she would ever compose–an entry that appeared to show that Mary had feared for her life just before she and her sister were murdered. Interestingly, the page had been removed from the diary and was found inside a box of greeting cards. Her words were a further indication the killer had specifically targeted Mary:

To my family, should I die, I ask that my stuffed animals go to my sister. If I am murdered, find my killer and see that justice is done. I have a few reasons to fear for my life and what I ask is important.

Mary's friend Anne Kinney, who had gone shopping with Mary just two days before the murders, said Mary tried to tell her about something that was bothering her but couldn't recall what it was. "I remember she was talking about something that day, and my mind was on something else," Kinney recalled. "I'm just beginning to wonder if I missed something, if there was anything she said that could have given me a clue as to what was going on."

On Tuesday, September 24, St. Cloud Mayor Alcuin Loehr, State Senator Jack Kleinbaum, and area law enforcement officials met to discuss the disappearance of Mary and Susanne Reker. Following the meeting, Loehr obtained approval from Minnesota Gov. Wendell Anderson to use National Guard and State Patrol helicopters to search for the girls. The helicopter search commenced later that day. Despite rumors to the contrary, the aerial search of the city and nearby quarries turned up nothing.

Intent on finding his daughters, Fred Reker organized search parties on his own. Family, friends, and neighbors of the Rekers scoured through a wooded area south of the Zayre shopping center, but the search yielded no clues to the whereabouts of Mary and Susanne. Rita Reker spent countless hours on the phone calling friends and acquaintances, reaching out to anyone who might have information about the girls. They put up reward posters and sent tapes to radio stations all around the area.

On Saturday, September 28, 1974, Rita Reker heard a knock at the front door. When she opened it, their family pastor and a man from Murphy's Ambulance Service were standing at her doorstep. She read the grim look on their faces, and in an instant Rita sensed why they were there.

Earlier in the day, a pair of teenage boys made a grisly discovery while walking along the edge of the abandoned Meridian quarry, just west of St. Cloud. They stumbled across the badly decomposed body of Susanne Reker lying under a bush. The boys hurried to the nearby home of Delbert Gillitzer to call police. It was one of four homes that lined the area between the highway and the quarry.

Stearns County deputy Al Ahlgrim was patrolling an area near the quarry when he heard the radio call that a body had been found there. He was the first member of law enforcement to arrive. After securing the scene he called Stearns County Sheriff Pete Lahr and deputy Lawrence "Brownie" Kritzeck.

Investigators responding to the scene found Susanne's body lying face down in a boggy area at the top of the quarry. She was partially covered with leaves and brush, and was fully clothed. One of her sleeves had been stretched out over her hand, indicating Susanne may have been dragged to the location where she was found. After a subsequent search by divers, Mary's body was found submerged near the bottom of the quarry, on a ledge about 40 feet under water. It was apparent both girls had been stabbed multiple times in the fronts of their bodies. Mary's slacks and underwear were found hanging on an exposed ledge, and her army jacket was in the water, indicating at least some of her clothing had been tossed into the quarry after her body. The front of her sweater had been cut open in a jagged line. Her bra had been cut into four pieces. The girls' bodies were sent to the Hennepin County Medical Examiner's Office in Minneapolis for a thorough autopsy.

Local law enforcement immediately launched an intensive investigation. Up to that point the case had been handled by the St. Cloud Police Department. With the deaths of the girls apparently occurring outside of the cities of St. Cloud and Waite Park, the investigation shifted to the Stearns County Sheriff's Department. Investigator Lawrence Kritzeck took over as the lead investigator in the case. He would lead the investigation from the Stearns County Attorney Office, reporting directly to Stearns County Attorney Roger Van Heel. Another Stearns County investigator would assist, along with an agent from the Minnesota Bureau of Criminal Apprehension and an officer from the St. Cloud Police Department.

Kritzeck established a special telephone number for the investigation and hired a secretary to take messages and notes about the case. He immediately appealed to the public for their assistance to help solve the crime. "We are asking every person who was at the Zayres or at Shopko between the hours of 10 a.m. and 3 p.m. on September 2nd, to call us," Kritzeck told the *St. Cloud Daily Times*. "We want to talk to everyone who was there, whether they think they have information to give us or not. They might have information we could use without knowing it."[9]

One witness reported seeing a tall man wearing a cowboy hat walking out of the Zayre store at about the same time Jacob Yunger had seen a suspicious-looking man in the parking lot. It was not clear whether the two men were one and the same.

Another man claimed he saw Mary and Susanne Reker enter the Briggs Lake Tavern on the east side of St. Cloud with two young men at about 2:00 p.m. on the day they disappeared. He was certain Mary was there because he saw her wearing the Army jacket with the name R-E-K-E-R sewn on the front. The witness said one of the men, the taller of the two, looked like he was about 28 years old. The other man, who was shorter, looked about 16 years old. He said the girl he believed to be Mary was enjoying herself, laughing and joking with the two men. She played foosball with them. The younger girl, however, stood off by herself and appeared to be uncomfortable. She didn't speak or engage with anyone.

Another witness said he saw two girls fitting the descriptions of the Reker girls walking toward the quarry from the north at about 3:00 p.m. He said he paid close attention to them because they passed very near his tool shed. "One of the girls was wearing one of those Army jackets," he said. "So I figured they were hippie types and I watched them until they went out of sight into the quarry."[10]

A woman who lived on the south side of the quarry said she saw two girls and a tall man walking across her yard and enter the quarry from that side at about the same time.

The timing of the sightings seemed to coincide with their apparent time of death. Again, autopsy results indicated the girls died between 3:00 and 4:00 p.m. that day. Furthermore, when Mary's body was recovered from the quarry, her watch was found to have stopped at 3:25.

On Sunday, September 29, 1974, investigator Kritzeck led a team of about 20 county deputies and city police officers as they searched the crime scene in vain for evidence. Investigators got down on their hands and knees, combing every square inch of the ground above the quarry in a desperate search for clues. No murder weapon was found near the murder scene.

The quarry where the bodies of Mary and Susanne Reker were found nearly four weeks after their disappearance. Photo courtesy of St. Cloud Daily Times

Funeral services for Mary and Susanne Reker were held on Wednesday October 2, 1974, at St. John Cantius Church in St. Cloud. The St. Francis Choir, the choir to which Mary had belonged, sang during the funeral. Memorial gifts were split between Father Beiting's Appalachian Mission in Lancaster, Kentucky, and the Franciscan Missions at St. Francis Convent in Little Falls. Two of the girls' siblings, Betsy and Martin, presented offertory gifts during the funeral ceremony that included Susanne's violin, a sweater Mary had been knitting and the butterfly she captured just before her death. Mary and Susanne were buried side by side in Assumption Cemetery in St. Cloud.

The nearly four weeks of waiting and the subsequent finding of Mary and Susanne's bodies were heart wrenching for the Reker family to endure. Their grief was soon amplified to include the added stress of being viewed by investigators as possible suspects in their own daughters' murders. It was a common, logical reaction by the police, but understanding that did not make it any less a painful burden to bear.

Investigator Kritzeck reported his office had received a good response to his plea for potential witnesses to come forward with information. He had specifically requested that anyone who had seen something near the Shopko and Zayre stores, or near the quarry, to contact a special number at the Stearns County Attorney's Office. "We have been following up on the calls we have received, and it's time consuming," Kritzeck said. "So I hope the people who have called don't get disgusted–we will get to them."[11]

Kritzeck also announced investigators were to do additional diving at the quarry in an attempt to locate the murder weapon. A preliminary search by a diver from the Minnesota School of Diving failed to produce the knife used to stab the girls. The diver was uncertain if he would need to utilize special magnetic equipment in a future dive.

Such equipment may have been necessary due to the rock ledges and formations at the bottom of the quarry.

Kritzeck cited an unconfirmed report the girls had been seen with two young men at a restaurant in Sauk Rapids on the day of their murders. He said he would consider it to be a rumor until the lead was checked out. He discounted another rumor that had been circulating about a 15-year-old boy, someone Mary Reker knew. He had been reported to be missing since September 4th, just two days after the murders of the Reker sisters.

Autopsies confirmed Mary and Susanne Reker had died of multiple stab wounds from a small, double-edged knife. Mary had been stabbed six times in the abdomen. Susanne had been stabbed twelve or thirteen times. Neither girl's body showed any signs of defensive wounds—no cuts, no bruises, no broken nails. The lack of defensive wounds seemed to indicate the possibility there was more than one person involved in their deaths.

Although Fred and Rita Reker had been questioned about their daughters' disappearance from the beginning, an apparent misunderstanding on the part of investigators precluded the Rekers from taking a polygraph test until nearly a year after the murders. The Rekers had never been asked to take a test until that point, but Kritzeck had apparently been of the misunderstanding that they refused to take polygraphs. Once they were asked to, the Rekers immediately agreed to take a test. BCA agent Les Loch drove them to St. Paul and subsequent test results revealed no indications of deception. The miscommunication by investigators was just one more miscue in a long, long line of problems that dogged the investigation.

As the first anniversary of the murders of Mary and Susanne Reker passed in 1975, the lives of Fred and Rita Reker and their other four children had finally settled into a normal routine–or as normal as could be expected given the tragic circumstances. Pictures of the girls still adorned the walls of their home. A memory box filled with items that belonged to the girls hung on a wall in the living room. Despite a massive investigative effort, there had been little in the way of progress in solving the murders, and evidence remained elusive.

Case investigators were not immune to the heartache felt by the family and their close friends. Investigator Kritzeck estimated that frustrated investigators had sifted through some 700-800 leads over the 12 months since the girls were murdered. Kritzeck had led the investigation since the girls' bodies were discovered, and for four months he had the assistance of a pair of Stearns County investigators to count on. However, Sheriff James Ellering was compelled to remove those two deputies from the case in January due to lack of leads to follow up on.

BCA agent Les Loch spoke of the lack of progress in the case, citing scant physical evidence at the rain-torn scene of the crime. Workload was also an issue, with Loch himself covering an eight-county area of the state. "Frankly, I don't think we've gotten one good lead so far," he lamented. "As far as I could go on this is that a number of people have been checked out but no information was gained to connect them to the case. I don't think we've had a good suspect since this thing broke."[12]

Despite the apparent lack of progress in the investigation, officials did reveal on the first anniversary of the deaths that they had about five good suspects. Those individuals had been identified for some time, but investigators lacked evidence to connect them directly to the crimes. One item of note investigators did reveal publicly was their assertion that the girls had been murdered at the scene where their bodies were discovered. Additionally, investigators believed the person(s) responsible for the murders was familiar with the area, and he probably knew at least one of the girls.

"You don't just drive along the highway and pull off and find that quarry," Loch offered. "There's a complete void from the time they were seen in the shopping center until the bodies were found. No one saw them getting in the car or anything. It's unfortunate that so much time elapsed between the disappearance of the girls and the time the bodies were found. People forget things in that time."[13]

For their part, the Rekers were hopeful the case would be kept in the public eye. They had been quite disenchanted with the early investigation, but in the fall of 1975 they were encouraged by the recent progress, especially in light of the lack of evidence. Still, they held on to hopes investigators would release more information to spur leads. The family's belief, and what may have been the only way to find truth, was the killer might feel remorse and give himself up.

By September 1976, another year had gone by without an arrest or word of key suspects. With little to no communication coming from investigators, the Rekers remained frustrated at the lack of progress in the case.

"Two years," Fred Reker pondered. "Yet we know no more, or very little more, than we did when our girls were killed. The authorities seem to be at a standstill. Sometimes it even seems like we must convince them anything ever happened. I think they should start fresh and try to find the person who killed our girls."[14]

Rita Reker agreed. To her knowledge, investigators had never had a serious suspect. "We've never been informed about how the investigation is going or what is happening," she declared. "The investigators seemed to have lost interest."[15]

Kritzeck defended the investigation, citing the importance of guarding the details of the crime and subsequent investigation. He said he didn't believe he had been overly uncommunicative with the family, although he conceded he had kept most information confidential from them. Kritzeck contended that investigators were making significant progress, and in fact, he said they were about to interview a man who claimed to have knowledge about who killed the girls.

"What really happened? I guess your guess is as good as mine," Kritzeck said when asked about current suspects as of the 2nd anniversary. "Right now we are looking for that one right piece of evidence that might blow the case open. Just last week we ran a check on two people arrested elsewhere to see if there might be a possible connection. We run a check on everything."[16]

Although the 2nd anniversary of the girls' murders passed without resolution, or even promising leads, another terrible crime was about to be committed in the city of St. Cloud. It was a crime that would bear striking similarities to the Reker murders, and it came at the hands of a pair of teenage boys.

It was Saturday night, September 25, 1976. Bernard Dukowitz, owner of the 25th Avenue Dairy Bar & Liquor Store, was minding the liquor store portion of the business. The liquor store and the convenience store shared the same building, but were divided into separate establishments by a common wall. When he was not waiting on customers, Mr. Dukowitz would peek through a hole in the wall to monitor activities in the convenience store. His 14-year-old daughter, Suzie Dukowitz, was working in the Dairy Bar that night.

At about 9:20 p.m., Herb Notch, then 17, walked into the Dairy

Bar. As he approached the counter another 17-year-old boy, James Wagner, walked into the store. Suzie stepped away from the soda cooler to tend to her customers. Then Wagner pulled out a handgun and ordered Suzie to take all the money from the register and put it inside a paper bag. Suzie complied. Wagner then ordered the girl to come outside with them.

Notch led the way to a station wagon parked on 7th Street. He climbed into the driver's side of the car while Wagner ordered Suzie to get in from the passenger side. Bernard Dukowitz called the police after realizing his daughter had probably been kidnapped from the store. St. Cloud police officer Winscher Kittridge arrived in his squad car just two minutes later. He interviewed a pair of witnesses who had seen Notch and Wagner leave the area in a station wagon. An investigation began immediately.

Meanwhile, Notch and Wagner had taken Suzie Dukowitz to a remote location southeast of Luxemburg. Herb parked the car near an old gravel pit and ordered Suzie to get in the back. The boys tied her arms and legs up with tape, and then Notch used a buck knife to cut open her sweater and cut off her bra. Both men then sexually assaulted the girl, took her outside, stabbed her in the back four times, and left her for dead.

Suzie lived. She was able to crawl and walk to a nearby home and ask for help. Back in St. Cloud, police officers on patrol were on the lookout for a station wagon with wood grain panels down the sides, and a burnt out headlight. Patrol officer Stephen Brockway was sitting in his patrol car in the parking lot of the First American Bank near downtown at about midnight when he observed a car matching that description heading east on Main Street. As he watched the station wagon drive by, he noted one of its headlamp covers was closed and he realized it resembled a burnt out headlight. He pulled the car over, and when he approached the vehicle he saw that the two young male occupants matched the general description of the young men who had kidnapped Suzie Dukowitz a couple hours earlier.

The young men were identified as Herb Notch, Jr. and James Wagner, and were arrested on suspicion of robbery and kidnapping. A subsequent investigation by St. Cloud police officers, the BCA, and Stearns County deputies found evidence of the station wagon at the location where Suzie was assaulted, stabbed, and abandoned. BCA agent Les Loch located Suzie's footprints and the tire tracks left behind by the station wagon, as well as a pair of freshly smoked Marlboro cigarettes. Stearns County investigator Jack Kritzeck later found the knife at the bottom of Keppers Lake near Luxemburg, where Notch had tossed the weapon along with a bag full of evidence. The knife was a stainless steel folding buck knife–its blade had been badly ground on a rough emery wheel. Deputy Bob Kunkel located Suzie's white bra.

Both Notch and Wagner cooperated with investigators and admitted to burglarizing the 25th Avenue Dairy Bar, kidnapping Suzie Dukowitz, stabbing her, and abandoning her near the gravel pit outside Luxemburg. Notch told investigators he wanted counseling and acknowledged he had previously been in a mental hospital, in 1974–the same year the Reker girls were stabbed to death.

Notch and at least one other young man were also implicated in a pair of unrelated purse-snatching incidents near the downtown area of St. Cloud in August 1976. In each case Notch used a knife and had at least one accomplice. Notch's connection to the purse-snatching had never been documented in media accounts during the time.

Herb Notch Booking Photo

Fred Reker visited Suzie Dukowitz's parents on Sunday, the day after she was stabbed. He said only parents of an abducted child could understand what they had to be going through at that time. The crime became known locally as the Dairy Bar case. Reker used the opportunity of that case's publicity to ask Stearns County officials to share more information about his own daughters' investigation, suggesting additional information might bring new facts out in the open and spur some new leads.

After a series of court hearings debated by defense lawyers and Stearns County Attorney Roger Van Heel, Notch and Wagner were eventually certified to stand trial as adults. Notch was charged with a total of six counts. He pleaded guilty to two of those counts–one count of kidnapping and another count of burglary. The remaining counts were dropped but were read into the court record. He was sentenced to a maximum of 40 years in prison, yet only served ten.

Due to several striking similarities between the stabbing of Suzie Dukowitz and the stabbing deaths of Mary and Susanne Reker, investigators naturally investigated Notch and Wagner for a possible connection to the Reker murders. On October 7, 1976, Herb Notch was administered a lie detector test to determine if there was any indication of involvement in the murders of the Reker sisters on Labor Day 1974. St. Cloud police officer Howard Paulson accompanied Notch for the test, which was conducted at the BCA office in St. Paul. Officer Paulson verbally reported back to Stearns County Attorney Roger Van Heel that Notch passed the test.

"I have only had a brief conversation with our investigator," Van Heel said. "But he indicated the test showed no involvement. I am waiting now for the written report on the polygraph test."[17]

According to James Wagner's attorney, his client was not asked to take a polygraph test in connection with the Reker killings, presumably because Wagner did not live in the St. Cloud area until September of 1975, a year after the murders.

As the third anniversary of the Reker murders approached in the middle of August 1977, Stearns County Sheriff Jim Ellering announced his office was taking over control of the investigation. The move effectively relieved Kritzeck from the investigation altogether. In announcing the change, Ellering reasoned that Kritzeck had run the investigation from the Stearns County Attorney's Office as a practical matter, and he downplayed sentiments of hostility between the departments, saying the change was merely an administrative move.

Sheriff Ellering also announced he had brought former FBI special agent Frank Sass into the case. Sass was an expert on sex crimes and an instructor at the FBI Academy in Quantico, Virginia. He was a highly regarded consultant for sexually deviant crimes. Ironically, Sass was one of the instructors who had taught the courses that future St. Cloud Police Chief Elwood Bissett was attending at the time of the Reker murders. Prior to his role as an instructor, Sass worked as an FBI agent for 29 years, with most of his experience investigating sex crimes.

Despite the hiring of a sex-crimes expert, Ellering declined to label the girls' murders as sex related. "It is possible, although at this exact time and date, there are no immediate plans for it, that other persons of expertise might be called in as well," Ellering said.[18] He noted there were active suspects in the case and he was hopeful the case could still be solved.

Although Sheriff Ellering's announcement of the changing of the guard in the Reker investigation appeared to be motivated by decisions internally, there may have been external pressure to make changes. That pressure came in the form of a thorough investigative journalism effort by Dave Anderson of the *Minneapolis Star* newspaper. Anderson, who began digging into the Reker investigation in July 1977, produced a 5-part series of articles in the *Minneapolis Star* that presented an unflattering, if not scalding, review of the investigation. The series was particularly critical of lead investigator Lawrence Kritzeck and apparent political infighting in Stearns County.

Anderson's series opened with an article titled *Search Reopened for Sisters' Killer*, on August 19, 1977. In the article, Anderson contended that Kritzeck had been very possessive of the Reker investigative file, refusing to share information with Sheriff Ellering or Chief Bissett. In fact, he pointed out when Ellering took over the case three years after the murders, neither he nor Bissett had ever seen the files relating to the investigation.

After reviewing the Reker file, Sheriff Ellering said he felt confident about the case. "If we have to go back to day one and start this case all over again, we will," Ellering declared.[19] He made a public appeal to citizens and law enforcement officials to come forward if they believed they had relevant information about the case, whether their information was new or old.

The political climate in Stearns County may have played a role in hampering the investigation, according to Anderson. He pointed out at the time of the Reker murders, while then-sheriff Pete Lehr was in the hospital battling cancer, Stearns County deputies Jim Ellering and Brownie Kritzeck, as well as Waite Park police chief Charlie Grafft, were all busy campaigning to be elected as the next sheriff. The implication was that Kritzeck had been leveraging his role as the lead investigator on the Reker case to his advantage politically.

The *Star's* first article cited a number of early missteps made by investigators. For example, one source familiar with the location where the bodies were found told the paper the crime scene was a virtual stampede of investigators and other agencies running amok over potential evidence. One police officer picked up Susanne's eyeglasses with his bare hands and shoved them in his pocket, possibly contaminating potential evidence. The articles alleged Kritzeck himself jeopardized the investigation when he draped blankets over the girls' bodies out of decency–before the bodies had been photographed and examined for evidence.

St. Cloud police chief Elwood Bissett took office in January 1976, two years after the Reker murders. Those close to Bissett said he quickly became upset at how the investigation was being handled. He was particularly angered by the political climate that surrounded the case. To change the course of the investigation, Bissett crafted a proposal to bring together himself, Kritzeck, Sheriff Ellering, and other investigators who had worked on the case to a summit meeting. The plan was to rent a hotel meeting room for a weekend, lock themselves in, and create a cohesive and comprehensive team to study the case in detail and move forward. The meeting failed to materialize, and another year would go by before Ellering or Bissett would see the Reker investigative file.

Some law enforcement officials who were discouraged at how Lawrence Kritzeck and the Stearns County Attorney's Office handled the case spent a lot of their own time investigating details. Frank Klatt, a highly experienced St. Cloud police officer began working on the case off the clock immediately after the girls disappeared. Klatt was one of the best detectives on the force. He was said to be as hard working, dedicated, and straightforward as they come. Rick Daniels, a young new BCA agent, worked the case quickly and efficiently on his own, identifying one man as an early suspect even before the girls' bodies were discovered. That man eventually became a top suspect in the case, but has since been cleared.

The Rekers appreciated the efforts of investigators who took initiative to investigate their daughters' case. "Rick Daniels was the first one with the courage to tell us that our girls are probably dead," Rita said. "He was also the first one to take us seriously and to listen to us. And that was almost three weeks after they disappeared."[20]

The *Minneapolis Star* articles included details about the girls' murders that were reported for the first time. For example, both girls had been stabbed in the stomach and abdomen. The cuts were 2 1/2" to 3" deep, 3/4" wide, and appeared to be made with a knife or instrument that was sharp on both edges. That information suggested the knife was small and double-edged. The *Star* claimed to have gathered more than 800 pieces of information about the case, and investigators had as many as 25 suspects.

Stearns County officials rebuked the *Minneapolis Star* for how they reported on the Reker investigation, saying the series accomplished nothing, and in fact, may have worked to hinder the three-year-old investigation. "I think you are interfering with an ongoing investigation," Roger Van Heel said of *Star* reporter Dave Anderson.[21]

The *Minneapolis Star* was not alone in publishing criticism of how the Reker murder investigation had been handled. The *St. Cloud Daily Times* ran a story in September 3, 1977, echoing many of the same concerns. That story alleged that a pair of law enforcement officials had approached Stearns County Judge Paul Hoffman with concerns about the investigation, specifically about a woman who said she had information about the case that had been ignored by investigators.

The *Times* article provided further insight to factors that led to the investigation changing hands from Kritzeck to Sheriff Ellering. According to Stearns County Attorney Roger Van Heel, the "straw that broke the camel's back" came in the form of outside pressure from the BCA. The BCA approached Stearns County officials after they discovered Kritzeck had been working on his own time in defense of a pawnshop owner who was being prosecuted for gun violations.

Sheriff Ellering confirmed the BCA had approached him about the issue with Kritzeck, but he maintained the decision to remove him from the case was his own and not affected by the BCA's ire. "It is unfortunate that this came at the same time as renewed interest in the Reker killings," Ellering said. "I want to make it clear that I have found nothing unusual, illegal, or suspicious in the investigation into the killings. My decision was an administrative decision."[22]

And so the Reker investigation began again, this time refocused in the hands of the Stearns County Sheriff's office. Although Lawrence Brownie Kritzeck was removed from the investigation as part of the change, his alleged efforts to conceal information about the case would resurface years later.

The Dairy Bar kidnapping and stabbing case was not the only stabbing case in the St. Cloud area in 1976, and Herb Notch was not the only young man in the area to have committed such a crime and draw the interest of Reker murder investigators. A teenage boy by the name of Michael Bartowsheski, who lived just six blocks away from the Reker family in September 1974, was charged in the October 1977 kidnapping and sexual assault of Bev Servio of rural St. Cloud. Bartowsheski allegedly kidnapped Servio and her 9-month-old daughter. The woman said Bartowsheski threatened her with a knife and forced her to drive her 1973 International Scout to an area near the Thrifty Scot Motel in Waite Park. Bartowsheski stripped his clothes off below the waist and held Servio at knifepoint while she drove the car at his command. He then sexually assaulted her.

Servio was lucky; she was able to escape Bartowsheski by driving the car off the road, taking her infant daughter in her arms, and running to freedom. Bartowsheski fled the St. Cloud area, ending up in Colorado with another man, Boyd Tarwater. One night in December 1978, Bartowsheski and Tarwater were implicated in the stabbing death of an eight-year-old girl who lived at a ranch where the pair had been staying.

As with the Servio case in St. Cloud, Bartowsheski claimed no memory of what happened when he murdered Michelle Talbott. Stearns County investigators examined the details of the Talbott murder in an effort to determine if there was any link to the Reker murders that had occurred four years earlier. Michael Bartowsheski was 15 years old at the time of the Reker murders. His age and physical proximity fit the profile of their likely killer. Like Mary and Susanne Reker, Michelle Talbott had been stabbed in the chest, but she was also stabbed in the neck and head–key differences between the crimes.

Bartowsheski insisted he had nothing to do with the Reker slayings. He claimed he had little recollection of his actions in the Talbott and Servio cases because he was extremely drunk when he committed those crimes. He reasoned that in 1974, at the time of the Reker murders, he was 15 years old and didn't start drinking alcohol until at least one year after those murders. He claims to have taken and passed a lie detector test in the case, although that is an assertion Stearns County investigators declined to confirm or deny.

As of the third anniversary of the stabbing deaths in September 1977, Sheriff Jim Ellering announced new information had come forward in the case. Although he declined to specify the nature of that information, he expressed optimism the case could still be solved. Others were more doubtful, saying the lack of physical evidence in the case meant the only hope of solving the case would be through a confession.

Sheriff Ellering announced yet again in December 1978 his department had received new information in the Reker slayings. Although he was not sure how significant the information would turn out to be, he declared his office continued to utilize all resources and efforts to solve the murders.

"A considerable number of interviews and re-interviews in the community, outside the community, throughout the state and out of the state as well, have been conducted by elements of the investigation team," Ellering wrote in a prepared news release. "We have requested a number of individuals to submit to polygraph examinations and most of them have willingly agreed and have taken the same. Some have declined or refused. We have cleared or dismissed a number of individuals who previously attracted our attention through the course of our investigation."[23]

Waite Park police chief Charlie Grafft challenged Sheriff Jim Ellering in the fall 1978 Stearns County Sheriff race. The election was a rematch of the 1974 election, which Ellering won by a thin margin just a few weeks after the Reker sisters' bodies were discovered at the quarry. Just prior to the 1978 election, rumors swirled that Sheriff Ellering was about to announce a major break in the Reker case and it was all but solved. Charlie Grafft ultimately won the election for Stearns County Sheriff in November 1978, and took office in January 1979.

In February 1979, Rita Reker's work with the families of other murdered children inspired her to support the proposed formation of a major crime unit involving detectives from multiple investigative agencies. In her conversations with other families she learned coordination between multiple investigative agencies was paramount to solving crimes. St. Cloud police chief Elwood Bissett formerly proposed a special team of investigators from Stearns, Benton, and Sherburne counties, as well as the St. Cloud police department.

Benton and Sherburne counties had already approved the effort, and approval by Stearns County and the St. Cloud Police Department would soon follow. Each agency would assign one officer to the team, whose members would be special deputies with arrest powers in all three counties. "I think it's a long overdue unit that will really work well," Bissett said. "We've been doing it for years but without official sanction."[24]

By the time the Reker investigation crossed the 5-year anniversary in September 1979, it was competing for investigative resources with the more recent December 1978 murders of Alice Huling and three of her children. Sheriff Grafft met with Fred and Rita Reker just before the anniversary and said his office was still actively investigating the case. "Whenever we get a chance, we'll be working but again, we're kind of hamstrung because of the shortage of help," Grafft said.[25]

He added that the Huling case had taken resources away from the Reker investigation. "They're both number one (priority) but we're looking at the freshest one first," Grafft said, downplaying public speculation about the murder cases being connected. "No connection at all unless something would come way out of left field."[26]

As the 10th anniversary of the murders approached in fall 1984, after all the public speculation about personalities and politics getting in the way of justice and interfering with the investigation, after all the uncertainty swirling about the original lead investigator, Lawrence Brownie Kritzeck, Reker investigators were about to reveal the discovery of new information–information that had been locked away in a drawer, unknown for nearly 10 years.

When Lawrence Brownie Kritzeck died in May 1983, he had still been working out of the Stearns County Attorney's Office. He hadn't been investigating the Reker case for several years at that point. About a year after his death, his old desk was finally cleaned out, and in his desk was found a mysterious pair of glasses and files filled with information and evidence from the Reker investigation. Investigators didn't know why Kritzeck kept the files, but speculated perhaps he thought he was close to solving the case.

Soon after the discovery, in August 1984, Tri-County Crime Stoppers released a description of the men's glasses, which investigators believed were connected to the murders. The gold-colored, metal-framed glasses were manufactured in West Germany and resembled a style that was popular in the early 1970's. The wide frames indicated the owner had a broad face, and the prescription was for someone who would have been nearsighted.

In 1987 the FBI created a profile of the likely murderer of the Reker Sisters. The profile suggested the killer was about Mary's age–a teenager. The type of weapon used–a small, double-edged knife, and other information about the crime led them to the conclusion the killer was young.

"If that's true, I feel it must have been more than one person," Rita Reker reasoned. "How could a 15 or 16 year old have done that alone? And if it was young people, how could it have been kept a secret all these years? The biggest mystery to me is how it could have been kept quiet for such a long time."[27]

By the fall of 1989, 15 years had passed since the girls' murders. Although investigators had many suspects over that time there had never been an arrest in the case. Throughout their ordeal the Rekers had never given up hope, but they acknowledged finding answers after so much time had passed would be challenging. Sheriff Charlie Grafft said investigators had one main suspect in mind at the 15th anniversary. At that time, the 1974 murders of Mary and Susanne Reker had been the biggest mystery in the St. Cloud and Stearns County area for years. But then something happened just a few miles from St.

Cloud to change all of that–a masked stranger kidnapped 11-year-old Jacob Wetterling at gunpoint. The abduction occurred on a quiet, dark, dead-end road just south of St. Joseph. News of the Wetterling abduction rapidly grew throughout the state, then the Midwest, then across all of America and beyond. The Wetterling case commanded the full attention of the Stearns County Sheriff's Department for years to come.

Despite the public focus of attention on the disappearance of Jacob Wetterling, Stearns County investigators continued pursuing answers in the Reker double murder case. Some leads in the Reker case actually resulted from publicity about the Wetterling abduction. In one example, a man came forward to tell investigators his former brother-in-law had suggested to his then-wife that he might have killed the Reker girls. The man lived in Belgrade, but had several relatives living in the Luxemburg area. Another unusual coincidence came up while officials investigated this man. A neighbor of the Rekers had their home reroofed a few weeks prior to the murder of the Reker sisters. It turns out the man who had allegedly told his wife he killed the girls was working on that roofing crew in the summer of 1974. If indeed he was working on the neighbor's roof, it could explain how he came to know Mary.

In June 1990, Sheriff Grafft announced that a new suspect in the Reker killings had emerged. Ironically, the publicity surrounding the Wetterling case is what prompted someone to come forward with information. The tip, which was received by telephone, suggested a former St. Cloud resident who was Mary's age at the time of the girls' murders should be looked at as a suspect. Neither Grafft nor assistant sheriff Jim Kostreba offered much in the way of details about their new suspect, but they did confirm the man was in his 30's and lived and worked in Minnesota. Investigators were piecing together whether or not the suspect knew Mary Reker.

Simultaneous to announcing the new suspect in the Reker case, Sheriff Grafft announced he would soon be retiring from his post as sheriff, a position he had held for nearly 12 years. Grafft cited his frustration of the unsolved Wetterling case as a primary factor in his decision to retire. Grafft retired at the end of 1990 and was replaced as Stearns County Sheriff by Jim Kostreba.

One of Sheriff Kostreba's first actions to refresh the Reker murder investigation was to enlist assistance from the BCA cold case team. The BCA spent months reviewing the case files. They organized an index of all the names that had come up over the course of the investigation. They even reviewed the roster of all the people who had attended the girls' funeral, looking for clues about their possible killer. Investigators developed a detailed timeline of the girls last few days and all their activities.

A lawsuit alleging sexual abuse of children was filed in 1993 against Rev. Richard Eckroth, a monk living at St. John's Abbey in nearby Collegeville. The lawsuit accused Eckroth of sexually assaulting multiple children at a monastery-owned cabin near Cass Lake. Hundreds of children had gone to the cabin for weekend getaways between 1972 and 1976. The trips typically included six or seven children, sometimes including Mary and Susanne Reker. After their first trip, the girls returned home and said they had a lot of fun. After the second trip, they didn't talk much about it.

"I thought they didn't have any fun and they just seemed so relieved to be home," Rita Reker recalled. She said Mary, who was 13 years old at the time, told her mother she had refused to go into a sauna with Eckroth and other children.

Abbey spokesperson John Klassen said Eckroth denied the allegations of sexual abuse and said he had no involvement in the Reker murders. Eckroth took and presumably passed a polygraph test in the murder case.

By the fall of 1994 another five years had gone by with no answers in either the Reker murder case or the Wetterling abduction. Although there had been little progress made public during the preceding years, the Rekers felt that significant work had been done behind the scenes in terms of clearing people who had not been cleared before. That list included several friends and acquaintances. Although those people had never been considered serious suspects in the case, their inclusion as possible suspects had been painful for the family to endure.

"In the last five years they've done a lot of work on our case. For me, it has settled a lot personally," Rita Reker said, in expressing the family's relief. "Questions were answered for us that had not been answered 15 years before."[28] Besides clearing a number of people in the case, the Rekers were allowed to see Mary's clothing for the first time, and that was important to them.

Sheriff Kostreba revealed investigators had about 10 suspects in the Reker murders. All of them had "qualities or circumstances" that put them on the suspect list, but in all cases investigators lacked the evidence necessary to make an arrest or institute grand jury proceedings. Although Kostreba did not name them publicly, he referred to similar crimes committed by Herb Notch and Michael Bartowsheski shortly after the Reker murders as examples of suspects in the unsolved case. Interestingly though, he indicated neither man was a top suspect in the Reker investigation.

Kostreba added that the BCA crime lab was utilizing new technology to determine if the killer left his DNA on the clothing of Mary or Susanne. Testing would be an ongoing process because advancements in DNA technology were continually evolving. When asked about the early murder investigation, Kostreba acknowledged it wasn't handled well but said it was difficult to say how much impact that had on the inability to solve the case. The nearly four weeks which passed from the time the girls went missing until the day their bodies were discovered precluded investigators from gathering solid physical evidence.

Suspicions about Rev. Richard Eckroth's possible involvement in the Reker murders resurfaced in May 2002. Sheriff Jim Kostreba announced plans to interview Eckroth again. The Rekers were skeptical about the resurgence of interest in Rev. Eckroth.

"It was just more suspect, the fact our kids had been to the cabin. We have no evidence whatsoever to connect him to our girls' murders," Rita Reker said. "And murder cases are based on evidence."[29]

In 2002, Sheriff Jim Kostreba again referenced the similar crimes committed by Herb Notch and Michael Bartowsheski, and once again said neither Notch nor Bartowsheski was an 'active' suspect in the Reker murder. Kostreba retired as Stearns County Sheriff in 2003, and long-time deputy John Sanner was elected to the post, taking over the reins of the investigation. Along with the change in administration came a reprise of former suspects back to the forefront of the investigation.

As the 30th anniversary of the Reker murders approached in the fall of 2004, Rita Reker attended the National Conference of Parents of Murdered Children and learned about the Vidocq Society–a members-only club made up of 150 experts, including professional FBI profilers, homicide investigators, scientists, psychologists, prosecutors, and coroners. The organization met monthly to review cold murder cases. Rita asked Sheriff John Sanner for his support in requesting that the Vidocq Society review her daughters' case. He agreed. Rita then penned a letter to the Philadelphia-based Vidocq Society and asked them to hear the case.

While waiting for a response from the Vidocq Society, investigators continued to work any and all angles on the case. On September 2, 2004, local radio stations played a song Rita had written about Mary and Susanne. Musician friends of the family recorded the song.

"There have to be people in this area who know, and all we need is for that person to call," Rita Reker pleaded. "It doesn't count unless he tells someone."[30]

"We hope it will ignite a spark of remorse in someone," Sanner said, in agreeing with Rita. "To get someone to come in and talk about something they haven't talked about for years."[31]

Asked about problems with the early investigation and whether the case had been bungled from the start, Sanner declined to elaborate. "Some of the obvious frustrations of working a cold case are playing the hand you're dealt," he said. "Investigative techniques that are routine today were not even considered 30 years ago." Sanner encouraged people with information to contact investigators. "I've always thought that this was a very solvable case. Please call. Let us make the determination (of whether information is important)."[32]

The Vidocq Society agreed to honor Rita Reker's request to review her daughters' murder case. Lead investigator Timothy DesMarais, along with KARE 11 reporter Rick Kupchella and a cameraman, traveled to Philadelphia for the May 19, 2005 meeting. By sheer coincidence, the meeting was on Mary Reker's birthday. Stearns County was said to have presented the Vidocq Society with case information about just two suspects–Herb Notch and Michael Bartowsheski. The group did not provide the Stearns County Sheriff Department with a written report of its findings, but did advise investigators they were on the right track with their investigation, an apparent endorsement of the suspects they had in mind.

The Vidocq Society read police reports, reviewed photographs, and asked questions of DesMarais in an effort to help provide a path for Stearns County investigators to find a killer. "In this case I believe the perpetrator made some mistakes," said Vidocq Society co-founder Richard Walter. "And my advice to them (investigators) is to capitalize on those mistakes."[33]

Meanwhile, the Rekers were very grateful the Vidocq Society had heard their case, and they reiterated what they had been saying for years–that someone probably knew what happened to their daughters. "We're very fortunate that they heard our case," Rita said. "It's another set of eyes and ears. We have so many unanswered questions."[34]

Media reports of the Vidocq Society's involvement in the Reker case prompted about 20 fresh leads in the case. The leads referenced individuals who had been in the focus of the investigation for years and did not identify any new suspects. Sheriff Sanner acknowledged the new attention to the case had reinvigorated the investigation. "A lot of it comes from the investigators themselves," Sanner said. "And more from the information we receive generates more interest in the case."[35]

In October 2005, Sheriff Sanner announced Reker case investigators were seeking George H. Beilke to determine if he had information relevant to the murders. Beilke was on Stearns County's Most Wanted list and had a pair of outstanding felony arrest warrants for receiving stolen property and escaping custody, but Sanner said Beilke was not considered a suspect in the Reker case. Beilke's whereabouts were not known exactly, but Stearns County investigators thought he was near one of two places–Willmar in Kandiyohi County, or Floodwood near Duluth.

Sanner declined to specify why Beilke had suddenly come to investigators' attention, but did acknowledge he was being sought for information he might have about a possible suspect in the case. Given that Reker investigators had recently directed their attention to Herb Notch as a suspect, it's likely they were seeking Beilke in connection with information he may have had about Notch. "We do need to try to locate him now," Sanner said of Beilke.[36]

Beilke lived in the St. Cloud area and was 17 years old at the time of the Reker murders. According to Sanner, he was questioned in the early stages of the investigation. He was not a close friend or boyfriend of either Mary or Susanne, although Mary might have been familiar with him given their proximity in age.

Beilke turned himself in to Kandiyohi authorities in mid-January 2006. He was questioned by Reker investigators but it was determined he did not have additional information about the case or suspects. "What he said has no impact on the investigation one way or the other," Sheriff Sanner said.

Following feedback from the Vidocq Society, Stearns County investigators submitted clothing worn by Mary and Susanne Reker to the BCA laboratory for DNA analysis. The goal was to compare DNA from the clothing to known suspects. Investigators hoped some of the blood found on Mary's sweater belonged to someone other than her.

DesMarais explained investigators were hopeful that Mary's body, which had been relatively well preserved, would provide clues to her killer's identity. "That was probably something that worked to our advantage because it was cold water, so Mary's body was more intact than Susanne's body was," he said. "There was more information available there."[37]

The lab results were revealed to be inconclusive in late January 2006. Although Sanner was disappointed with the results, he said investigators would not be deterred and would continue to search for answers in the Reker girls' murder case. "This will not deter us from exploring other avenues," Sanner declared.[38] He suggested investigators would be looking at other physical evidence to determine if DNA samples could be recovered.

BCA agent Ken McDonald focused his efforts on the Reker case by studying the life of Mary and Susanne. He concurred with early investigators' theory that whoever killed the girls knew Mary. "She was somewhat troubled," McDonald said of Mary. "Prior to Mary and Susanne's disappearing, she had concerns. She wanted to speak to a teacher about some problems, but didn't have a full chance of doing that. And she expressed in her diary some concerns that if anything would happen to her, you 'find the person that did this.'"[39]

Fred Reker died in 2013 at the age of 84. He had spent nearly half of his life searching and praying for answers to the question of who was responsible for murdering his beloved daughters.

WJON, a news radio station in St. Cloud, ran an aggressive story about the Reker case in August 2016. Dan Debaun's story suggested Stearns County investigators were on the verge of solving the Reker case. The WJON story indicated the case was just a few witness accounts from resolution. "Somebody knows something that they're either hiding on purpose or are just afraid to say what they knew at the time," said Stearns County Chief Deputy Bruce Bechtold. "We'd like to know what happened from the time they left to go to the store until they were murdered. If someone saw certain people together, and I can't say who those certain people would be, but we have witnesses who saw the girls at the store and we have witnesses who saw them in different places."[40]

"There are people out there who have never come forward that know what happened, know who did it and are not telling what they know," added Rita Reker. "People who have never come forward before."[41] Rita told WJON she believed that the girls' killer had an accomplice. Bechtold offered no opinion on the matter, but declined to rule it out.

In September 2016, just days after the 42nd anniversary of the Reker murders, KMSP TV produced a remarkable 10-minute news story centered around the strong circumstantial evidence linking the 1976 Dairy Bar stabbing case with the 1974 Reker murders. In doing so, the piece painted Herb Notch as the chief suspect in the murders. The story earned the station a regional daytime Emmy award for crime reporting.

Stearns County Chief Deputy Bruce Bechtold declined to say whether Notch was a top suspect in the Reker case. "I can agree with you that there are similarities in both cases," Bechtold said.[42]

KMSP's story presented a detailed history of other crimes Herb Notch had been accused of since serving 10 years in prison (of his 40-year sentence) for the Dukowitz stabbing. Notch was released from prison in 1988. Soon after, a former girlfriend accused Notch of breaking into her home and raping her at knifepoint. He was convicted of false imprisonment and burglary but was acquitted on the charge of sexual assault.

In 1992, another woman accused Notch of driving her out to a remote location, tying her wrists together with rope, striking her, and then assaulting her in the back of his truck. The woman reported that Notch said to her, "Shut up or I'll kill ya'." That incident landed Notch on the State of Minnesota's Most Wanted Fugitives list. The Minnesota Task Force began looking for Notch, a man who did not want to be found. Notch vowed that he would not be taken alive and law enforcement considered him to be armed and dangerous. They finally found Notch in Phoenix, Arizona more than a year later. He had been living there under the name of his brother, Steve Notch, who was serving prison time for murdering a roommate. Herb Notch was acquitted on the rape charges.

Retired BCA investigator Dennis Sigafoos at one time had been working as an active investigator on the Reker case. He told KMSP he had not been aware of the Dairy Bar case while he was investigating the Reker murders. "I would have been all over Notch and anybody that he knew and everybody that he knew," Sigafoos said, speaking of the similarities between the cases. "When you say about, you know, the cutting of the bra and the sweater up the front, that's a pretty big coincidence."[43]

In September 2016, Rita Reker approached author Robert, who had assisted KMSP with some of the research for their big story, about writing a book about the Reker Murders. The book, "Two Sisters Missing–The 1974 Reker Murders," was released in March 2017. The book presented a history of the investigation, and offered a glimpse of what Mary and Susanne were like as people.

One topic that Dudley speculated about in the Reker case, something that had not been addressed by news media over the years, was motive. With little evidence to go on, finding and understanding the motive for the murders was essential to solving the case or identifying a likely suspect. Dudley noted three elements that stand out about crimes committed by the main suspect, Herb Notch. First, in nearly all the crimes Notch committed as a youth in the 1970's, he was seeking money. Second, his crimes almost always involved a knife. Finally, he always had at least one accomplice.

Within weeks of the book's release, Dudley received tips from several readers. One reader was a victim of one of Notch's 1976 purse snatch attacks. But the most significant tip came in April 2017, when a reader informed Dudley that Herb Notch was hospitalized in St. Cloud with terminal liver failure.

Dudley contacted Rita Reker and Stearns County about Notch's hospitalization. They were not aware of Notch's condition. Rita shared with Dudley that she had long hoped for a deathbed confession from Notch, but had never thought it possible that she would outlive him. Rita did arrange a meeting with Notch in the hospital and confronted him in his hospital room, but Notch refused to admit to killing Mary and Susanne. He did, however, tell her that he would be going to hell when he died. As far as Rita was concerned, that statement by Notch and the strong circumstantial evidence connecting him to the murders was confession enough. She was finally at peace knowing she had confronted the man who murdered her daughters on Labor Day 1974.

Herb Notch died on May 11, 2017. At the time of his death, Stearns County investigators were reengaged with the case, and had gone back to the beginning to see if any clues were missed.

The Labor Day 1974 murder of sisters Mary and Susanne Reker was one of the most horrific tragedies in the history of the State of Minnesota. While investigators believe Notch was responsible, the case remains open because it's likely another suspect was involved. If you or someone you know has information that may be relevant to the investigation, please contact the Stearns County Sheriff's Department at 320-259-3700.

Bibliography – Two Sisters Missing

Adcock, L. (20174, September 30). Reker Still Sees Girls Wave Goodby. *St. Paul Pioneer Press Dispatch* , pp. 1-2.

Ahlgrim, A. (1989, September 15). Letter To The Editor: Former Deputy Recalls Tragedy Of Reker Girls. *St. Cloud Times* , p. 6A.

Anderson, D. (1977, October 7). Discord Held Back Murder Probe. *Minneapolis Star* , pp. 1A, 8A.

Anderson, D. (1977, October 5). Doubts Delayed Probe Of Slayings–Murder Clues Erased By Time. *Minneapolis Star* , pp. 1A, 12A.

Anderson, D. (1977, September 22). Minneapolis Star. *Slain Girl Knew Death Near, Diary Hints* , pp. 1A, 8A.

Anderson, D. (1977, August 19). Search Reopened For Sisters' Killer. *The Minneapolis Star* , pp. 1A, 5A.

Anderson, D. (1977, September 1). Slain Girls' Final Hours Retraced. *Minneapolis Star* , pp. 1A, 4A.

Baillon, J. (2016, September 19). Reker Murders: Connection Or Coincidence. *KMSP Television* . Eden Prairie, MN.

Brown, C. (2002, May 9). Details Still Eerie 28 Years After Girls Were Slain. *Minneapolis Star Tribune* .

Daley, D. (1978, December 18). City Man Faces Murder Charges In Colorado. *St. Cloud Daily Times* , p. 37.

Daley, D. (1979, September 3). County Hasn't Written Off Reker Murders. *St. Cloud Daily Times*, p. 1.

Daley, D. (1978, October 25). Investigators Probe New Information In Reker Case. *St. Cloud Daily Times*, pp. 1,6.

Daley, D. (1978, October 4). Rematch Takes Center Stage – Close Race Seen For Stearns Sheriff Vote. *St. Cloud Daily Times*, pp. 1, 6.

Dalman, D. (2011, November 4). Reker Recounts Daughters' Murders. *St. Joseph Newsleader*, pp. 1, 4-5.

DeBaun, D. (2016, August 1). WJON Cold Cases: 1974 Reker Murders Still A Mystery. St. Cloud, MN.

Haukebo, K. (1989, August 27). Investigators Hope Girls' Killer Will Slip Up. *St. Cloud Times*, pp. 1A, 4A.

Haukebo, K. (1989, August 27). Note Haunts Friends, Family. *St. Cloud Times*, pp. 1A, 4A.

Kupchella, R. (2005, November 14). KARE 11 Investigates: Reker Case. MN.

Kupchella, R. (2005, May 29). Seeking A Killer – A Cold Case Gets New Life Part 1. *KARE 11 News Extra*.

Kupchella, R. (2005, May 29). Seeking A Killer – A Cold Case Gets New Life Part 2. *Kare 11 News Extra*.

Lewis, D. (1976, August 31). 2 Years Later, Parents Ask: 'Who Killed Them?'. *St. Paul Pioneer Press Dispatch*, pp. 17-18.

Louwagie, P. a. (2002, May 8). Priest Is Among Suspects in '74 Deaths. *Minneapolis Star Tribune*.

Mattson Halena, S. (1984, August 30). Parents Still Seek Girls' Murderer – Glasses Released As Possible Clue In 10-Year-Old Case. p. 1C.

Pearson, M. (1976, September 4). 2 Years Later: Reker Trail Remains Cold. *St. Cloud Daily Times*, p. 1.

Pearson, M. a. (1976, September 27). County Eyes Charges In Stabbing Incident. *St. Cloud Daily Times*, p. 1.

Pearson, M. (1977, September 3). Reker Slayings Unsolved But Not Forgotten. *St. Cloud Daily Times*, pp. 1-2.

Pearson, M. (1977, August 8). Sheriff Takes Control of Reker Killings Probe. *St. Cloud Daily Times*, p. 1.

People v. Bartowsheski, 661 P.2d 234 (1983) (Colorado April 18, 1983).

Peters, Dave. (1975, September 29). Year Sheds Little Light On Murders – Memories Thick, But Clues Sparts. *St. Cloud Daily Times* , pp. 1-2.

Petrie, K. (2005, July 11). Investigators, Rekers Maintain Fight For Answers. *St. Cloud Times* , pp. 1A, 7A.

Petrie, K. (2006, January 19). Man Unable To Add Insight On Reker Deaths. *St. Cloud Times* , p. 1B.

Petrie, K. (2006, January 27). Rekers' Clothes Provide No Clues. *St. Cloud Times* , p. 1A.

Petrie, K. (2005, October 11). Stearns Seeks Man For Information On 1974 Reker Slayings. *St. Cloud Times* , p. 1A.

Reker, F. a. (1997, August 6). Letter To The Editor: Acknowledge City's Other Murders. *St. Cloud Times* , p. 6A.

Reker, F. a. (1998, November 28). Letter To The Editor: Convene Grand Jury On Unsolved Murderes. *St. Cloud Times* , p. 14A.

Reker, F. a. (1982, September 8). Letter To The Editor: Grafft Has Done All He Could. *St. Cloud Times* , p. 4A.

Reker, F. F. (1974, October 15). Letter To The Editor: Response Unbelievable. *St. Cloud Daily Times* , p. 6.

St. Cloud Daily Times Staff 09/14/1974. (1974, September 14). Area Man Dies In One Car Mishap. *St. Cloud Daily Times* .

St. Cloud Daily Times Staff 10/08/1974. (1974, October 8). Investigation Into Murder Of Reker Girls Takes Time. *St. Cloud Daily Times* , p. 15.

St. Cloud Daily Times Staff 12/20/1977. (1977, December 20). Sheriff Says New Information Received In Murder Probe. *St. Cloud Daily Times* .

St. Cloud Daily Times Staff, 10/01/74. (1974, October 1). Search Begins For Reker Killer; Reward Fund Set. *St. Cloud Daily Times* , pp. 1-2.

St. Cloud Daily Times Staff, 10/02/76. (1976, October 2). Stabbing Victim Remains In Hospital. *St. Cloud Daily Times* , p. 1.

St. Cloud Daily Times Staff, 10/03/74. (1974, October 3). Family, Friends Join To Bury Reker Girls. *St. Cloud Daily Times* , p. 1.

St. Cloud Daily Times Staff, 10/07/77. (1977, October 7). Reker Investigation Defended. *St. Cloud Daily Times* , p. 1.

St. Cloud Daily Times Staff, 10/08/76. (1976, October 8). Kidnap Suspect Tested For Role In Reker Killings. *St. Cloud Daily Times* , p. 1.

St. Cloud Daily Times Staff, 10/11/77. (1977, October 11). Ellering Calls Reker Press Coverage 'Hindrance'. *St. Cloud Daily Times*, p. 13.

St. Cloud Daily Times Staff, 9/04/74. (1974, September 4). Police Search For Two Missing St. Cloud Girls. *St. Cloud Daily Times*, p. 1.

St. Cloud Daily Times Staff, 9/24/74. (1974, September 24). Helicopters, Reward Added To Search For Reker Girls. *St. Cloud Daily Times*, p. 1.

St. Cloud Daily Times Staff, 9/27/76. (1976, September 27). Slain Girls' Father Comforts Clerk's Kin. *St. Cloud Daily Times*, p. 1.

St. Cloud Daily Times Staff, 9/30/74. (1974, September 30). Reker Girls Found Dead Near Quarry. *St. Cloud Daily Times*, pp. 1-2.

St. Cloud Daily Times, 10/04/74. (1974, October 4). Reker Reward Goal Set At $10,000. *St. Cloud Daily TImes*, p. 1.

St. Cloud Daily Times, 2/13/79. (1979, February 13). Mrs. Reker Urges Major Crime Unit. *St. Cloud Daily Times*, p. 3.

Unze, D. (1999, September 2). 25 Years Later, Rekers Continue To Wonder Who Killed Their Children – St. Cloud Couple Use Anniversary To Publicize Case. *St. Cloud Times*, pp. 1A, 7A.

Unze, D. (2004, September 2). Rekers Hope For Clues In Killings. *St. Cloud Times*, pp. 1A, 5A.

Unze, D. (2005, October 12). Sheriff: Beilke Isn't A Suspect. *St. Cloud Times*, p. 1B.

Welsh, J. (1994, September 9). Double Murder Still Baffles Family – Even After 20 Years, The Pain Is Still There. *St. Cloud Times*, p. 1A.

Chapter Three

The Postman

Victim: Ivend Holen

Date: May 13, 1976

Status: Unsolved

Location: Kimball

Author's Note: This chapter is condensed from Robert M. Dudley's book, *Tragedy on the Prairie—The Story of the 1976 Kimball Post Office Bomb.*

Ivend Holen, the assistant postmaster of the Kimball Post Office, reported to work bright and early on the morning of Thursday, May 13, 1976. He had just turned 60 years of age two days earlier, and his family had eaten the last of his birthday cake after supper the night before. Ivend was officially scheduled to start work at 7:00 a.m. daily, but it was customary for Holen and other Kimball post office employees to arrive early, at 6:30 a.m. Their goal in getting an early start was to get a jump on sorting the inbound mail that arrived overnight from the postal bulk station in Minneapolis.

Ray Covert was the driver of the first of two bulk mail delivery trucks that delivered mail daily from Minneapolis to Kimball. Covert's truck had three sacks of mail for Kimball, the last stop on his route that morning. He dropped them off in back of the building at 1:00 a.m. Since Kimball was the last stop on Covert's route, any and all mail dropped off there would be addressed to someone residing within the Kimball Post Office service area.

The lobby of the Kimball Post Office opened for business at 8:30 a.m. daily. Home delivery of personal mail, a luxury that most folks in other Minnesota cities took for granted, was not available in Kimball in 1976. City residents would instead filter into the post office throughout the day to pick up their daily mail. The lobby was usually the busiest during the first hour or so of opening, as many residents stopped in on their way to work.

Under normal circumstances, there would have been three additional post office employees accompanying Holen to sort through the sacks of mail that day. However, a recent strike by UPS workers led to a surge in the mailing of small packages through the U.S. Postal Service. The sudden influx of parcels resulted in a "clogging" of the mail processing service. The net effect was a disruption of mail processing that resulted in a reduction in packages coming in on the 1:00 a.m. truck from Minneapolis. Accordingly, Postmaster Clayton Linn altered the schedule for Thursday morning so that only Ivend Holen would be arriving early.

Ivend began the task of sorting the daily mail promptly upon his arrival. He apparently forgot to raise the American flag in front of the post office, a task normally performed by the first employee reporting to work each day. Ivend sorted letters and small packages for city residents into their respective post office boxes. He placed mail destined for the 300 postal patrons that lived north of Kimball onto a staging cart for Rural Route 1. Mail for customers that lived to the south of Kimball was put onto a staging cart for Rural Route 2.

The exact sequence of events that occurred as Ivend was sorting out the mail remains unclear, but it is believed that he came across a heavy bag of booklets destined for delivery to a local school north of town, and he tossed it on the Route 1 pile. It was 6:42 a.m., and Holen's seemingly innocuous toss of the mailbag would be the last bit of work that Ivend Holen would ever do.

The impact of that bag of books hitting up against another package was enough to jostle what was inside, triggering a powerful bomb that exploded with so much force that it thrust Ivend Holen across the floor and through the steel door at the back of the post office. A clock hanging on the wall of the Kimball Post Office recorded the exact time of the blast. The explosion riveted the clock's hands at 6:42 a.m., and the clock fell to the floor.

Twelve-year-old Paul Schoenfelder was across from the post office building delivering the early morning paper to the Knaus Sausage House when the bomb went off. Paul's older brother, fourteen-year-old

Joe, was much closer to the post office when the bomb exploded. He had just put the newspaper inside the handle of the post office's front door when the bomb went off. The blast launched Joe about twenty feet into the street, and he narrowly escaped serious injury.

Jan Arntsen, who owned the boutique shop next door to the post office, was in her store when the explosion occurred. She and her husband, a Kimball volunteer firefighter, heard the explosion and went to investigate immediately. They were the first to find a badly injured Ivend Holen barely clinging to life. Holen's injuries were massive. He had cuts and severe burns across his face, hands, and legs. Some of his clothes were still on fire as his body was dragged away from the post office building. One foot and part of a leg had been severed from his body.

An ambulance arrived minutes later and Holen was rushed to the hospital in St. Cloud. He was near death when the paramedics arrived, and he died in route.

Meanwhile, Kimball postmaster Clayton Linn woke up usual at 6:45 a.m. on that morning. He was getting himself dressed for work when the Kimball town fire chief called to notify Linn that there had been an explosion at the post office, and he should get to work as soon as possible. Linn arrived at the post office and found a scene of carnage and destruction. Sheriff's deputies would not allow Linn to enter the post office building because they were afraid there could be another bomb among the packages.

Alton "Stretch" Greeley, the substitute postal carrier who would be delivering the daily mail to the 300 residents of Kimball's Rural Route 1 that day, was already in route to the post office when the bomb exploded. Greeley was just minutes away from being a victim himself.

Likewise, postal clerk Betsy Stelton was just about to report for duty at the Kimball Post Office when the bomb exploded. She would later say that there was always an element of fear associated with working as a postal clerk. She recalled a time that a packaged arrived and had the word "Balm" scribed across the outside of the package. Postal inspectors were called to investigate after workers realized the sender might have been a bad speller. After a brief investigation the package was determined to contain cow udder balm.

A slow but steady drizzle of rain added emphasis to the collective somber that swept over the town of Kimball as the death of its beloved Ivend Holen was absorbed. A gathering of forty or so residents looked on in shock as investigators sifted through fragments of metal and glass strewn about piles of wet and fire-damaged letters and packages.

"Mr. Holen was a real good guy," said Clarence Kamber. Kamber, like Holen, was a farmer and lived a few miles from town. "When you went in to see him at the post office, he always had a smile, he was always jolly and was always kidding. And this town is really going to miss him."[44]

The Kimball Post Office bomb of 1976 was not the first explosion to rock the otherwise peaceful prairie town. In fact, the bomb was not even the first explosion to occur at the very site where the post office had been built in 1973. The site was formerly the home of a creamery building that was destroyed by a gas boiler explosion on Christmas Eve 1954.

For many Kimball residents the shock of the post office bomb rekindled memories of uneasiness following the creamery explosion. But this time things were different, for Kimball had now lost one of its finest human beings. Ivend Holen was a well-liked man by all who knew him, and he was someone who always seemed to make fast friends with new people.

While everyone in Kimball was speculating about who may have been the intended target of the bomb, it was universally accepted that Ivend Holen could not have been the target. He was liked by everyone and held no enemies.

"Everyone knew Holen," said Kimball Bank President Ellwood Erickson, "and he was certainly not the person anyone would try to harm. Kimball was at first mostly in a state of shock and then after the shock wore off we wondered what motive is behind all this. We're kind of running scared right now."[45]

Born in Cherry Hill, Canada, Ivend Holen was raised in nearby Starbuck. He graduated from high school there and later served in World War II. He was father to five children of his own from his first marriage. His first wife died of a hemorrhage. He was married to his second wife, Irene, in 1963. Irene brought five children of her own into the union with Ivend.

Holen was a key part of the Kimball community. He had lived in the area for the last fourteen years, after moving there in 1962 from Minneapolis, where he also worked as a postal worker. He commuted from Kimball to the Minneapolis area for years before finally transferring to a lower paying job as a post office clerk in Kimball in 1969. He was later promoted to assistant postmaster at the Kimball Post Office.

Ivend was actively involved in his family's church, St. John's Lutheran Church. He served on the local school board, was a member of the American Legion Post in Kimball, as well as the Sons of Norway. He was also known for the significant amount of volunteer work he did for the young people in town.

The Kimball Post Office

Everyone who knew Ivend Holen was quick to point out that he always had a smile for everyone he came across. When children wrote letters to Santa Claus at Christmas time, it was Ivend Holen who would answer those letters, writing back to the children as if he were Santa himself.

Ivend and his large family lived on a modest forty-acre hobby farm about three miles south of Kimball. He was known for his gardening prowess and also as a beekeeper. He utilized his gardening experience and influence to assist the Kimball High School in building a greenhouse for its students to utilize. He wanted the younger generations to have the tools available to learn how to grow vegetables and flowers for themselves.

Some Kimball residents were in denial about the target of the bomb, suggesting that the package containing the bomb had been delivered to the post office by mistake. "It wasn't meant for Kimball," said city resident Dan Erger. "It was meant for someone else. I don't think it was meant for anyone here."[46]

Holen's coworkers were deeply affected by the sudden and senseless act that took him away from their team. "He was very gracious, very accommodating," postal clerk Betsy Stelton said of Holen. "He would always go out of his way to give people service. He loved life and he loved people. His death is a great shock to this community."[47]

Clayton Linn, the longtime postmaster of the Kimball Post Office, was set to retire in October 1976. He had recommended to his superiors that Ivend Holen take over his role as postmaster after Linn's impending retirement. He was as shocked and shaken as anyone about the blast that killed his friend and coworker.

"I think we're all going to be a little bit gun shy," Linn said of his fellow post office workers. "I wish we didn't have to be that way, and I hope it's not part of a pattern because we never dreamed it would happen here. The townspeople are shocked. Yes, I think that would be the best word."[48]

Tragedy or not, Clayton Linn was the postmaster of the Kimball Post Office, and he understood the loss of his friend could not deter him from carrying out his duties. He and Mabel went to work quickly to set up a temporary post office in a mobile trailer brought in from the Minnesota State Fairgrounds in St. Paul. The temporary post office was equipped with 140 post office box sorts, well short of the 240 boxes that were needed to properly service the Kimball community. Once the temporary post office was set up and ready to resume operations, Ivend Holen's coworkers observed a moment of silence in honor of his contributions to the post office and the Kimball community.

Stearns County Sheriff's Deputy Bob Kunkel was the first member of law enforcement to arrive at the scene of the Kimball Post Office bomb. Kunkel was also a part-time police officer on the staff of the Kimball Police Department. Upon his arrival, Kunkel found shattered glass had been sprinkled all over the sidewalk and part of the street in front of the post office. Debris had projected as far as 60 feet away from the building. Ivend Holen's blood could be seen on the bottom of the heavy metal door at the back of the post office.

The Kimball Fire Department was called upon to extinguish the small fires that lingered about the post office building after the bomb's blast. The water used to battle the fires complicated the investigation by damaging or moving evidence of the blast.

"Important evidence may have been destroyed by the blaze or by firemen putting out the blaze," Dave Madden, the Assistant Postal Inspector from St. Paul, advised. Nevertheless, he acknowledged that the firemen were just doing their jobs, and that the fire had to extinguished.[49]

Investigators from the U.S. Postal Inspector's Office, the FBI, and Stearns County descended upon Kimball within hours. By noon there were a dozen investigators on the scene. They roped off an area to keep onlookers away from the post office. Privately, investigators were concerned about the possibility that there may be another bomb among the remaining packages.

Dave Madden was one of the first Postal investigators to arrive in Kimball. He initially speculated the building's gas system had caused the explosion, but that possibility was quickly ruled out. Investigators understood very quickly that they had a legitimate bomb case on their hands. The Kimball Post Office was a crime scene.

Authorities began the tedious task of sifting through the debris of mail, searching for bomb components and any other clues they could identify. Magnets were used to separate metal fragments from other debris. Investigators searched for clues to identify the intended target of the bomb and the components used to make it. Ultimately, the goal of investigators was to identify the two most critical components of the crime—the sender, and the intended target.

"The location of the explosion is such we're reasonably sure he (Holen) pushed a cart in with a mail bag containing the explosive device," said Bill McClanahan, Chief Postal Inspector from the St. Paul district. "While he was sorting the mail the parcel exploded."[50]

Investigators sift through bomb debris. Photo courtesy of St. Cloud Daily Times

Investigators worked around the clock to sort through all the evidence. By 4:00 a.m. on Friday May 14th, they had completed their first sweep through the debris. McClanahan said they found enough components of the bomb package to reconstruct the bomb, but that the process would probably take several days or even weeks. It was quickly determined that Ivend Holen was not the intended target of the bomb, and that the bomb was not intended to detonate at the post office at all.

James Upton, the top investigator from the US Postal Service crime laboratory, was summoned to assist with the investigation. Upton had recently headed up a mail bomb investigation that led to the arrest of a man who mailed a bomb that killed a judge in Pasco, Washington. Upton's specialty was in the chemistry field. He had investigated more than 50 bombings over his career. His main mission in Kimball was to determine the type of device that had been used. Within hours of his arrival, it was clear to Upton that this particular investigation would not yield any quick and easy answers.

"We've got a championship jigsaw puzzle on our hands," Upton declared, as he directed the investigation from the remote command center that had been set up in the back of the Kimball City Hall.[51]

The collected fragments of the bomb were sent off to Washington, DC for laboratory analysis. Pieces of mail that survived the explosion were sent to St. Paul for further testing and inspection. Officials said that "everything loose" had been retained for further investigation. Investigators determined that the bomb was inside of a parcel package, and that the bomb was likely made up of some sort of smokeless explosive powder.

Investigators came to the preliminary determination that the bomb had been set off by some sort of timing device. That was a point of confusion for many, because it seemed that controlling such a bomb with a timer would be an unusual strategy given the uncertainty of the time that mail would be delivered to the intended target. Furthermore, there were no assurances that the package would remain unopened before the timer set off the bomb. Investigators quickly reversed their opinion and said the bomb was designed to explode upon opening of the package.

Within a couple days of the explosion, investigators determined that the bomb had been mailed from outside of Kimball and was probably intended for a patron living in Rural Route 1, north of Kimball. That delivery area included about 300 customers across nearly 50 square miles. Officials mailed notices to 3,500 people requesting their assistance and cooperation in providing leads to investigators.

Inspector Madden disclosed that the bomb was well constructed and probably contained a low-grade explosive, possibly a smokeless powder. Authorities were convinced that someone experienced in making bombs was responsible for the crime–this was not the work of an amateur.

On May 17, 1976 a reward of $3,000 was established for information leading to the arrest and conviction of the person or persons responsible for the bomb. Investigators quietly began searching for sources of several of the bomb's components, including a tackle box, putty, orange electrical wire, and a small but powerful 12-volt battery. The battery was considered somewhat rare due to its relative size and power. It was similar in size to a lantern battery, but at 12 volts, it was much more powerful than a 6-volt battery that was more consistent with the bomb's physical size.

Hardware store owners in the surrounding area confirmed that they were questioned specifically about sales of batteries and putty. "Yes, we were asked if we sold any putty and batteries to customers," said an unnamed Kimball area store employee. "We told them we did, but we couldn't remember to whom, since they were cash sales."[52]

One hardware store owner indicated that investigators were comparing retail price tags on his store's products to one they had apparently found on the battery that was used as the energy source to detonate the bomb.

"They (the inspectors) had a little (price) tag that they probably got from the post office," said the storeowner, who declined to allow his name to be published in newspaper accounts. "They matched it up with the tags on the batteries we sold, but the tags were different. The type of battery they were looking for is a rare type."[53]

Investigators were pursuing any and all angles in their efforts to identify potential suspects and possible targets of the bomb. They were looking for anyone who may have had a grudge held against them, whether that was from a family or neighborly dispute, a quarrel between businessmen, or some other motive that would have prompted someone to take such a violent and drastic step to retaliate. One possibility that investigators considered from the very beginning was the idea that a 'love triangle' may have been at the root of the bomb.

"Eight out of ten mail bombings can eventually be traced to a 'love triangle'. I don't mean to imply that is what we are looking for or what we suspect in this case," said Dave Madden. "But in the last ten years, the cases of this type I can remember occurring throughout the country, eight of ten have been traced to some sort of 'love triangle' where someone is out to get someone."[54]

Madden was clear that investigators had not yet developed any specific clues as to a motive for the bomb, but that all possibilities were being looked at. That included looking at possible suspects that may be from outside the area. He indicated that this was a complex case that could take considerable time to solve because the bomb debris did not yield a lot of good clues.

Postal service investigators completed their interviews of postal patrons in the Kimball area within a week of the blast, and subsequently relocated their investigation headquarters from Kimball to St. Cloud. From then on, the investigative team worked out of a room at the St. Cloud Post Office.

At that point, a total of nearly 3,000 customers within the city of Kimball and in both of the rural routes had been interviewed. A survey conducted by the *St. Cloud Times* revealed that bomb investigators actually interviewed all Rural Route 1 patrons twice, and also interviewed Rural Route 2 customers, south of Kimball, once. That finding further reinforced the idea that investigators believed the bomb had been intended for someone in Rural Route 1.

Inspector Madden explained that investigators were going into more depth with persons they had already interviewed and who might have information about the bombing incident. He said that some of the best leads from the initial round of questioning did not prove to be productive, so they were doing another round of interviews to develop more leads. Among other factors, investigators sought to identify postal patrons who had been expecting to receive a package.

Postal investigators asked mail customers about people who may have had a problem with them or may have mailed a bomb with the intent to harm or kill them. Customers indicated that investigators' lines of questioning indicated they were seeking information about anyone who had severe marital problems.

With very few solid tips coming in about possible victims or targets, the U.S. Postal Service increased the reward in the Kimball Post Office bombing case from $3,000 to $10,000 on May 26, 1976. The increased reward was designed to motivate potential witnesses or persons with information to come forward. There was concern that the failed first attempt could mean that whoever had mailed the bomb would probably try again.

According to a June 16, 1976 article in the *Eden Valley Journal*, U.S. Postal Inspectors had interviewed two men from Eden Valley on Friday June 4th. Assistant Inspector Dave Madden said that the suspects were questioned in Eden Valley and St. Cloud. Madden indicated that the men were eliminated as possible suspects in the bombing case after their interrogation.

While investigators did not reveal exactly what led them to question the Eden Valley men, they did say the questioning had resulted from information that investigators had received. Neither man was charged or arrested, but Madden did indicate that investigators had obtained a court order to question the men. He said the men voluntarily complied with the interrogations.

By mid-June 1976, investigators had mailed out 60,000 flyers to Kimball area residents to announce the $10,000 reward and to give them an opportunity to submit tips anonymously. Recipients of the flyers included postal customers in Meeker, Wright, and Stearns counties, as well as select towns in other counties. Anonymous tipsters would still be eligible to receive reward money if their information led to the arrest and conviction of the person responsible for the bomb.

The tip forms were unique because they allowed informants to make up a secret six-digit code to identify the form as theirs without giving their name. Informants were directed to write the code on opposite corners of the form. They were to tear off one corner of the form, keep it, and mail the form to the postal inspectors. If someone was subsequently arrested due to an informant's tip, the informant could claim the reward money by turning in his or her secret code. According to Inspector Madden, the secret witness program generated a good amount of tips from the public, identifying several individuals as potential suspects as well as possible intended victims.

Investigators generally kept mum about the suspects and bomb targets they identified over the course of the investigation. Over the years they did reveal that they had identified as many as a handful of suspects and had executed about that many search warrants.

In early July 1976, investigators released a rarely seen composite sketch of a man they said might have information about the May 13, 1976, bombing of the Kimball Post Office. Inspectors were careful to specify that the man in the sketch was not being sought as either a suspect or an intended target of the bomb. They simply believed that the man might have information relevant to the investigation. The man was described as being 23-26 years old, standing 5' 8" tall, with a medium build and a light skin complexion. He had sandy colored hair with a slight reddish tint. His hair was not thick and appeared to be blow-combed down over his forehead. One of the man's more notable features was that his cheekbones stood out noticeably.

By February of 1977, nine months had passed without an arrest or a suspect being named in the Kimball Post Office bombing case. The investigative team had been reduced to two agents working out of the St. Paul office, having completely withdrawn from the St. Cloud area. Dave Madden said that the remaining investigators were going back

$10,000 REWARD!

FOR CONFIDENTIAL INFORMATION LEADING TO THE IDENTIFICATION AND CONVICTION OF THE PERSON WHO MAILED A PARCEL CONTAINING A BOMB TO KIMBALL, MINNESOTA.

On May 13, 1976, a bomb went off in the Kimball, Minnesota Post Office and killed a postal employee. It is indicated the intended victim of this explosion has a Kimball, Minnesota mailing address. You can now help in this investigation and qualify for a reward of up to ten thousand dollars by furnishing the information you have on a confidential basis without using your name. Fill in the information as shown below. Then make up a six digit number and write the same number in both the lower left hand and lower right hand corners of this page. Tear off the lower right hand corner containing the number and hold it for your reward claim. Mail the remaining portion to the Postal Inspector in Charge, P. O. Box 3558, St. Paul, MN 55165. You do not have to furnish your name unless you want to.

NAME AND ADDRESS OF THE PERSON YOU SUSPECT.

_____

_____

_____

NAME AND ADDRESS OF THE PERSON WHO MIGHT BE THE INTENDED VICTIM.

_____

_____

_____

Write in the following spaces the reasons you believe the above people may be involved in the mailing of this bomb parcel. Use extra pages if needed.

_____
_____
_____
_____
_____
_____
_____
_____
_____
_____

Secret Number   Secret Number

THIS DOCUMENT CIRCULATED AROUND THE KIMBALL AREA IN 1976.

Man sought for bomb case information

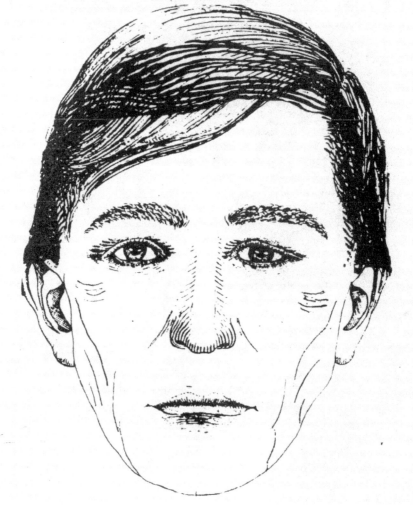

This sketch of a man wanted as a witness in the Kimball Bomb case appeared in the Tri-County News

through all the materials, re-examining everything again to see if investigators had missed any clues. He reported that the $10,000 reward that had been posted had failed to result in new developments in the case. Madden indicated that investigators had no plans to conduct further interviews with Kimball area residents.

"If we felt we could solve the case we would go out with another appeal for information," Madden said. "But we feel like we've probably gone out to people at Kimball enough. If we go too much more, we feel we will just get them down on us."[55]

As the one year anniversary of the Kimball bomb approached in May 1977, U.S. Postmaster General Benjamin F. Bailar announced that the reward for information leading to the arrest and conviction of those responsible for the Kimball bomb was being increased from $10,000 to $50,000.

Postal Inspector Madden announced that investigators had narrowed the number of possible intended targets to just a few people and the number of likely suspects to less than five. They believed someone in or near Kimball made the bomb and that the intended target of the bomb was definitely living in the Kimball postal delivery area. The decision to raise the reward was made to encourage someone who had information to come forward to authorities.

A full year into the bomb investigation, postal inspectors had conducted more than 3,000 interviews and logged 11,000 hours of time into the effort to find answers for Ivend Holen, his family, and the community of Kimball. Over the course of the investigation investigators developed a profile of the person likely to have made the bomb. They were also able to determine how the bomb had been constructed, although investigators declined to divulge details about the profile of the bomber or the makeup of the bomb.

Postal investigators employed a number of unusual methods in their efforts to elicit information from the public. One of the more bizarre tactics was an offer from a former private investigator and church minister. Kimball resident Harlow Robinson offered to speak with the person who mailed the bomb so he could persuade him against sending a second bomb. Robinson said that although no one admitted to sending the bomb, he did develop what he thought was a solid lead and he forwarded that lead to investigators. Robinson himself was investigated as a suspect in the case.

Don Deeble took over as the postmaster of the Kimball Post Office in March 1977. Deeble noted that the increased award amount had spurred further interest in the case. He said he believed that investigators were getting closer to solving the case. He also acknowledged that he experienced a certain level of uneasiness since he came to the Kimball Post Office.

"There's an awful lot of talk about the bombing in town," Deeble said. "When I dump parcels in the morning I don't throw them around too much."[56]

In May 1978, on the two-year anniversary of the Kimball Post Office bomb, Dave Madden issued a brief update on the investigation. In doing so, he noted that the combined number of hours spent investigating the case had swelled to 14,000.

"We have several suspects in mind," he said. "We know the details of how it was done. We need that one piece of information, that one key, to tie together the case."[57]

Hope of finally solving the Kimball bombing case was rekindled in 1996, when Unabomber suspect Ted Kaczynski was arrested. Kaczynski was eventually found to have mailed a total of sixteen bombs, killing three people. Don Deeble was still the postmaster at the time and he acknowledged that Kaczynski's arrest elevated his level of hope, and that many other Kimball residents felt a resurgence in belief that the Kimball case would finally be solved. Despite that hope, anniversary after anniversary continued to pass without progress in the case.

Perhaps investigators did have suspects and targets in mind, but if they did, word of their identities was a well-kept secret. The 1976 Kimball Post Office bombing case essentially went cold after two years of intense investigation. By 1996 the case was still classified as an open investigation, but according to the Postal Inspection Service it was not being actively investigated.

Henry DeFord was a bomb specialist for the Postal Inspection Service and led the investigation of the Kimball Post Office bomb until he was transferred to the Los Angeles office in 1981. In a 1996 interview, he indicated that he became convinced of who had made and mailed the bomb but was unable to prove it.

"As far as I'm concerned, it would pretty much take a confession because we exhausted all possibilities and there was no place to go," DeFord said. "Without a confession, I don't know what to do. As far as I'm concerned, I know who did it, but I was never able to prove it."[58]

Determining the type of explosive used in the bomb was a key objective of the investigation, but DeFord said that was something that early investigators were unable to achieve. He said that he personally ran tests with a variety of explosives and believes that a commonly used military explosive, Composite C-4, was used to make the bomb. The laboratory was unable to confirm that, however. Inspector DeFord left no doubt as to whether or not the bomb was on a timer or was set to go off when opened.

"It was a premature explosion, no question about that," DeFord said. "And I can tell you it was designed to go off when it was opened, it was not a timed device. It also could have gone off at any point along the delivery route if it was manhandled."[59]

Investigators did disclose the nature of the basic components of the bomb, and they did reveal that some of the bomb's components were purchased in St. Cloud. Based on investigators' keying their search on finding the source of the 12-volt battery, it's likely that the component traced to St. Cloud was the battery.

Whatever the explosive material was, it was likely molded into a block by mixing the material with a plastic binder, thereby producing a malleable, formable material. Composition C-4, popularly known as C-4, was a commonly used bomb making material in the Vietnam War. A typical C-4 brick measured eleven inches long, two inches wide, and one-and-a-half inches high. One or two such bricks, also known as Claymore mines, would have easily fit inside the metal fishing tackle box that the Kimball Post Office bomb was mailed in. Additionally, C-4 is very stable and resistant to physical shock. For example, the impact of a gun's bullet would not detonate a C-4 bomb. C-4 bricks are detonated only by a combination of heat and an electric shockwave fired from a power source such as a battery.

The Vietnam War ended on April 30, 1975—almost exactly one year before the Kimball bomb of May 13, 1976. Given that the person who sent the bomb was likely an experienced bomb-maker, and that the explosive material was likely to have been C-4, and with the recent return of soldiers from Vietnam, it's reasonable to conclude that the profile of the Kimball bomb maker would include veterans of the Vietnam War. Of particular interest to the profile would be soldiers who were demolition experts or otherwise had access to C-4 explosives in Vietnam.

After DeFord transferred out of St. Paul, the reigns of the investigation were turned over to Sterling McKusick. In 1996, at the twentieth anniversary of the Kimball Post Office bomb, McKusick confirmed that the bomb was inside a fishing tackle box and that batteries designed to detonate the bomb when it was opened were what triggered the bomb.

"You take your leads from who the device was intended for," said McKusick, "and we did not know that, and in that case it is difficult to determine what a motive might be. It is like you are investigating the world when you don't know who the intended victim was."[60]

"We had three to four leads that we considered good, and we conducted three to four major search warrants," McKusick said, "none of which gave us enough information that we could proceed with that individual."[61]

In the summer of 2012 as the case had just turned thirty-six years old, the Postal Inspector's office went public for the first time, giving detailed information about the fishing tackle box that was used to package the bomb. The green colored tackle box was a popular box that was sold in area hardware stores at the time of the Kimball bomb. The words "Old Pal" were etched onto the top and there was a picture of a fish on it. The all-metal tackle box measured thirteen inches long, six inches wide, and 4 inches deep. A photograph of a replica of the tackle box was published in various media outlets.

Virginia Lalley was the postal inspector who had been assigned the case of the Kimball bombing since 2006. She went public with information about the tackle box, hoping that someone would remember seeing a similar box in someone's garage, boat, or vehicle. Lalley suggested that perhaps early investigators' conclusion that the bomb was intended for someone living in Rural Route 1, north of Kimball, was premature. She indicated that the assumption may have limited the early investigation, but she did acknowledge that investigators investigated all possible targets in the Kimball postal service area.

Lalley said there was at least one person who had been a suspect in the case but had been cleared. Publicity about the tackle box led to a pair of tips being generated, but they were investigated and cleared. In 2012, the reward for information leading to the arrest and conviction of the person responsible for the Kimball Post Office was increased to $100,000.

The U.S. Postal Inspector's office in St. Paul has so many files on the Kimball bombing case that it has a special room, called 'The Kimball Room,' dedicated to the case. It is the only case investigated by the postal service that has such a room.

In 2012, postal inspectors had replica made of the tackle box that the Kimball Post Office bomb was mailed in. Details about the bomb were released publicly for the first time ever.

Speculation about possible targets of the bomb seemed to be plentiful, but investigators have released very little information in that regard. A group of amateur sleuths led by Dan Becker developed a few theories about possible targets. One such theory centered on former Stearns County Coroner R. Lawrence Thienes and his wife Suzanne. Thienes served as the county coroner from 1971 to 1992, overseeing several high profile murder cases, including those of Alice Huling and her children, the Reker sisters, and Ivend Holen. The Thienes divorced in 1980, with the court approving a $1 million divorce settlement payable to Suzanne. Stearns County court documents revealed that in January 1981, St. Cloud police informed Suzanne Thienes that they had obtained credible information that Dr. Thienes had put out a murder contract on Suzanne. Police said they were aware of the name and address of the alleged contract killer but had been unable to locate him. Dr. Thienes eventually faced a grand jury that heard testimony related to the alleged murder-for-hire scheme. The grand jury rejected the charges, but the case remained open for some time after.

Becker, who put together several mini-books of newspaper clippings, including one about the 1976 Kimball Post Office bomb, discovered that the Thienes owned a cabin near Pearl Lake in Rural Route 1 north of Kimball. The cabin was situated on a one-half acre parcel of land near the southeast portion of the lake. Becker theorized that since Dr. Thienes had allegedly attempted to have Suzanne murdered in 1981, perhaps he had unsuccessfully tried to murder her with the Kimball bomb.

In September 2014, the U.S. Postal Inspector's office was given information from an amateur sleuth and author Robert Dudley, about a man named Duane Hart. Hart had been investigated in 1990 for the kidnapping of Jacob Wetterling, and was ultimately convicted of sexual assault crimes against four juveniles in Kandiyohi County. A private investigator spent 60 hours in Hart's jail cell and kept a series of handwritten notes of the interviews. Dudley had come across a copy of the long forgotten notes, and noticed the reference to the Kimball Bomb. In a subsequent interview with Dudley, one of Hart's juvenile victims made unsolicited comments that Hart would often get drunk and brag about being investigated for the Kimball Post Office bomb. The man said that Hart had talked about it several times in the late 1980's, and said that Hart claimed he had gotten away with the crime.

Hart lived in Eden Valley when the bombing occurred in 1976. He had experience with bomb munitions as a 'tunnel rat' during the Vietnam War, including the use of C-4. In the series of interviews with the private investigator, Hart acknowledged that the FBI had searched his house after the bomb went off. He said that agents removed bomb-making materials from his Eden Valley home. Soon after, the person holding the deed to his home forced Hart to move out, and he relocated to Paynesville.

Dudley took interest in the Kimball Post Office bomb after reading the private investigator's notes. Dudley's books about the Jacob Wetterling kidnapping case referenced the notes as the 'Hart Notes.' In April 2016, Dudley reviewed all the newspaper archives about the Kimball Post Office bomb and noticed that one man's name kept coming up—Stearns County Sheriff deputy and part-time Kimball police officer, Robert Kunkel. Dudley contacted Kunkel to ask him about the case. In that interview, Kunkel acknowledged that he had once been considered a target of the Kimball Post Office bomb. Kunkel said that about three weeks before the blast, he and the Eden Valley police chief arrested a man who had an outstanding warrant for writing a bad check. A scuffle ensued, and after finally placing the suspect under arrest, the man told Kunkel that he was going to bomb him out of his house. That man's name was Duane Hart.[62]

The use of the tackle box to mail the bomb led to speculation locally that the intended target of the bomb was an avid fisherman. That information was never disclosed or suggested publicly by investigators, but sources said it was a common topic of conversation among locals at the time. Robert Kunkel, incidentally, was an avid fisherman. Furthermore, he lived on Beaver Lake north of Kimball, in the Rural Route 1 delivery area.

Kunkel was not aware that Duane Hart had been a 'tunnel rat' and demolition specialist in the Vietnam War. He was aware that Hart had been questioned in the Kimball bomb case because he had made a direct bomb threat to Kunkel. Kunkel's understanding was that Hart had been cleared because he did not appear to be aware of Kunkel's identity as the man who had arrested Hart in April 1976. However, the 1990 Hart notes include comments made by Hart referring to Kunkel by name.

Whether or not U.S. Postal investigators had ever considered the possible connection between Hart and Kunkel is unclear. What is clear, based on the admissions of both men, is that they were individually viewed as a potential suspect in the bombing, and a potential intended target of the bomb, respectively.

WCCO Television in Minneapolis ran a story about the Kimball Post Office bomb in May 2016, at the 40th anniversary of the tragedy. Liz Collin's story focused on the possible link between Duane Hart as a possible suspect and Robert Kunkel as a potential intended target of the bomb. The day after the story aired, a local FBI agent contacted Kunkel.

Robert Dudley wrote a short book about the case, *Tragedy on the Prairie—The Story of the 1976 Kimball Post Office Bomb*. Profits from the sale of the book were used to purchase a granite memorial to Ivend Holen. The granite memorial was dedicated at the Kimball Post Office in October 2016, and was mounted on a wall at the American Legion, where Ivend Holen had served as a member.

The 1976 Kimball Post Office bomb remains unsolved, and is under investigation by the U.S. Postal Inspector's Office. Postal authorities are asking anyone with information about the incident to contact the 24-hour National Law Enforcement Communication Center at 877-876-2455 or the postal inspector at 612-884-7880.

Bibliography – The Postman

Chicago Tribune Staff. (May, 20 1976). Fear Strikes Small Town After Mail-Bomb Death. *Chicago Tribune*, p. 1.

Coffman, J. (1976, May 15). Experts Say Kimball Bomb Was Well Made, But For Whom? *Minneapolis Tribune*, p. 16A.

Coffman, J. (1976, May 14). Explosive Device Sent in Mail Kills Kimball Post Clerk. *Minneapolis Tribune*, pp. 1A, 12A.

Collin, L. (2016, May 12). 40 Years Later, New Suspect Identified in Kimball Bombin. *WCCO.com*

Daley, D. (1981, June). Grand Jury Rejects Thienes Charges. *St. Cloud Times*, pp. 1A, 12A.

Eden Valley Journal Staff. (1976, June 16). Two Questioned by Postal Inspectors. *Eden Valley Journal*, p. 1.

Furst, R. (1976, May 14). Kimball Bombing is Probed. *Minneapolis Star*, pp. 1A, 6A.

Kunkel, R. (2016, March 31). (R. Dudley, Interviewer)

Monn, B. (1976, May 18). Battery Sale Clues Sought. *St. Cloud Daily Times*, p. 1A.

Monn, B. (1976, May 26). Bomb Officials to Move Here After Quizzes. *St. Cloud Daily Times*, p. 1B.

Monn, B. (1976, May 20). Kimball Settling Down in Bomb Aftermath. *St. Cloud Daily Times*, p. 13A.

Monn, B. (1976, May 19). 'Love Triangle' Blamed for Most Mail Bombings. *St. Cloud Daily Times*, p. 1A.

Monn, B. (1976, May 20). Memories, Jitters Run High Week After Kimball Blast. *St. Cloud Daily Times*, p. 1A.

Nistler, M. (2012, November 30). Green Tackle Box May Hold Key to Post Office Bombing, Murder. *St. Cloud Daily Times*, p. 1.

Pearson, M. (1976, May 14). Blast Victim's Funeral Draws 200. *St. Cloud Daily Times*, pp. 1A-2A.

Pearson, M. (1976, May 14). Expert Joins Hunt for Mail Blast Clue. *St. Cloud Daily Times*, pp. 1A-2A.

Pearson, M. (1976, May 16). Kimball Bombing Remains Unsolved. *St. Cloud Daily Times*, p. 1A.

Pearson, M. (1976, June 5). Officials: No Leads in Bomb Inquiry. *St. Cloud Daily Times*, p. 9A.

Petrie, K. (2007, June 6). Kimball Bomb Case Still Open - Relative Works to Keep Man's Death Under Investigation. *St, Cloud Times*, pp. 1A-2A.

St. Cloud Daily Times Staff. (1976, June 10). Bomb Investigators Revisiting Kimball Area Postal Patrons. *St. Cloud Daily Times*, p. 23A.

St. Cloud Daily Times Staff. (1976, June 15). Informant System Tried in Probe of Kimball Mail Bomb. *St. Cloud Daily Times*, p. 17A.

St. Cloud Daily Times Staff. (1977, May 2). Kimball Bomb Reward Increased. *St. Cloud Daily TImes*, p. 2A.

St. Cloud Daily Times Staff. (1976, June 18). Kimball Probe Reportedly Narrowing Down to Specifics. *St. Cloud Daily Times*, p. 1B.

St. Cloud Daily Times Staff. (1976, May 13). Mail Blast Kills Kimball Man. *St. Cloud Daily Times*, p. 1.

St. Cloud Daily Times Staff. (1976, May 15). Postal Patrons Probed for Bomb Clues. *St. Cloud Daily Times*, p. 1A.

St. Cloud Daily Times Staff. (1976, May 14). Postal Workers Stay Calm After Bombing. *St. Cloud Daily Times*, p. 1B.

St. Cloud Daily Times Staff. (1976, May 22). Reward Upped in Kimball Bombing. *St. Cloud Daily Times Staff*, p. 1A.

St. Cloud Daily Times Staff. (1976, May 13). Shocked Citizens Watch; Grieve Loss of Town Friend. *St. Cloud Daily Times*, pp. 1-2.

St. Cloud Daily Times Staff. (1976, May 13). Temporary Service Disruption Seen. *St. Cloud Daily Times*, p. 1.

St. Paul Dispatch Staff. (1976, May 14). Bomb Expert Probes Explosion. *St. Paul Dispatch News*, p. 1.

St. Paul Pioneer Press Staff. (1976, May 14). Bombing Fatality Probed. *St. Paul Pioneer Press*, pp. 1-2.

Tri County Times Staff. (1976, May 27). Search for Suspects in Bombing Continues. *Tri-County News*, p. 1.

Tri-County News Staff. (1976, July 1). Man Sought for Bomb Case Information. *Tri-County News*, p. 1.

Tri-County News Staff. (1976, May 20). Tension Follows Bombing at Kimball Post Office. *Tri-County News*, pp. 1, 20.

Wangstad, W. (1996, July 30). 20 Years Later, Kimball Parcel Blast Still Unsolved - Post Office Bomb That Killed One Destroyed a Vital Clue. *St. Paul Pioneer Press*, p. 1B.

Wangstad, W. (1976, May 17). Blast-Shocked Town Now Calm. *St. Paul Pioneer Press*, pp. 1-2.

Welsh, J. (1996, April 12). Unabomb Case Stirs Memories of Kimball Blast - Retired Workers Recall Explosion in Post Office That Killed Man in '76. *St. Cloud Times*, pp. 1A, 4A.

Wilkins, C. (1977, May 13). Fears Still Linger in Kimball One Year After Fatal Bombing. *St. Cloud Daily Times*, pp. 1A, 12A.

Wilkins, C. (1976, May 13). Friend's Slaying Stuns, Frightens Kimball People. *St. Cloud Daily Times*, pp. 1A-2A.

Chapter Four

Lone Survivor

Victims: The Huling Family-Alice, Susie, Wayne, Patti
Date: December 15, 1978
Status: Solved
Location: Rural St. Augusta Area

It was Thursday, December 14, 1978. That was a school night, and it was bedtime for eleven-year-old Billy Huling. As he walked through the kitchen he set his Corgi Juniors Batmobile toy on the kitchen counter, then made his way to the staircase that led to the upstairs bedrooms where he and his brother and two sisters slept.

Billy's parents had been divorced for five years. For the last three years he and his siblings had lived with their mother, Alice Huling, on a small farmstead seven miles south of St. Augusta in rural Stearns County. The Huling property was an 18-acre farm property in an isolated area, with access to the home gained only by a long, winding road. Billy's mother put a lot of effort into the home. She worked hard to clear the home site, cutting down dozens of trees by herself to make room for the house. She then arranged to have the white, two-story house she bought moved to the property from another site.

Alice Huling, 36, had been raised on a family farm near Dassel, in Meeker County. She worked as an offset printer operator at ABC printing in St. Cloud, where coworkers and supervisors alike touted her work ethic. Alice was a quiet, religious woman who mostly kept to herself. She was active local school groups as well as the Fairhaven Go-Getters 4-H Club. All her children were active members of the club and pitched in with raising chickens and rabbits at their small farm.

Susie, 16, was a junior in high school and was the oldest of the Huling children. She was a top-notch student with a very outgoing personality. Her teammates selected her as captain of the Kimball High School's gymnastics team. She also participated in track and choir, and worked part-time as a waitress at the Cozy Cafe in Kimball.

Wayne, 13, was the quietest of the Huling children. He was a good student and competed for the wrestling team at school in Kimball.

Patti, 12, was the youngest of the Huling children. She was a very friendly girl despite her shy nature. She participated in gymnastics at school.

At about 4:00 a.m. on Friday December 15, 1978, an unknown man entered through the unlocked back door of the Huling home. He stepped through the kitchen and living room, and then walked into Alice Huling's bedroom. Alice was awakened by the man's presence. She got up from her bed and confronted him. Words were exchanged, followed by a brief struggle. Then the man beat her and fired his 12-guage shotgun into Alice's hip. The bullet ricocheted into her stomach as the blast thrust Alice back onto her bed. The man fired again, this time directly into her stomach.

The loud noises coming from downstairs woke Billy Huling from his sleep, and he was frightened. The next thing he knew, the lights in the hallway outside the bedroom he shared with his brother Wayne were turned on. He could hear the man's footsteps as he slowly made his way to the upstairs bedrooms. He heard him order his sister Patti to get back into bed and cover herself up–telling her that everything would be OK.

The unfamiliar stranger then stepped into the doorway of Billy and Wayne's room. All Billy could see was his dark silhouette against the lit hallway.

Wayne, lying on his bed across from Billy, was also awake and could see the man standing in the doorway. "Who are you? What do you want?" Wayne asked the man.[63]

The stranger then walked over to Wayne's bed. He pulled the shotgun up from his side and aimed it at Wayne's head. He pulled the trigger. The blast killed Wayne instantly.

The killer then stepped into Susie's room. She screamed as he walked in. Without a word, the man promptly shot and killed her. Billy heard the distinctive sound of the shotgun's pump-action.

The killer then returned to Billy's room. By this time Billy had buried his head under his sleeping bag. Boom! The killer fired at Billy's head. His ears were ringing, but he was uninjured because he had wriggled his way down into his sleeping bag, and the bullet narrowly missed him. The stranger poked Billy in the chest to see if he was dead. Billy reacted to the poke, so the man fired at Billy's head a second time. Again, the shot missed the boy. But this time, Billy played dead, and the man left the room.

"Don't cry little girl, this won't hurt"[64] was the next sound Billy heard as the man talked to Patti in her bedroom across the hall.[65] Then he shot her in the head. Patti curled into a fetal position and died.

The killer then walked downstairs and returned to Alice's bedroom. Billy's mother was still alive, and had been trying to crawl to the aid of her children upstairs. The man shot her a third time, this time into her jaw at close range. That third blast killed Alice Huling.

Too scared to move and unsure of what to do, Billy laid still in bed. His entire family had been shot. After several minutes he peeked out from his sleeping bag and looked at his digital alarm clock. It was 4:15 a.m. Billy slowly rose to his feet and peeked out through his bedroom window. The only vehicle he could see was his mother's car. Billy went from room to room to check on his brother and sisters–all appeared to be dead. Then he quietly crawled down the stairs, unsure of whether the killer was still in the house. Billy finally made his way over to his mother's room to check on her. She was dead, too.

Billy walked to the kitchen to call for help but when he picked up the telephone up off the receiver there was no dial tone. The man who killed his family had cut the phone line. He went back up to his bedroom and got dressed, putting on a pair of jeans, shoes, and a winter coat. Next, Billy looked around for the family dog, Dusty. He walked into Patti's bedroom where he found the Chihuahua hiding under her bed, shivering in fear. He scooped Dusty up in his arms and took him outside to find help.

Billy walked toward the next-door neighbor's house, where family friend and Stearns County Sheriff Deputy John Dwyer lived. As he approached the Dwyer residence, the light of a full moon revealed fresh footprints in the snow on a path that led to the home. Fearing that whoever had killed his family might now be inside Dwyer's home, Billy decided not to stop at the house. He ran another mile up the road to the next house, the home of Steve Dirksen.

Billy pounded on the Dirksen's front door. Mr. Dirksen got up from his bed and opened the door to find the freezing young Billy, his dog clutched in his arms. Billy told Dirksen that a man had shot his family and asked him he would go check on them. Dirksen brought Billy inside the house and then called John Dwyer. He drove over to his house while Billy stayed back at the Dirksen residence.

Dwyer and Dirksen went to the Huling home to investigate together. They found Alice's lifeless body in her bedroom. She was on the bed dressed in a nightgown and housecoat, facing the foot of the bed. They returned to Dwyer's home to call the Stearns County Sheriff's Department. It was 5:00 a.m.

Stearns County deputy Jim Kostreba was the first on-duty officer to arrive at the Huling home. He and Dwyer entered the Huling home to investigate. From the strong odor of gunpowder that he picked up as soon as he stepped on the front porch, Kostreba knew something terrible had happened inside the house. He walked into Alice's bedroom and found her lying on her bed. Even with the powerful beam of his flashlight, he wasn't able to see the shotgun wound to her head until he got close up to her.

Kostreba then went upstairs to check on Alice's children. He requested Dwyer's assistance, but Dwyer declined. "I'm not going up there," said an upset Dwyer. "I don't want to see them like that. They were like brothers and sisters to me."[66]

Deputy Kostreba went on alone. As he walked up the stairs, cautious to the possibility that a killer might still be hiding out somewhere in the house, he could hear Susie Huling still gasping for air. But there was nothing he could do for her. One by one, Kostreba checked all the rooms. By the time he went back to Susie's room she had stopped breathing altogether. Part of her thumb and wrist had been shot off. A ruthless murderer had wiped out Billy Huling's entire family.

Stearns County Sheriff Jim Ellering immediately launched a full investigation into the Huling murders, while shock spread throughout the rural area south of St. Cloud. Bruises found on Alice's face and her broken collarbone and several broken ribs led to the theory that the killer had beaten her with the butt of the shotgun before shooting her.

Patti Wayne Susan

The Huling family home on the day of the murders. Photo Courtesy of St. Cloud Times.

Ellering formed a task force of Stearns County investigators, agents from the Minnesota Bureau of Criminal Apprehension (BCA), and Stearns County attorneys. The 20-member group assembled for a meeting in St. Cloud on Saturday, December 16, to review details of the case and develop a list of potential suspects. Waite Park Chief of Police Charlie Grafft, who had just defeated Sheriff Ellering in the November 1978 election for Stearns County Sheriff, was invited to participate as well.

Investigators questioned Billy Huling multiple times, but he was unable to offer many details about the man who killed his family. In one interview, he described the killer as tall and thin, but upon reviewing transcripts of the interview officials downplayed that description on the grounds the interviewer had asked Billy leading questions in an effort to draw out a description. Later, Billy told investigators that the killer appeared to be about 35 years old and was wearing a blue jean jacket and a stocking cap with a tassel. A sketch of the suspect was made, but because of the varying descriptions given by Billy, Stearns County authorities decided not to release the sketch. One interview session with Billy did produce some helpful information, however. Using details of what Billy said he saw as the killer stood in the doorway to his room, investigators were able to determine the man probably stood about 5' 7" tall.

"He could be blocking it out mentally," one investigator speculated. "Look what the kid went through. You'd probably want to forget about it too."[67]

Fr. Paul Folsom, the priest of St. Anne's Catholic Church in Kimball, to which Alice Huling and her children were new members, established a fund for Billy Huling's future education. Donations were initially scarce though, partly because many people considered Billy to be a suspect in the slayings. "I want to give to this fund but I sure don't want to find out later the kid is the one that did it," one person told the *St. Cloud Times*.[68]

People were skeptical that Billy could have survived not one, but two shotgun blasts directed at his head. The likelihood seemed remote, especially considering that all of Billy's siblings had been shot just once each. Investigators acknowledged that Billy's story seemed incredible, but they had all but ruled him out as a suspect almost immediately. They noted that when the killer fired at Billy he used slugs, similar to regular bullets with a small, narrow trajectory. The other Huling family members were shot with buckshot, which produces a wide-angle spray of projectiles. At close range, such ammunition is almost certain to strike its target. Additionally, the severe beating injuries suffered by his mother were such that it would have been nearly impossible for Billy to inflict them.

"We've not ruled anybody out yet but I just can't see Billy doing it from the evidence we've got," said one investigator.[69]

Stearns County authorities kept Billy in seclusion, moving him between multiple locations in St. Cloud for several weeks. Part of the reason for this was to protect Billy from a killer who was still on the loose, but also to keep him from being recognized and possibly harassed.

As investigators worked to piece together the sequence of events that occurred in the Huling home on the night of the murders, one key element of the crime eluded them—motive. Robbery was ruled out quickly because there had been nothing of value taken from the home. The killer left behind a television, a record player, and a chainsaw–the only valuable items in the home. None of the victims had been sexually assaulted, so that motive was ruled out as well. As far as anyone knew, no one held a grudge against Alice Huling. In fact, she and her children were well liked in the Kimball community.

"Whoever went in there, went in there with the express interest in killing the Hulings," said an official close to the investigation.[70]

Charlie Grafft was sworn in as Stearns County Sheriff on January 2, 1979, and took over the reigns of the investigation from Jim Ellering. Grafft declined to speculate on whether investigators thought the Huling murders had been premeditated. He began his term with a full plate, as the Huling murders were just the latest of unsolved murders in Stearns County. Others included the 1974 murders of sisters Mary and Susanne Reker and the 1976 Kimball Post Office bomb that killed Ivend Holen. Grafft offered few details on progress in the Huling case, saying only that an arrest in the case could be made at any time.

"I will be personally very actively involved in the Huling investigation," Grafft promised his constituents. "We're going to spend as much time as possible on the Reker case, but the Huling murders will come first."[71]

Investigators developed a number of suspects early on in the Huling murder investigation. Alice Huling's ex-husband, Darrel "Tex" Huling was naturally investigated as a suspect. Darrel was a truck driver and living in Norcross, Minnesota at the time of the murders. He worked at the Pepsi Cola bottling plant in St. Cloud when he and Alice were together, but moved to Norcross soon after their 1973 divorce. The day after the murders, investigators tracked him down driving an over-the-road truck in Ohio. They determined that he could not have been in Minnesota at the time of the murders, and was quickly ruled out as a suspect.

There were several other suspects in the mix, however. John Dwyer, the off-duty Stearns County deputy who lived next door to the Hulings, was among them. He had been out rabbit hunting until 2:30 a.m. with Steve Dirksen. Dwyer confided in another friend that he was at the Huling home in bed with Alice about 45 minutes prior to the murders. Stearns County Deputy Jim Kostreba was highly suspicious of Dwyer's behavior and the comments he made when the pair entered the Huling home shortly after the murders. Kostreba noted that Dwyer, despite admitting he had not gone upstairs during his first visit to home after the shootings, seemed to know that all the children were dead.

Fr. Paul Folsom, the priest at St. Anne's Catholic Church in Kimball and pastor of the Huling family, was also a suspect in the gruesome murders. Investigators' interest in Folsom as a suspect was piqued when he misled them about how long he had known Alice Huling. He had met Huling just a few days prior to the murders, but in interviews with detectives he indicated he had known the woman much longer. Additionally, Folsom had sharply criticized Alice for what he considered immoral behavior. But what kept investigators going back to Folsom as a suspect in the murders was that he was the only suspect interviewed to have failed polygraph tests. The priest failed as many as a dozen tests and owned a pair of 12-guage shotguns. However, laboratory tests concluded that neither of Folsom's guns had been used in the murders.

Another major suspect was a man named Joe Ture. Wright County Deputy Gary Miller responded to a complaint of a man harassing customers at a restaurant in the Clearwater Travel Plaza. Deputy Miller questioned Ture, who appeared to be living out of the 1971 Chevrolet Impala he was driving. Upon further investigation, Deputy Miller learned that the car had been reported stolen. He arrested Ture, who asked the officer to retrieve a newspaper from the back seat of the car. While getting the paper, Miller found a leather-wrapped club, a toy car, a ski mask, and a booklet containing the names, addresses, and license plate numbers of dozens of women. Those items were confiscated and turned over to Stearns County investigators as possible evidence in the Huling slayings.

Without a motive for the killings or physical evidence tying any known suspects to the crime, the Huling murder investigation seemed to have stalled out. Concerned residents of the rural area where the Hulings were murdered were pessimistic the case would ever be solved. In the past five years several unsolved murders had occurred within a five-mile radius, including the 1976 Kimball Post Office bomb that killed Ivend Holen and the 1974 Reker sisters murders.

Despite being as suspect in the slayings himself, John Dwyer defended the investigation, urging rural Stearns County residents to be patient. "There may never be a legitimate time to criticize an investigation," Dwyer said. "This is not TV. Criminal investigations involve a lot of legwork, a lot of knocking on doors."[72]

Two months after the murders, Sheriff Grafft reassured the public that progress was being made in the case, and vowed that the killer would be caught. He declined to comment on criticism of the investigation, including from law enforcement insiders who complained anonymously about how the crime scene had been handled initially. He said that nearly 300 people had been interviewed so far, and a number of 12-guage shotguns had been confiscated and tested by the state crime laboratory. He said there was much more work to be done.

Investigators working the Huling murder case were just as frustrated as the public by the lack of progress in identifying the killer. "We talked to everybody that knew Alice and the kids and nobody hated her," said one Huling task force investigator. "She had no enemies, nobody with any reason to kill her. So you come to the conclusion that we've got some psychopath out there. And it's really hard to put yourself in his shoes, to try and figure out why he did it."[73]

By March of 1979 detectives had focused their attention primarily on Fr. Folsom. To date he had been the only suspect to have failed lie detector tests in the Huling case. Folsom had also been questioned in regard to the 1974 Reker murders, but he passed a handful of lie detector tests in that case. In the Huling investigation, Folsom had initially agreed to undergo a psychiatric examination and turn the results over to investigators. However, as investigators turned up the heat in their questioning of Folsom, the suspect hired a well-known defense attorney, John Simonett from Little Falls. In doing so, Folsom also became the only suspect to date to hire a lawyer. Simonett quickly ordered that investigators were to cease interviewing his client.

Detectives were not able to glean much physical evidence from the Huling crime scene, and what little evidence they did collect was slow in getting processed due to a February 1979 strike by state crime laboratory workers. A dispute about workers' salaries led to the work stoppage, and Sheriff Grafft wasn't shy about sharing his dismay about how the lab strike was hurting his investigation.

"Reports that we should have, we don't have," said a disappointed Sheriff Grafft. "We don't know exactly what they'd say but they sure could put us on the right track. We're still looking for that little key that could unlock this case for us."[74]

Stearns County investigators turned their attention to a new suspect in March 1979. Billie Ray Davis, formerly from Houston, Texas, was a truck driver who murdered a military police officer near Detroit in October 1978. He also stole two shotguns from the officer at the time of the shooting. Davis, 23, was arrested the same day the Hulings were killed. He had been in central Minnesota at the time of the murders, and was charged in Wright County for the rape and beating of a woman near Monticello.

Stearns County detectives Jim Kostreba and Ross Baker flew to Detroit to interview Davis. They collected blood and hair samples from the suspect. They also confiscated a blue quilted ski jacket with stains splattered across the front. Billy Huling had told investigators that his family's killer was wearing a blue jacket. Investigators also went to Arkansas and Missouri to document Davis' movements in those states in the days leading up to the Huling murders.

"Davis is a strong suspect," Sheriff Grafft declared. "He's as strong as any of them until we can clear them. We're hoping, but I'm not putting all my marbles in one bag. There's no telling which way it'll go."[75]

Laboratory test results of the samples collected from Davis were sent to Stearns County in May 1979. They revealed no connection between Davis and the Huling crime scene. Davis was ultimately cleared in the case.

On December 15, 1979, at the one-year anniversary of the Huling family murders, Sheriff Grafft hinted that new clues had come up in the investigation and there could be a major break in the case by Christmas. According to a *St. Cloud Times* report, confidential sources from within the Stearns County Sheriff's Department said that the suspect list, which had started out with as many as 25 suspects, had been whittled down to a single top suspect. He was the man who had failed multiple lie detector tests, the only one of the lot to fail any such tests– Fr. Paul Folsom.

"When you talk to him, you get the idea it's like a chess game with him," said one investigator, who characterized Folsom as highly intelligent. "He's talking to you here, but he's two steps ahead of you."[76]

Sheriff Grafft made a public appeal for anyone with information about the Huling murders to come forward. "I'm hoping that if anybody in the county has some information, that they've been afraid before to come forward, that they will now," Grafft said. "Their names will be kept out of it."[77]

Despite Sheriff Grafft's outward optimism, Christmas of 1979 passed without an arrest. Then another month went by, and still there was no apparent forward progress in the case. In a January 1980 story, the *St. Cloud Times* posed a survey question to readers:

Do you expect that the Huling murders of December 1978, still under investigation by the Stearns County Sheriff's Department will ever be solved?

The Center for Human and Community Development at St. John's University in Collegeville conducted the poll for the newspaper. The results reflected the public's low level of confidence in Stearns County's crime-solving abilities, as only 19 percent of respondents said they thought the Hulings' killer would be captured.

Another year went by. With the case then two years old in December 1979, Sheriff Grafft said the suspect list in the case had swelled back to five individuals. Although he declined to discuss specifics of the man they had considered the top suspect all along, he did acknowledge the case against Folsom was weak, and the focus of the investigation had shifted.

"We're switching all over. Until we get somebody in jail, we've got four or five suspects we're still checking out," said Grafft. "It's been a long time now but I feel just as confident now as I was two years ago. We're taking this real slow. It's a grind, grind thing. I'll be damned if I want to lose this in court."[78]

Huling investigators turned their attention to Joe Ture in late 1981. By then, Ture was already in prison for the 1980 murder of Diane Edwards, a waitress at Perkins in West St. Paul. According to a KSTP television news report, Ture signed a written confession admitting responsibility for the Huling murders and other unsolved crimes. The confession was actually penned by a fellow prison inmate, Tony Krominga, and was signed by Ture. The letter stated that Ture had poor spelling, and that was the reason it was written by someone else. According to the document, Ture's original intention upon entering the Huling home was to rape one of Alice Huling's daughters, but after arguing with Alice he shot the woman.

"She told me to 'leave my house, you pervert.' Then I shot her above the knees with the shotgun," Ture said to his fellow inmate. "I then went upstairs. By this time I was really crazy. I shot two girls and a boy. I let the other boy live."[79]

Joe Ture attempted suicide by taking an overdose of tranquilizers on Friday, January 8, 1982. He was rushed from the Sherburne County Jail to the hospital in Elk River. Ture was treated and released hours later, and transferred to the state prison in Stillwater to serve out his prison sentence. Prior to his suicide attempt, Ture claimed that he fabricated his confession to the Huling murders in an attempt to get assigned to a mental hospital instead of Stillwater prison. Joe Ture denied killing the Huling family, claiming that he actually hated guns. He said the only time he ever used a shotgun was at his father's farm in Prescott, Wisconsin. He shot a raccoon that was harassing chickens.

"I hated guns," Ture said. "I could never shoot nobody. Don't you think that would make me go crazy? I'd go nuts if I ever killed anyone."[80]

Despite Ture's change of heart regarding his alleged confession, it seemed the Huling investigation was finally looking up. But that apparently wasn't the case. Years would roll by and the Huling case continued to go on unsolved. Billy Huling grew up, moved to California, and got married. By the age of 21, he was enlisted in the Navy and had fathered two children.

Billy returned to St. Cloud in 1988 to collect the fund that had been set up for him by Fr. Folsom ten years earlier, but was disappointed to learn the money was gone. Meryl and Georgia Huling, Billy's uncle and aunt, were administers of the $20,000 worth of certificates of deposits that had been reserved for him. Bankruptcy court documents indicated that Billy's relatives used the money as collateral on a business loan for their True Value store in Sartell.

A cold case unit from the BCA re-opened the Huling case in late 1994, 16 years after the killings. Everett Doolittle, leader of the investigative team, said the agency's goal was to review the case to see if anything was missed during the early investigation. He would re-interview witnesses in an effort to develop new information.

"One of the keys to old homicides is that witnesses and cohorts may be more open," Doolittle explained. "The allegiances that were strong long ago weaken or don't exist. Here, time isn't your enemy, it's your ally."[81]

Doolittle went to work immediately. He revisited the investigative files, going back to the beginning of the case to see if anything had been missed. He noted that several items from Ture's car had been held in evidence. There was the leather colored billy club, the notebook, a ski mask, and a toy car. Doolittle called Billy Huling and asked him if he recalled if anything had been missing from his home after the night of the murder.

Billy, though he had never returned to his family's home following the killings, responding to Doolittle out of reflex. "Why? Did you find my Batmobile?"[82]

And that's when agent Doolittle knew he had his man–Joe Ture. Still, it took another five years for Stearns County Attorney Roger Van Heel to agree to convene a grand jury to seek an indictment against Ture in 1999. Ultimately, Ture was tried for the murders and was convicted in the Huling case. Court proceedings leading up to Ture's indictment and trial included testimony that revealed shocking details about how Ture got away with the murders for more than two decades.

Van Heel hired Dr. Daniel Davis, a medical examiner from Edina, to testify as an expert witness against Ture. Dr. Davis testified that the metal bar wrapped in a steering wheel that was found in Ture's vehicle a few days after the Huling murders was the weapon used to beat Alice Huling before he shot her to death. He employed digitally enhanced photographs to demonstrate that the bruises on Alice's ribs matched markings on the bar.

Jeff Morris, a former inmate of Ture's at the Minnesota Correctional Facility in St. Cloud, testified about the details of Ture's confession to the Huling murders and other crimes. Morris had written Ture's confession on paper, which Ture apparently signed. Morris told the court details that only the Huling killer could know, including that one of the bullets fired at Billy's head went through his pillow before exiting through the wall behind his bed. Sheriff Charlie Grafft testified that handwriting analysis proved that the signature on the confession was in Joe Ture's handwriting. Another former fellow prison inmate, Randall Ferguson, also testified that Ture had confessed to him about committing the murders.

The prosecution called on Billy Huling to recount the murder of his mother and siblings. Ture's defense team tried to divert the court's attention to other suspects in the case. While Billy was unable to identify who killed his family, he did testify to who he was sure didn't kill them–Stearns County deputy and family friend, John Dwyer. He explained that Dwyer's physical size and voice were simply not consistent with the man he heard and saw kill his siblings.

The prosecution brought several items of physical evidence found in Ture's car after the murders, including Billy's Corgi Juniors Batmobile car. Apparently, investigators had never asked Billy about the car when it was taken into evidence in 1978. Testimony about the car was the first direct evidence in the case against Ture that place him in the Huling home. Stearns County deputy Jim Kostreba testified that Ture became agitated when questioned about the toy car in December 1978.

"I would say he became confused, maybe a little rattled," Kostreba said of Ture's demeanor. "Later he became more defensive."[83]

Prosecutors played portions of the 1978 interrogation of Ture conducted by Kostreba and detective Ross Baker. They asked Ture about the car and where he got it:

"I noticed a little toy there, a little thing with Batman. Was that in the car when you go it, too, or do you recall where that might have come from? " one of the detectives asked Ture.

"It's mine. I got grandkids," said Ture, then 26 years old.

"Oh, you have grandkids?" the investigator asked.

"My daughter does. I'm an uncle, or whatever," Ture replied.

Baker and Kostreba had Ture flustered, and kept at him. "Well, if your daughter has children, well then you would be a grandfather then, huh? How old are you?"

"No, I mean my sister," Ture said, correcting himself. "I'm the uncle. My sister's got kids. I'm the uncle, right?"[84]

Despite objections from the prosecution, Ture's lawyers were able to present information about John Dwyer as a possible suspect in the Huling murders. Patrick Burke, a friend of Dwyer's, testified that in 1980 Dwyer told him words to the effect that he killed Alice Huling, and that he was responsible for her death because he had encouraged her to move to the rural Stearns County area next door to him. Burke had made statements about Dwyer to Stearns County investigators in 1984, but his information did not come to light until June 1998, when he contacted Ture's lawyers. Burke claimed that Dwyer told him that he was in bed with Alice Huling 45 minutes prior to the murders.

On Tuesday, February 1, 2000, a Stearns County jury convicted Joe Ture of the December 1978 murders of Alice, Susie, Wayne, and Patti Huling. Jurors polled after the trial cited Dr. Davis' testimony about the metal bar used to beat Alice Huling as the crucial piece of physical evidence presented in the trial. They also relied on the testimony regarding the confessions Ture relayed to fellow inmates.

Stearns County District Court Judge Richard Ahles sentenced Joe Ture to four life terms in prison for the murders. Ture was already in prison for the murders of Diane Edwards in 1980, and the 1979 murder of Marlys Wohlenhaus of Afton. His conviction for the Huling murders meant that Joe Ture would never again walk as a free man. Marlys' mother, Fran Wohlenhaus-Munday, attended Ture's sentencing hearing. She had two words for Ture as he was escorted from the Stearns County courthouse: "Happy Birthday."[85]

Bibliography – Lone Survivor

Aeikens, D. (1988, June 30). Huling Tells of Family's Murder. *St. Cloud Times*, pp. 1A, 6A.

Aeikers, D. (1998, June 30). Huling Tells of Family's Murder - Prosecution Aims to Link Ture to 4 Local Killings. *St. Cloud Times*, pp. 1A, 6A.

Associated Press. (1979, January 10). Report Says Bill Tells More Details. *St. Cloud Daily Times*.

CBS News. (2000, September 27). A Cold Case Heats Up - A Forgotten Confession is Revived. Retrieved from CBSNews.com.

Daley, D. (1979, May 3). Angles Probed in 'Murder Triangle'. *St. Cloud Daily Times*, pp. 1, 10.

Daley, D. (1978, December 23). Billy Holding Key to Puzzle. *St. Cloud Daily Times*, pp. 1, 11.

Daley, D. (1979, January 11). Billy's Information Met with Some Skepticism. *St. Cloud Daily Times*, pp. 1, 7.

Daley, D. (1978, December 22). Fear Haunts Neighbors Week after Huling Family Murders. *St. Cloud Daily Times*.

Daley, D. (1979, April 27). Huling Probe Turns to Michigan Inmate. *St. Cloud Daily Times*, pp. 1, 8.

Daley, D. (1978, December 20). Huling Victims Reportedly Were Awake When Killed. *St. Cloud Daily Times*.

Daley, D. (1979, April 12). Lab Strike Crimps Huling Probe. *St. Cloud Daily TImes*, p. 1.

Daley, D. (1979, January 6). Motive for Huling Case Puzzling. *St. Cloud Daily Times*, p. 1.

Daley, D. (1979, January 11). Mrs. Huling First Beaten. *St. Cloud Daily Times*, pp. 1, 7.

Daley, D. (1978, December 16). Murder - Police Hunt Family's Killer. *St. Cloud Daily Times*, pp. 1, 3.

Daley, D. (1979, January 2). New Sheriff Grafft to Take Reins on Murder Probe. *St. Cloud Daily Times*, p. 1.

Daley, D. (1979, March 2). Officials Have Strong Suspect in Huling Murders. *St. Cloud Daily Times*, pp. 1, 5.

Daley, D. (1979, December 15). One Suspect Emerges in Year-long Huling Murders. *St. Cloud Times*, pp. 1, 6.

Daley, D. (1979, February 15). Strong Clues Lacking in Huling Case. *St. Cloud Daily Times*, pp. 1, 5.

Daley, D. (1978, December 18). Task Force Starts on Murders. *St. Cloud Daily Times*, p. 1.

Daley, D. (1979, May 10). Tests May Clear Suspect in Huling Case. *St. Cloud Daily Times*.

Daley, D. (1980, December 15). Two Years Later, Huling Murder Probe Drags On. *St. Cloud Daily Times*, pp. 1A, 6A.

Haukebo, K. (1988, December 11). Evidence, Survivor Tell Horrific Story. *St. Cloud Times*, p. 1A.

Haukebo, K. (1988, December 11). Surviving Son Builds New Life. *St. Cloud Times*, pp. 1A, 12A.

Monn, B. a. (1978, December 16). Slain Children Excelled. *St. Cloud Daily Times*, pp. 1, 3.

St. Cloud Daily Times Staff Report. (1980, January 21). Only 1 in 5 Say Huling Murderer Will be Found. *St. Cloud Daily Times*, p. 1.

St. Cloud Daily Times Staff Report. (1978, December 15). Woman Described as Quiet. *St. Cloud Daily Times*.

State of Minnesota, Repondent, v. Joseph D. Ture, Appellant, C8-00-798 (Supreme Court of Minnesota August 16, 2001).

Tri-County News Staff Report. (1978, December 21). Community Shocked by Four Huling Murders. *Tri-County News*, p. 1.

Tri-County News Staff Report. (1994, November 24). Huling Case Re-opened. *Tri-County News*, p. 1.

Unze, D. (2000, January 27). Inmate Testifies About Ture Statements. *St. Cloud Times*, p. 1B.

Unze, D. (1999, November 25). Judge Admits Key Evidence into Ture Trial. *St. Cloud Times*, p. 1B.

Unze, D. (1999, December 30). Judge Narrows List of Ture Suspects. *St. Cloud Times*, pp. 1B, 5B.

Unze, D. (2000, February 2). Jurors: Metal Bar, Medical Examiner Testimony Helped Sway Decision. *St. Cloud Times*, p. 4A.

Unze, D. (2000, January 14). Jury Gets 3-D Crime Scene Tour. *St. Cloud Times*, pp. 1B, 4B.

Unze, D. (1998, July 2). New Evidence Ties Ture to Slayings. *St. Cloud Times*, pp. 1A, 4A.

Unze, D. (1998, July 1). Officer Briefly Suspected Deputy in Huling Killings. *St. Cloud Times*, pp. 1A, 5A.

Unze, D. (1998, July 3). Toy Car Queries Angered Ture. *St. Cloud Times*, pp. 1A, 4A.

Unze, D. (2000, February 2). Ture Guilty in 1978 Killings. *St. Cloud Times*, pp. 1A, 4A.

Unze, D. (2000, February 8). Ture Sentence Please Huling Family, Doesn't Diminish Anger. *St. Cloud Times*, pp. 1A, 5A.

Werder, C. (1982, January 6). Police Checking Ture Links. *St. Cloud Daily Times*, pp. 1A, 14A.

Werder, C. (1982, January 9). Ture Tries Suicide as Route to Heaven. *St. Cloud Daily Times*, pp. 1A, 8A.

Zack, M. (1998, August 7). Ture Witness Says Deputy Took Blame for Huling Killings - He Said He Doesn't Want to See an Innocent Person Accused in the 1978 Slayings. *Minneapolis Star Tribune*.

Chapter Five

A Tick Short of Justice

Victim: Joanie Bierschbach
Date: November 5, 1979
Status: Likely suspect already in prison
Location: St. Cloud

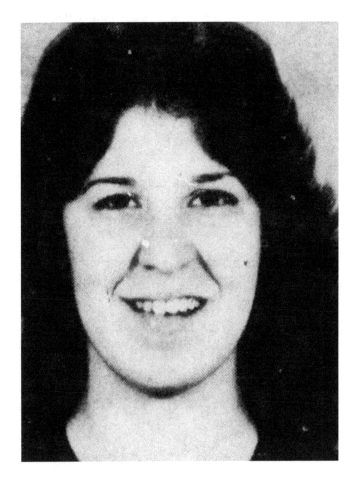

Joanie Bierschbach left her Ninth Avenue home in St. Cloud on Monday night, November 5, 1979, to play volleyball in nearby Waite Park. The match was scheduled to start at 7:30 p.m. at the elementary school gymnasium. The 20-year-old Melrose native looked forward to the weekly tilt with her friends and teammates. On this particular night, Joanie planned to stop first at the Perkins restaurant on Sixth Avenue South, where she worked part-time.

Joanie was expected to return to her apartment right after the volleyball game because she was due in to work early Tuesday morning at her full time job at Stearns County Social Services. She had worked there as a clerk for six months since graduating from the Area Vocational-Technical Institute in Alexandria.

Joanie drove her recently purchased, red-colored Ford Gran Torino into the parking lot at the Perkins restaurant and pulled into a parking stall. She failed to show up for her volleyball game that night, and didn't report to work the following day, either. After Joanie Bierschbach left the Perkins restaurant that night she was never seen again.

On Tuesday night, Joanie's boyfriend, 22-year-old John Fischbach of Melrose, made the 40-mile drive from his Melrose family's farm to Joanie's St. Cloud apartment. It was a drive he made to see her nearly every Tuesday evening after finishing his farm chores. Joanie would drive home on the weekends and spent much of her free time with John. Although they weren't officially engaged, lately they had spent a good deal of their time discussing marriage.

Joanie wasn't home when John arrived at her apartment. Her roommates informed him they hadn't seen her since she left to play volleyball the night before, and they didn't know where she was. Fischbach promptly called the St. Cloud Police Department to report

Joanie missing. Fischbach then phoned Joanie's family to let them know he couldn't find her in St. Cloud. Everyone was flabbergasted by her sudden disappearance. John had spoken with her by telephone on Monday night, just minutes before she left for her volleyball match.

Fischbach spent much of Tuesday night driving around St. Cloud searching for Joanie and her car. He drove up and down all the streets he could think of to look for her, and finally found her Gran Torino parked in the lot shared by the Perkins restaurant and another business. Joanie's purse was sitting in plain view on the front seat. Inside the purse were her glasses, contact lenses, money, and checkbook. Nothing was missing—except for Joanie, that is.

Police promptly issued a news release with Joanie's description–5 feet 4 inches tall, 120 pounds, and with black shoulder-length hair. They asked that anyone with information about her whereabouts contact them. An investigator took Joanie's eyeglasses to an optometrist for evaluation, and learned that the woman's prescription was strong. Joanie needed her glasses or contacts just to be able to get around and function normally. That information and the fact she had left her purse behind in the car were strong indications to police that Joanie had not just run off somewhere on her own.

One week after she had vanished, on November 12, police used a State Patrol helicopter to search for Bierschbach along the banks of the Mississippi River near St. Cloud. St. Cloud Police Chief Jim Moline declined to say what lead them to search the river, and he refused to reveal whether he suspected foul play in the woman's disappearance. He would only say that Joanie was considered to be a missing person at that point. The parking lot where her car was found was very near the river, so the search was likely prompted by a theory that Joanie might have gone into the water.

"We're looking at all the avenues," Chief Moline said. "We don't know what happened to her."[86]

Another ten days passed by, and neither St. Cloud police nor Joanie Bierschbach's family had developed any new information to explain what happened to her. By then, police had given strong consideration to the idea that Joanie either committed suicide or was the victim of foul play. The problem was they had no evidence of either, and nothing to work from. They had interviewed several of Joanie's friends, her family, and John Fischbach. They conducted tests on her car for fingerprints and other evidence, but came away with nothing.

Lorraine Bierschbach, Joanie's mother, asked several Twin Cities television stations to broadcast a picture of her missing daughter. She said that Joanie had not acted unusual in any way during the time leading up to her disappearance. During their last conversation, Joanie gave her mother no indication of anything troubling going on in her life.

"She was very happy," Lorraine Bierschbach said. "Right now we've got to think anything could happen. But we hope for the best."[87]

Those first few weeks of relentless worry gradually turned into a full year of more of the same. Despite investing thousands of hours of investigative effort, St. Cloud police were unable to develop any more clues to finding Joanie Bierschbach than they had since the day she disappeared. One hopeful lead that developed during that time was in July 1980 when someone reported seeing a woman resembling Bierschbach riding a Greyhound bus. Police investigated the report but it quickly fizzled out.

Later in the summer of 1980, someone called Joanie's parents' home claiming to be Joanie. Ray Bierschbach, Joanie's father, took the call. "Dad, this is Joanie," said the woman on the other end of the line. Then the woman screamed and the line was cut off. Mr. Bierschbach said the voice sounded like Joanie's, but the contact later proved to be a cruel crank call.

On October 27, 1980, Charles LaTourelle raped and murdered St. Cloud State college student Catherine John, and dumped her body in the Mississippi River. He called police to report the killing soon after and was subsequently convicted of her murder. LaTourelle was living in St. Cloud in 1979, and Ms. John worked at a pizza restaurant, so his confession for her murder naturally prompted police interest in LaTourelle as a suspect in the Bierschbach case as well. Years later, LaTourelle would confess to the June 1972 killing of an Arden Hills, Minnesota woman. He wasn't cleared in Bierschbach's disappearance, but wasn't considered a top suspect either.

As the one-year anniversary of Joanie's disappearance passed by in November 1980 John Fischbach still held out hope that his girlfriend was alive. He had a theory that Joanie might have been kidnapped into a prostitution ring in Minneapolis. He said he had heard several stories about young women in the Melrose area being propositioned by strangers attempting to lure them to the Twin Cities.

"I feel there are such things as the Minnesota pipeline," Fischbach said. "I've checked out three or four incidents with parents of kids that have been approached in this area, and it's true."[88]

In January 1982, Joe Ture was sentenced for the October 1980 murder of Diane Edwards. Edwards was a waitress at a Perkins restaurant in West St. Paul. The day after his conviction Ture was said to have signed written confessions to the 1978 murders of Alice Huling and her family in Stearns County, as well as the 1979 slaying of Marlys

Wohlenhaus in Afton, Minnesota. KSTP-TV claimed to have obtained copies of those confessions. But the confessions didn't stop there, as Ture reportedly told a fellow prison inmate that he was also responsible for the murder of Joanie Bierschbach. The inmate suggested he could tell investigators where to find her body. Ture's apparent motive in confessing to all these murders, effectively admitting that he was a serial killer, was to persuade authorities to have him committed to Minnesota Security Hospital in St. Peter rather than send him to prison.

St. Cloud Police Chief Woody Bissett acknowledged that his office had received new information in the Bierschbach investigation but he declined to elaborate. He said he took the information seriously and that his investigators would be following up on it immediately. Ture's statements implicating himself in Joanie's disappearance were met with a good measure of doubt, however. One St. Cloud police official categorized the information as "skeptical at best."

That officer's skepticism was soon reinforced when Ture denied the confessions in an interview with the *St. Paul Pioneer Press* a few days later. Specific to Bierschbach's case, Ture acknowledged that investigators had questioned him about her disappearance but he denied having any involvement. The *Pioneer Press* story named Ture's inmate as 36-year-old Tony Krominga.

"It's B.S.," Ture said of Krominga's claim. "Krominga is a snitch. He's here for protective custody because he had something to do with a drug bust at Stillwater."[89]

Divers from Smith Divers of Minneapolis searched for Joanie's body in the waters of a quarry in Waite Park for two days beginning on July 14, 1982. Several Stearns County Sheriff Office (SCSO) deputies assisted with the search of the quarry, commonly known as Dead

Man's Quarry. Stearns County Sheriff Charlie Grafft said the search had actually begun on a smaller scale a few months earlier. Stearns County divers had made four separate dives of their own into the quarry waters, but Grafft ultimately called upon the more experienced and better-equipped team at Smith Divers. He said his department had received information last winter that Bierschbach's body might have been dumped into the quarry, an apparent reference to information that had been provided by Tony Krominga.

"If we don't find her today, I don't know what we'll do," Grafft said on the second day of the search. "We waited until the ice went out and the water cleared up before we made our dives."[90]

The dive search for Bierschbach was very near where the bodies of sisters Mary and Susan Reker were found in September 1974. Divers concluded their search without finding any evidence of Bierschbach, casting further doubt on the information provided by Krominga about Ture's possible involvement in her disappearance. The case went cold again.

In the late summer of 1984 serial killers Henry Lee Lucas and Otis Toole were implicated in as many as 200 murders of women between 1974 and 1983. A pair of officers from the Tri-County Major Crime Investigative Unit traveled to Louisiana to meet with detectives there to determine whether the pair might be responsible for several unsolved Stearns County cases, including Bierschbach's. They left without developing any solid information that either of the men was responsible, even though Lucas said he was in Minneapolis at the time of Joanie's disappearance.

In October 1984, nearly five years after Joanie Bierschbach disappeared without a trace from St. Cloud, a youngster played a major role in finally finding answers to what happened to her. A seven-year-old boy was hunting along the Mississippi River in Wright County when he discovered bones in a dry part of the riverbed. While media reports suggested that the boy then told his mother about the bones and that she subsequently contacted Wright County authorities about the find, a source familiar with the investigation said that the bones actually came to light when the boy brought them to show-and-tell at school. The school's principal, realizing the bones were probably human, contacted the boy's mother.

The Wright County Sheriff's Department searched the area of the river where the boy found the bones, about five miles west of Monticello. Searchers found more bones there, along with teeth, jewelry, and a women's sweater. Suspecting that the remains belonged to Joanie Bierschbach, Wright County Sheriff Darrell Wolff contacted SCSO. The teeth, bones, and sweater were sent to the Minnesota Bureau of Criminal Investigation (BCA) for testing and to compare with Bierschbach's dental records. On October 9, 1984, authorities announced that the remains indeed belonged to Joanie Bierschbach but the BCA was still in the process of determining her cause of her death.

Lorraine Bierschbach reacted with to the news of her daughter's remains being found with mixed feelings.

"It was terrible—almost five years," Mrs. Bierschbach lamented. "We don't know what happened to her. We had just a little hope left. But it's better to know, if she has to be gone."[91]

Ray Bierschbach cried and fell to his knees when he delivered the news to his remaining children and grandchildren. For many in his family it was the first and only time they had seen the man cry.

Authorities suspected foul play in Bierschbach's death, but until the cause of her death would be determined, St. Cloud Police Chief Woody Bissett said he could not yet rule out the possibility her death had been accidental. He noted the Perkins parking lot where Joanie's car had been found was only a short distance from the steep banks of the Mississippi River. He reiterated they still had no witnesses or information to indicate why Bierschbach's car was parked at the Perkins restaurant. One clue that diminished the likelihood that Bierschbach had entered the water near the Perkins, however, was that her jewelry was found near her skeletal remains and clothing. Jewelry is one of the first items that separates from a body in water, meaning that her body was likely put in the water very near the location where it was found.

Any doubts about foul play in Joanie's death were soon allayed. In January 1985, Dr. Janis Amatuzio, a pathologist from Hastings, Minnesota, revealed her findings—Joanie Bierschbach died as the result of at least one stab wound to the chest. Her conclusion came after she found cuts in two of the woman's front ribs. A two centimeter long cut in Bierschbach's sweater was consistent with a knife cut, and appeared to correspond to the location of the cuts to her ribs.

In 1996, BCA investigator Everett Doolittle was reviewing the files of another former BCA investigator when he discovered letters written in 1984 by Jeffrey Morris, another former inmate of Joe Ture's. Much like the information provided by Krominga, Morris's letters detailed Ture's confessions for the murders of Huling, Wohlenhaus, and Bierschbach.

According to the letters, Ture met Bierschbach at the Perkins restaurant and asked her to give him a ride to an automotive service station where his car was being repaired. He then held Joanie at knifepoint and forced her to drive her car to an area of the Mississippi near Monticello, in Wright County.

"He said he raped her and stabbed her in the chest because he didn't want her to live to tell the story," Morris told the *Minneapolis Star Tribune*.[92]

But there was one significant detail in the Morris letters that really piqued investigators' attention relative to the Bierschbach case. Morris said that Ture told him Joanie's speedometer made a loud ticking sound and it irritated Ture. Written reports in the BCA file from 1984 suggested that the clue about the ticking sound should be investigated, but apparently it was not. Investigators said that only Joanie Bierschbach, her family, close friends, and her killer could have known about the unique noise.

"He said the ticking drove him crazy," Morris said of Ture's confession.[93]

Doolittle continued to follow up on long-lost clues in the case. It turns out there had been witnesses to Joanie Bierschbach's disappearance after all. What's more, one of those witnesses later identified Joe Ture as the man seen with Bierschbach at the Perkins restaurant on the night she disappeared in November 1979. A woman and her four children were dining at the restaurant when one of her daughters saw a man who caught her attention. The girl said that as she and her family were leaving Perkins she saw Ture and Joanie Bierschbach near the pay phone in the restaurant entryway, and that Ture grabbed Bierschbach by the wrist and forced her to look away from the family.

"The reason she remembers this was that shortly after that she heard about the disappearance of Joan Bierschbach," Doolittle said.[94]

The alleged confessions communicated by Ture to Krominga and Morris, coupled with the strong clue about the ticking sound from Bierschbach's speedometer, led investigators to focus on Joe Ture as the primary suspect in Joanie's case. Their theory was that Ture had been stalking Bierschbach before kidnapping her from the Perkins restaurant.

At Ture's June 1998 trial for the murder of Marlys Wohlenhaus, Tony Krominga testified that Ture kidnapped Bierschbach and took her to a cabin near the Mississippi River.

"She was talking about God all the way to the cabin and saying the Lord's Prayer while he raped her," Krominga told the court. "He slapped her and told her to shut up. Then he tied her up and had her three or four days at the cabin."[95]

Krominga said that Ture strangled and stabbed Bierschbach to death after she tried to escape from the cabin. Later in the trial, a third former prison inmate of Ture's testified that Ture bragged about killing someone in Afton (a reference to Marlys Wohlenhaus) and had killed someone else in St. Cloud.

In January 1999, Wright County Attorney Tom Kelly said that he would soon make a decision on whether to convene a grand jury to charge Ture in Bierschbach's murder case.

"In my heart, do I think he had something to do with the death of Joan Bierschbach? Absolutely," Kelly said. "But it's a whole different ballgame trying to get back 20 years now and rehash what happened. We've got to take that evidence with what we have and what we don't have and make a decision."[96]

In March 2000, Kelly announced that he would not seek a grand jury indictment against Joe Ture for the murder of Joanie Bierschbach. He cited the lack of evidence necessary to achieve a high probability of a conviction.

"The double jeopardy clause of the Fifth Amendment only gives us one shot of prosecuting Joseph Ture for the Bierschbach homicide," Kelly explained. "It was our opinion that to do so at the present time with the evidence we have would not be prudent."[97]

Kelly said the case would remain open, and that if more evidence developed in the future he would reconsider pursuing charges against Ture.

Bierschbach's family took some comfort in knowing that Joanie's likely killer would never walk as a free man again, even if he would never be held directly responsible for the murder. Lorraine Bierschbach seemed to understand the decision not to charge Ture.

"Right now, they don't know," she said. "But who knows, maybe they will in the future. He's already in prison for life."[98]

The November 5, 1979 murder of Joanie Bierschbach technically remains an unsolved crime because no one has ever been charged with her murder. Anyone with information about the kidnapping death of Joanie Bierschbach is asked to call St. Cloud Police Department at 320-345-4444 or the Stearns County Sheriff's Office at 320-259-3700.

Bibliography – A Tick Short of Justice

Adams, J. (1998, June 22). Inmate Testimony is Key to Tying Man to Several Unsolved Killings. *Minneapolis Star Tribune*, pp. B1, B3.

Adams, J. (1998, June 23). Woman Allegedly Slain by Ture Was Suicidal, Suspect's Lawyer Says. *Minneapolis Star Tribune*, p. B2.

Darlin, D. (1979, November 22). Few Clues in Disappearance of Local Woman. *St. Cloud Daily Times*, p. 17.

Geiber, B. (1984, October 5). Bones May Belong to Missing Woman. *St. Cloud Daily Times*, p. 1C.

Mattson Halena, S. (1985, January 30). Evidence of Foul Play - Pathologist Says Bierschbach Suffered Stab Wound in Chest. *St. Cloud Daily Times*, pp. 1A, 8A.

Minneapolis Star Tribune Staff. (1984, October 10). Skull, Bones Found Near Monticello. *St. Cloud Daily TImes*, p. 32.

Ruff, G. (1980, November 6). Still Missing - Family, Friends Hold Out Hope That 20-Year-Old Will Return. *St. Cloud Daily Times*, pp. 1A, 3A.

St. Cloud Daily Times Staff. (1984, October 9). Authorities Identify Remains of Area Woman. *St. Cloud Daily TImes*.

St. Cloud Daily Times Staff. (1982, July 16). Diving for Missing Woman Called Off. *St. Cloud Daily Times*, p. 16.

St. Cloud Daily Times Staff. (1979, November 8). St. Cloud Police Search for Woman Reported Missing. *St. Cloud Daily Times*, p. 35.

St. Cloud Daily Times Staff. (1979, November 14). Young Woman Still Missing After Nine Days. *St. Cloud Daily Times*, p. 31.

St. Cloud Times Daily Staff. (1984, October 9). Authorities Idenity Remains of Missing Woman. *St. Cloud Daily Times*, p. 13.

Unze, D. (1999, January 23). Attorney: Grand Jury Decision Will Come Soon in Huling Case. *St. Cloud Times*, pp. 1A, 5A.

Unze, D. (1998, June 24). Doctor: Bierschbach Died in Homicide. *St. Cloud Times*, p. 3A.

Unze, D. (1998, June 26). Investigator: Witness Saw Ture, Slaying Victim. *St. Cloud Times*, p. 1A.

Unze, D. (1999, October 22). Police Look for Inmate's Connection to Unsolved Case - New Confession From SCSU Woman's Killer Sparks Interest in 1979 St. Cloud Slaying. *St. Cloud Times*, p. 1A.

Unze, D. (2000, March 17). Ture Won't be Indicted for 1979 Killing - For Now. *St. Cloud Times*.

Werder, C. (1982, July 25). Divers Probe Quarry for Body of Woman Missing Since 1979. *St. Cloud Daily Times*, p. 1B.

Werder, C. (1982, January 6). Police Checking Ture Links. *St. Cloud Daily Times*, pp. 1A, 14A.

Werder, C. (1982, January 7). Ture Denials Won't Cancel Huling, Biersbach Probes. *St. Cloud Daily Times*, pp. 1A, 6A.

Chapter Six

The Beloved Maid of Fairhaven

Victim: Myrtle Cole
Date: December 12, 1981
Status: Unsolved
Location: Village of Fairhaven

Milo Cole made the short, two-mile drive from the farm where he lived to his Aunt Myrtle Cole's house at about 9:30 a.m. on Saturday December 12, 1981. Milo had been checking in with his 81-year-old aunt daily to see if she needed his assistance with anything. Sometimes he would call her, and other times he would stop in for a visit. On that particular morning, Milo first tried to phone Myrtle but she didn't answer, so he drove over right away. He pulled into his Myrtle's driveway, got out of his vehicle, and plodded his way through the freshly fallen snow to the back door of his aunt's house. As he approached the house, Milo noticed the window on the back door had been broken. Concerned, he went inside and found shattered glass spread across the kitchen floor and on top of the stove.

Milo looked around the kitchen as he passed through, but he didn't see anything else out of order. He proceeded through the living room, where again nothing seemed out of place. But when entered Myrtle's bedroom he discovered his apparently lifeless aunt lying face down on her bed. She was naked from the waist down, her legs dangling over the edge of the bed. A quilt covered her head. Milo reached out to touch her hip with his hand to determine if she was alive or dead. Then he hurried back to the kitchen to call police.

Within an hour, the small Township of Fairhaven was swarming with Stearns County deputies and curiosity seekers. A thorough investigation was launched immediately. Investigators scoured the ground of the corner lot around Myrtle's rundown two-story home. Deputies sealed off the area to keep curious onlookers from disturbing the crime scene. By late afternoon, members of the Tri-County Major Crimes Unit of Benton and Sherburne Counties, as well as the sheriff's departments of Wright and Hennepin Counties, the State Patrol, and the Bureau of Criminal Apprehension joined Stearns County investigators.

Deputies took many photographs inside and outside Cole's home. Surveyors from the Stearns County Highway Department were called in to make detailed measurements that could be transferred to a map of the crime scene. Inside the home, investigators searched for fingerprints, hair samples, and other evidence of the killer. A State Patrol helicopter hovered above the house, a Stearns County deputy on board took aerial photographs and video footage. Deputies searched the ground around the house with metal detectors, looking for the murder weapon or some other clue to the crime. Nothing was found.

Several Stearns County deputies involved in securing the crime scene had been trained in crime scene preservation by Hennepin County investigator Ken Christenson. Christenson was present on Saturday and applauded investigators for how they handled the initial investigation, saying they secured the crime scene "almost flawlessly." However, a source close to the crime scene investigation said many officials had trampled through the house with snow on their shoes, and onlookers had been allowed access to the yard around Myrtle's home.

The Township of Fairhaven lies barely within the southeastern confines of Stearns County. To many of the 200 or so people living there, Myrtle Cole was a stranger. She had lived alone in her run-down house for many years, but she was beloved by the friends who knew her well. To them, she was a friendly, caring, and deeply religious person. Myrtle did not have much money, relying solely on her monthly social security check and food stamps to make ends meet in her run-down home. Close friends lamented Myrtle Cole's hard life. She had grown up in Litchfield, where she cared for her mother. She finally married at the age of 48, exchanging vows with 59-year-old Roy Cole in 1958. She had been unable to work for most of her adult life due to chronic, severe headaches that kept her from holding down a steady job. However, she did manage to earn a little money performing housekeeping duties for others.

Myrtle was known as a good cook, and she often prepared a feast for friends who helped her out with chores. She cooked meals for Milo, too. He raved about Myrtle's Sunday chicken dinners. She was active in her church despite being unable to drive herself to and from. Myrtle hosted a weekly Bible study group on Wednesdays. The group was unable to meet the previous Wednesday, December 9th, so she cooked up a pot of soup for her good friend, Ruth Salmela, instead. Myrtle Cole loved cats. She had fed dozens of stray cats for years, and on that Sunday morning there were a few of them sitting on her porch waiting for Myrtle to feed them.

Just a couple of days before her murder, Myrtle Cole had cooked dinner for the three young men from the Tri-County Action Program. They spent the morning at her house, installing plastic film over her home's windows and putting tarpaper on the base of the house to help keep out the cold. She insisted on cooking a large meal for them, even though the young men had brought their own lunches to work that day. The workers were friendly with her in return, fetching her mail from the box, and taking her garbage out to the street.

Despite being a strong-willed woman, as many would characterize her, Myrtle Cole was also known as a persistent worrier. She often expressed the fear of someone breaking into her home to harm her. Her frightened disposition was not the result of any specific threat—it was just in her nature.

"She used to worry about intruders," Milo Cole said. "But I always told her, you don't have to worry about that in Fairhaven, a little town like this."[99]

On more than one occasion, Milo had offered Myrtle the opportunity to live with him, but she always declined. She didn't want to leave her home of more than 20 years, and reasoned she would simply stay safe by keeping her doors locked. After her murder, Milo told the *Minneapolis Star Tribune* that it appeared to him his aunt had been strangled or smothered to death. Although he apparently didn't notice it when he found her body, Myrtle had been stabbed multiple times in the genitals.

Sheriff Charlie Grafft kept mum about a possible motive in Myrtle's murder, but friends and neighbors universally ruled out theft. Anyone who knew Myrtle, they reasoned, was aware she had very little money or items of value. The house was furnished with electricity, but had no running water. For a would-be burglar who didn't know Myrtle, one look at the outside of her sagging, paint-worn house would have them think twice about going inside to rob whoever lived there.

Myrtle's husband Roy died in 1970 at the age of 70. The couple never had any children together. When Myrtle died she left just two significant survivors—her sister, Elsie Maher, and a stepdaughter, Dorothy Belka. Her death brought with it the fading of a family's history.

"She had a memory of an elephant," Milo Cole recalled. "I would always go talk to her when I needed to know something about the old family. Now there's nobody left who knows."[100]

The shocking murder left Fairhaven residents unsettled, and it brought back memories of the yet-unsolved 1978 murders of the Huling family that occurred just five miles away. Area residents had finally started to feel at ease again in their homes, but Myrtle Cole's murder resurrected their collective feeling of fear. The eerie fact that

Myrtle Cole's run-down house as it appeared days after her murder. Photo courtesy of Minneapolis Star Tribune.

Myrtle's murder happened just three days shy of the third anniversary of the Huling killings only added to the heightened sense of fear.

"It makes me sick to my stomach to think things like this can happen in our backyard." Neighbor Phyllis Thompson said. "After that Huling deal, and now this. You have to wonder what's going on."[101]

Another common element that Myrtle Cole's murder shared with the Huling slayings is that both crimes occurred on a night of a full moon. The coincidence worried some Fairhaven residents even further.

"You just begin to wonder if there's a psychopathic killer around," said Meta Rucks. "Whoever did it had to be one big coward to attack an 81-year-old lady."[102]

That Saturday night was the first of several sleepless nights for many people in town. Some who lived alone spent the next few nights with neighbors or friends. Most everyone began locking their doors at night—something almost no one in town had done before the murder.

As the investigation into Myrtle Cole's murder began, rumors of unusual activity from that Friday night swiftly spread through town. Fairhaven resident Lloyd Lehse lived just one block away from Myrtle's house. He was one of three witnesses who told investigators they saw a car with its lights on parked in front of her house at about 2:00 a.m. on Saturday. Further investigation revealed the car had been stuck in the deep, fresh snow, but some people familiar with the case have questioned that explanation. An unidentified neighbor said she saw men peeking into windows along Myrtle's street after midnight. Some rumors focused on the possible involvement of drug-using transients who were known to hide out in abandoned buildings in Fairhaven.

On Sunday December 13th, Sheriff Charlie Grafft summoned a group of detectives to his office at the Stearns County Sheriff's Department. They reviewed the Cole case and created task lists for each investigator to follow up on. Other investigators continued to search for and gather evidence in Fairhaven.

On Monday, Sheriff Grafft was downplaying speculation that Myrtle Cole's murder had any connection to the unsolved Huling family slayings or the 1976 Kimball Post Office bomb case that claimed the life of assistant postmaster Ivend Holen. All three devastating crimes had taken place within a 5-mile radius, and during a five-year time period. Two days into the investigation, Grafft acknowledged that his office had no suspects in the Cole case. He did say, however, that his detectives had interviewed multiple people who had information about the crime. Grafft said no motive had been established in the murder, but he said he couldn't yet rule out robbery. He revealed very few details of the crime scene, choosing only to describe Myrtle Cole's killing as "vicious."

Grafft urged anyone with information to contact his office or Tri-County Crime Stoppers. He announced a $1,000 cash reward to be given to anyone providing information leading to an arrest and conviction.

Cole's autopsy report was released on Tuesday. Grafft was again reserved in his comments regarding the murder, saying only that Myrtle Cole died of multiple traumatic injuries. He declined to specify the weapon used, referring to it only as a sharp instrument. What was left open to speculation was whether Cole's multiple stab wounds were inflicted before or after her death.

Sheriff Grafft defended his decision to limit the release of information about the murder. "We already have seven unsolved murders in this county," he said. "I don't want it to become eight. I've been living with the pressure of the other unsolved murders 24 hours a day since I took office. With this new murder, the pressure is even worse."[103]

Many residents of Fairhaven were growing increasingly restless, and were demanding more answers from Grafft. Grafft sympathized with them, but offered them little else other than committing that a pair of deputies would be on duty in the town 24 hours a day.

"I'd like to do more for them, and I'd like to keep the people informed," Grafft reasoned. "But I can't release the details on what we're doing because it could hurt the case down the line."[104]

When Grafft scheduled a news conference for Wednesday December 16th, many interpreted it as an indication there had been a major development in the case. The press conference was suddenly canceled without explanation, however.

Myrtle Cole was buried on Thursday December 17, 1981 in Annandale, alongside her husband Roy. Several Stearns County investigators monitored the funeral ceremony. Sheltered from the cold inside a van, they took photographs of everyone who attended, while deputies walked the streets and recorded the license plate numbers of parked cars within a wide radius of area surrounding the Dingmann-Farrell Funeral Chapel.

Baffled by the gruesome nature of the crime, and stymied by the inability to develop good suspects in the case, Grafft enlisted the assistance of the FBI. A Behavioral Science Unit from Quantico, Virginia examined the available evidence to develop a psychological profile of the type of person who would commit that type of crime.

"I think these FBI agents have given us a very accurate picture of the kind of person we're dealing with," Grafft said. "I've been very pleased with the progress and I'm confident we're on the right track."[105]

Public grumbling and comparisons to the unsolved Huling case continued to dominate public perception. Grafft argued the Cole case was entirely different. "This case was handled altogether differently than the Huling case," Grafft countered. "I can understand their concern, but this case was handled the right way and that's why I can respond positively about the progress. If it's going to take 10 or 15 years to get this guy, then we'll do it. It won't take that long, of course, but if it did the case would remain open."[106]

By New Year's Eve, Sheriff Grafft revealed that investigators were looking at several suspects in the Cole murder. Eight county detectives continued to work full time on the case, putting in 16 to 18 hour days. By that point nearly all Fairhaven residents had been interviewed, many of them more than once.

Grafft said the BCA laboratory in St. Paul was conducting further testing and he was also waiting for additional information from the autopsy. He reiterated the need to keep tight-lipped about case information, but he did offer up a surprise revelation, that the cause of death had actually been strangulation—not stabbing.

"We don't want to give our cards away to the killer," he said. "We've got to hold our aces close to the chest so the killer doesn't know what we're doing."[107]

In early January 1982, the FBI was able to find crucial evidence—a bloodied palm print on a pillowcase from Myrtle Cole's bedroom. The discovery was made utilizing laser technology at the FBI laboratory in Quantico. The BCA had collected the evidence at the crime scene but were not able to detect the print with the technology available in their St. Paul lab. Sheriff Grafft expressed hope that the newly discovered evidence would help solve the case.

In mid-January, Sheriff Grafft reiterated that investigators had still not established a motive for the murder. However, most familiar with the case presumed robbery was not the motive, even though Grafft continued to indicate that possibility had not been officially ruled out. The fact that Myrtle had been stabbed in the genital area, that she was naked from the waist down, and that investigators quickly sought the assistance from the FBI, were all strong indications the murderer was sexually motivated. Also, the fact that her killer covered her head with a quilt was another key piece of information used in the FBI's psychological profile of the killer. It suggested the killer might have been someone known to Myrtle. Grafft again declined to specify the murder weapon, repeating what he had said from the beginning, that Myrtle Cole had been stabbed repeatedly with a sharp instrument. He acknowledged several suspects were being studied, and that tips from the public had led investigators to do follow-up investigation in Wright, Meeker, and Kandiyohi counties.

With little forward progress in the case after three months, Sheriff Grafft appealed to the public once again in mid-March, asking people with information about the case to come forward. He indicated leads in the case had also taken investigators to Mcleod County near Hutchinson. The case had grown cold though, and there were no longer any investigators working on it on a full-time basis.

"We have not run into a dead end," he said. "This still is an active investigation, and we don't want to reveal anything that may hurt us down the road. We just think it's a good time to ask people who may have some new information to come forward."[108]

After failing to match up the bloody palm print from Myrtle Cole's pillowcase to any suspects, investigators exhumed her body in March to verify that the print did not belong to Myrtle herself. Grafft was furious when the *St. Cloud Times* learned of the exhumation. Results indicated the print did not belong to Cole. Her palm print was not taken at the time of her autopsy because at the time there was no reason to believe it to be relevant evidence. The palm print from Myrtle's pillow was compared to 200 possible suspects in Minnesota and other states, as well as 2,000 prints on file at the Stearns County Sheriff's office. The comparisons yielded no matches.

Stearns County Sheriff deputies Jim Kostreba and Lou Leland flew to Seattle, Washington on March 22, 1982. They returned four days later with two men who had outstanding arrest warrants in Stearns County. Both men had been wanted on charges of theft-by-check. The men were 28-year-old Jesse Ray Dinkins and 26-year-old Donald K. Steinmeyer. Dinkins and Steinmeyer had been sought for questioning in Cole's murder from the beginning. Sheriff Grafft did not get into specifics as to why the pair was under investigation except to say they had been in the Fairhaven area at the time of Cole's death. The men fled the state soon after the murder.

Dinkins and Steinmeyer pleaded guilty to the theft charges and returned to Washington after their brief jail terms. Both men have extensive criminal records in that state. Grafft declined to say whether the men were serious suspects in the Cole case.

"They are still under investigation," Grafft said of Dinkins and Steinmeyer. "We haven't ruled anybody out."[109]

In May 1982, a rusty knife was found on the ground outside of Myrtle Cole's home. Grafft said the knife, which was described as six to eight inches long, should be considered the possible murder weapon due to it's close proximity to Myrtle Cole's house. His comments were remarkable on two accounts. First, it was the first public disclosure that Grafft made about the weapon used in Cole's slaying, other than to say the weapon was a sharp instrument. And second, because the cause of death in Myrtle's case had been determined to be strangulation—not stabbing.

Other investigators who were interviewed by a *St. Cloud Times* reporter were less certain the recently found knife was involved in the murder. They cited BCA test results, which found no blood or fingerprints on the knife. Additionally, since the knife hadn't been found prior to its discovery in May, they speculated the knife had only been placed there recently.

"There's no blood on the knife because it laid out in the weather for a period of time," Grafft said, pushing back on doubts expressed by other law enforcement sources. "The knife was rusty because it was covered by snow for so long. Until otherwise proven, the knife is the only thing found near the murder scene that could be the weapon."[110]

By June of 1982, six months had passed since Myrtle Cole's murder. The investigation had stretched out to a wider area than had been previously reported, with authorities investigating people from Hennepin, Benton, and Morrison counties. After a meeting of investigators who had worked the case since the beginning, Detective Lou Leland was to resume working the case on a full-time basis again. Sheriff Grafft subsequently revealed more information about the FBI's profile of the likely killer. He acknowledged the killing was sexually motivated, something most people familiar with the case had suspected all along. Grafft said the profile suggested the killer was acquainted with or knew of Myrtle Cole, and that it was likely a young, mentally disturbed, and sexually maladjusted male.

"The FBI has been doing this kind of psychological profiling for many years and I feel very comfortable with it," Grafft added. "We've been checking everyone, because we're not psychiatrists and we can't tell what the guy's like. And I'm not ruling out the motive may have been other than sexual. It could have started out as a motive of robbery. But when she woke up, maybe the killer panicked, killed her, and didn't take anything from the house."[111]

A pair of Stearns County investigators flew to Denver, Colorado at the end of July 1982 to interview a 25-year-old man in Littleton. Investigators had recently learned through follow-up interviews in the case that the man, who was from Fairhaven, had left Minnesota a few days after Myrtle Cole's murder. The detectives took finger and palm prints of the man and sent them to the BCA laboratory by airfreight. Subsequent analysis revealed the man's prints did not match the bloody palm print found on the pillowcase.

In November 1982, investigators cleared another possible suspect because his palm print did not match. The man was in jail in Kansas on unrelated charges. Once again, the man had again come to the attention of investigators because he had been in Fairhaven at the time of Cole's murder and left soon after. Grafft said the man was one of about 1,000 "remote" suspects who had been investigated in the case up to that point. Most of those remote suspects were investigated on the basis of having committed similar crimes or because they matched the psychological profile developed by the FBI.

The one-year anniversary of the murder passed in December 1982 without investigators identifying a main suspect. Despite the apparent lack of progress, Grafft remained optimistic that the murder would be solved. "We're still confident with the feeling that it's going to be solved," he said."[112]

Residents of Fairhaven disagreed with their Sheriff. Some had become so frightened by the unsolved crimes in the area that they purchased handguns to protect themselves. Others shuttered at the prospect of snowfall in the coming winter, which would serve as a grim reminder of the brutal murder of Myrtle Cole. The stigma attached to Stearns County because of so many other unsolved crimes led residents to become pessimistic about resolution in the case, and their displeasure manifested itself at the Township of Fairhaven polls in November 1982. Although Grafft was successful in his countywide reelection bid, in the town of Fairhaven only 45% of voters marked their ballots for the incumbent.

Late at night on Wednesday January 19, 1983, Stearns County investigators served a search warrant on the rural South Haven trailer home of Steven Berry. According to the warrant, Berry had bragged in detail to visitors how he had stabbed Myrtle Cole. He told them he went to Cole's home with a friend from Minnetonka and broke into her home through the back door. He claimed he held a knife to her throat, raped her, choked her, and then stabbed her to death. After telling the story, Berry pulled a knife out from between the cushions of his couch and told his visitors it was the very knife he had used to kill her. During the search of Berry's trailer, investigators seized a pair of knives and sent them, along with Berry's palm print, to the BCA lab for testing

Wright County authorities arrested Berry and his roommate, John Pederson, following the search of their residence. Their arrests were in connection to an armed robbery of the Fina gas station in Annandale on January 17th. Pederson had allegedly used a BB gun to rob the gas station attendant of more than $100, and Berry was charged with aiding Pederson. Berry had previously been convicted of robbing a home near Clearwater Lake in May 1981, and he had a history of mental disorders. Berry denied having any involvement in Cole's murder and further denied ever telling anyone he had killed her.

"I've never seen the lady," Berry told a reporter. "I don't know her. I don't know nothing about it and they have no proof I did it."[113] He claimed he was watching a Kung Fu movie at a bar in Hopkins at the time Cole was murdered. Berry was apparently cleared of the murder.

Stearns County deputies flew to Texas in June 1983 to interview convicted serial killer Henry Lee Lucus to determine his viability as a suspect in the Cole murder case. Lucas, who had killed his own mother in 1960, had been charged a week earlier for the murder of an 80-year-old woman in Texas. Lucas became a suspect in the Cole murder because he admitted to killing women all over the country, and his methods of killing were consistent with some elements in the Cole murder.

Lucas denied involvement in Cole's death. He explained he had been in the state of Minnesota only in 1971 and 1977. Cole was murdered in 1981, and Lucas claimed he was living in a halfway house in Florida at the time of her death. He admitted to murdering at least 100 women in at least 16 states, including the murder of one woman in Minnesota in 1971, and a pair of hitchhikers in the mid 1970's. Detectives also questioned Lucas about the 1974 Reker sisters murder, the 1978 Huling murders, and the 1979 murder of Joanie Bierschbach.

Despite Lucas' claim of innocence in the Cole murder, Stearns County investigators kept up their efforts to link him to the crime. Shortly after interviewing Lucas in Texas, officials learned Lucas had teamed up with a man named Otis Elwood Toole in committing dozens of murders. Detectives had previously collected finger and palm prints from Lucas, and collected the same from Toole in late 1983. Neither suspects' prints matched those found in Myrtle Cole's home.

The December 1981 murder of Myrtle Cole remains an unsolved crime. There have been no developments in the case made public since 1983. Anyone with information about Myrtle Cole's murder is asked to call the Stearns County Sheriff's Office at 320-259-3700.

Bibliography – The Beloved Maid of Fairhaven

Brenden, S., & Werder, a. C. (1981, December 31). Cole Was Strangled, Grafft Confirms. *St. Cloud Daily Times*, pp. 1B, 5B.

Coleman, N. (1981, December 16). Woman's Murder Shakes Up a Town. *Minneapolis Star Tribune*, pp. 1A, 8A.

Kennedy, T. (1983, December 22). Florida Suspect is Interviewed on Area Murder Cases. *St. Cloud Daily Times*.

Kennedy, T. (1983, January 24). Knives Could Be Break in Cole Murder. *St. Cloud Daily Times*, pp. 1A, 3A.

Kennedy, T. (1983, June 30). Man Says He Didn't Kill Area Woman. *St. Cloud Daily Times*, pp. 1C-2C.

Kennedy, T. (1982, December 13). One Year Later, Cole Murder Still Unsolved. *St. Cloud Daily Times*, pp. 1A, 9A.

Kennedy, T. (1983, October 18). Pair Probed in Widow's Murder. *St. Cloud Daily Times*, pp. 1C-2C.

Kennedy, T. (1982, November 9). Palm Prints Checked in Cold Murder Case. *St. Cloud Daily Times*, p. 17B.

Kennedy, T. (1983, January 27). Slaying Suspect No Killer, Says Friend. *St. Cloud Daily Times*, pp. 1A, 5A.

Kennedy, T. (1983, June 29). Suspect Denies Link to 1981 Cole Case. *St. Cloud Daily Times*, pp. 1C-2C.

St. Cloud Daily TImes Staff. (1983, June 28). Possible Link to Cole Case Probed. *St. Cloud Daily Times*, p. 17B.

Werder, C. (2918, January 13). A Month Later, Fairhaven Still Fearful Over Cole Killing. *St. Cloud Daily Times*, pp. 1C, 7C.

Werder, C. (1982, August 27). Campaign Focuses on Grafft - Challengers Attack Budget, Murder Probes. *St. Cloud Daily Times*, pp. 1A, 5A.

Werder, C. (1982, July 29). Cole Probe Sends Officers to Colorado. *St. Cloud Daily Times*, p. 15B.

Werder, C. (1981, December 15). Fairhaven Murder Not Being Linked to Other Slayings. *St. Cloud Daily Times*, pp. 1A, 6A.

Werder, C. (1981, December 18). FBI Compiles Personality Profile of Cole Killer. *St. Cloud Daily Times*, p. 19A.

Werder, C. (1982, January 7). FBI Helpful in Cole Slay Probe. *St. Cloud Daily Times* , pp. 1A, 6A.

Werder, C. (1982, June 18). Hand Print, Knife Clues to Unsolved Murder. *St. Cloud Daily Times* , pp. 1A, 5A.

Werder, C. (1981, December 14). Murder - Authorities Awaiting Autopsy. *St. Cloud Daily Times* , pp. 1A, 6A.

Werder, C. (1981, December 14). Murder - Victim a Worrier, Say Friends. *St. Cloud Daily Times* , pp. 1A, 6A.

Werder, C. (2918, December 16). Report Reveals Little About Cole's Death. *St. Cloud Daily Times* , p. 1A.

Werder, C. (1982, March 15). Sheriff Calls on Public to Help with Cole Killing. *St. Cloud Daily Times* , p. 1C.

Chapter Seven

Under the Radar

Victim: Cindy Schmidt and Ronnie Bromenschenkel
Date: August 16, 1986
Status: Unsolved, both are missing and presumed dead
Location: St. Cloud

Cindy Schmidt was missing, and her family was worried. She was 18 years old and had been living on her own since 1986. Cindy had been more than a handful for her mother, Elaine, to contend with when she lived at home. Elaine would often return home from work to find their apartment reeking of marijuana smoke, and empty beer cans scattered across the floor. Cindy's personality wasn't the easiest to accommodate, and she was often verbally abusive to her mother and her sister, Christine Midas. Despite that, her family was always supportive of Cindy.

Cindy was the youngest of six children in the family, her parents having divorced in 1979. Most who knew her saw her as an independent and abrasive personality.

"She was street-wise too soon," Christine reasoned. "She did not have enough restriction and that led her to the wrong crowd, but she always kept in touch with the family."[114]

By August of 1986, Cindy had already been living on her own for a few months in a mobile home at the Riverview mobile home park in St. Cloud. According to neighbors, a pair of men had been living there with her at various times as well. It was customary for Elaine to speak with her daughter by telephone on an almost daily basis. So it was natural that her mother had become increasingly worried about Cindy in September after the pair had not spoken to each other for about a month. Worried to the point she was upset, Elaine decided to call the St. Cloud Police Department to report her daughter missing.

Because Cindy was an adult, there was little the St. Cloud Police Department could do to find her without some evidence of a crime. They interviewed some of Cindy's friends and relatives, but were unable to find anyone with good information. One relative told police they thought they saw Cindy in August nearly 190 miles away in Worthington. Cindy's sister-in-law said she spotted someone who looked like her in Mankato. Neither lead panned out, and without a reason to suspect otherwise, police had no choice but to treat the situation with the assumption that Cindy had "disappeared" on her own free will.

By Christmas, more than four months had passed by without word from Cindy, and that's when the situation bottomed out for Elaine. Christmas was the most important time of year to Cindy. She would never had missed it

Cindy's family was deeply concerned about her well-being, and they had reason to be. They knew she had been struggling financially because she was behind on payments for her mobile home and her car. Cindy had a surgically implanted metal rod in the thigh of her left leg that resulted from an injury suffered in an April 1985 car accident. The rod was due to be removed in the fall of 1986, and doctors had advised Cindy that the leg would be painful if she were not in a warm climate.

According to some of Cindy's friends, she had been talking about going on a trip for a few days, but she had offered few details. One neighbor said she left the trailer park with two male friends, and another friend speculated the trio was involved in an illegal money-laundering scheme. Cindy left behind all her clothes, personal items, and her car, so it seemed unusual to her sister that she would have left for more than just a day or so.

St. Cloud police were able to locate one of the two men that Cindy allegedly left town with, but they were unable to find the other. The unidentified male they did find claimed he didn't have any knowledge of Schmidt's whereabouts. The other man, Ronnie Bromenschenkel, was also missing. Friends of Schmidt indicated that Cindy and

Bromenschenkel had been dating at the time of their disappearance.

Bromenschenkel, 26, of Sauk Rapids had a long record of criminal activity dating back to 1979. In May of that year he and 18-year-old Kevin Kurtz, also of Sauk Rapids, took a Pontiac Trans Am from the Baston Chevrolet dealership and ended up being the subject of a high-speed chase through Stearns and Morrison Counties. In a related incident, Kurtz was charged with burglary for breaking into the Pelican Lake Ballroom in the Township of Avon, where he stole a large amount of beer.

In March 1980, Bromenschenkel robbed a St. Cloud Yellow Cab driver at knifepoint. A city police officer on patrol witnessed Bromenschenkel attempting to force the cab driver, Kenneth Johnson, into the trunk of his cab. Bromenschenkel was arrested after a struggle with the officer.

The 1986 disappearance of Cindy Schmidt and Ronnie Bromenschenkel went completely quiet after receiving very little local media coverage to begin with. In 1987 the St. Cloud Police Department offered a $20,000 reward for information leading to answers about what happened to the pair. In releasing information about the reward, police finally revealed they believed that Schmidt and Bromenschenkel were dead, and that they believed they had been victims of foul play. St. Cloud police and the Minnesota Bureau of Criminal Investigation assigned full-time detectives to investigate their disappearance.

When the reward money was offered, BCA agent Dennis Flier and St. Cloud detective Ken McDonald revealed they had a possible suspect in the case, and felt the case may be close to closure.

"We're hoping with this exposure there are people who were well acquainted with Cindy and Ronnie that may have additional information that will help us with some answers," said McDonald.

Christine Midas reiterated investigators' beliefs that there were people who knew what happened to her sister, saying that Cindy hung out with people who likely had information that could solve the case.

"I think they have information and they have been apprehensive about saying it," Midas said. "I hope this reward will encourage them to take a risk."

The August 16, 1986 disappearance of Cindy Schmidt and Ronnie Bromenschenkel remains unsolved. Anyone with information about their disappearance or whereabouts is asked to call St. Cloud Police Department at 320-345-4444.

Bibliography – Under the Radar

Aeikens, D. (1997, July 30). $40,000 Offered for 2 Unsolved Crimes. *St. Cloud Times* , pp. 1A, 6A.

Norton, M. (1986, December 20). Family Fears for Missing Daughter. *St. Cloud Times* , pp. 1A, 10A.

St. Cloud Times Staff. (1979, May 19). 5 Arraigned in Court on Various Charges. *St. Cloud Times* , p. 10.

St. Cloud Times Staff. (1980, March 25). City Police Thwart Alleged Robbery of Yellow Cab Driver. *St. Cloud Times* , p. 24.

St. Cloud Times Staff. (1980, May 17). Man Admits to Robbing Cab Driver. *St. Cloud Times* , p. 14.

St. Cloud Times Staff. (1979, June 7). Man Given Prison Term fo Forgery Count. *St. Cloud Times* .

Chapter Eight

The Search for Jacob Wetterling

Victim: *Jacob Wetterling*
Date: *October 22, 1989*
Status: *Solved in 2016*
Location: *St. Joseph*

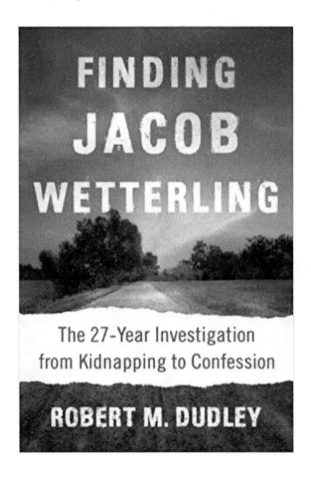

The October 22, 1989 abduction of Jacob Wetterling from a dark, dead-end road in St. Joseph is arguably the most shocking and mysterious crime the state of Minnesota has ever known. Jacob's abduction at the hands of a masked man toting a handgun was all sorts of rare. It was rare not only because a stranger took him, but also because the abduction happened in the presence of two witnesses—Jacob's brother Trevor, and his best friend Aaron Larson.

Word of the kidnapping of Jacob Wetterling spread quickly across the state and country—it seemed the boy was everywhere, but couldn't be found. The story went viral in a time long before the availability of cell phones, the Internet, and social media. Unfortunately, that widespread exposure actually proved detrimental to the investigation, sending detectives and police scrambling to check out thousands of leads all across Minnesota, other states, and even other countries.

It took more than a quarter of a century to solve the Jacob Wetterling kidnapping, but the answers turned out to be simple and were right there in the dirt driveway from where the young child was taken away. All along, the secret to uncovering what happened to Jacob Wetterling tied directly to well-publicized assaults on boys that happened in the nearby towns of Paynesville and Cold Spring from 1986-1989.

Robert M. Dudley's book, *Finding Jacob Wetterling*, chronicles the history of the investigation. The comprehensive and well-researched story begins with the day of the abduction and recounts the massive, multi-agency investigation that followed.

Dudley's interest in the case was piqued in 2010, when Stearns County investigators turned their attention publicly to Dan Rassier as a suspect in Jacob's kidnapping. Rassier was the man who lived at the end of the dirt driveway where Jacob had been abducted. Two years later, Dudley's casual dabbling into the case evolved into more serious research, and he ultimately resurrected several "old" pieces of information that cast doubt on Rassier as a suspect, and pointed to the actual abductor. Newspaper archives from the *Paynesville Press* and *St. Cloud Times* newspapers, a memoir written by one of the key investigators in the case, and a set of long-lost, handwritten notes from a private investigator proved to be the keys to unlocking the mystery of what happened to Jacob Wetterling.

In the fall of 2014, while social media, Twin-Cities television news stations, and Stearns County investigators were focusing again on early suspects in the case, including Delbert Huber and Duane Hart, amateur sleuth Robert M. Dudley believed they were after the wrong man. Unable to draw media attention to the information he had uncovered, Dudley turned his efforts to constructing a history of the case in the form of a book. The original book, *It Can't Happen Here — The Search For Jacob Wetterling*, debuted in March 2015. In the book, Dudley suggested that Duane Hart had pointed the finger at the actual kidnapper, Danny Heinrich, back in 1990. It turned out he was right.

Just six months after the release of Dudley's book, Danny Heinrich was arrested and named a person of interest in Jacob's case. The book also formed the basis for the research behind the popular, Peabody award-winning podcast series *In The Dark* in 2016. *Finding Jacob Wetterling* is the third edition of that book. It details the day of Jacob's abduction, the Paynesville series of assaults and other incidents that preceded it, and concludes with the stunning courtroom confession of Danny Heinrich.

Chapter Nine
Centennial Park Mystery

Victim: Herbert Fromelt
Date: August 3, 1994
Status: Unsolved
Location: 13th Avenue North in the City of St. Cloud

Herbert Fromelt, Sr. returned to his St. Cloud home from a meeting at St. Paul's Catholic Church Tuesday night, August 2, 1994. At the age of 81, Herb, who had retired from his hardware store business more than 20 years earlier, had been gradually deteriorating in terms of his physical health. Despite that, he remained quite active in community affairs. He wasn't feeling well that particular evening and for that reason he canceled plans to meet one of his daughters, Mary Ann May, for dinner. Mary Ann left a note on her father's kitchen counter, asking him to call her to make plans for lunch later in the week instead. He telephoned Mary Ann when he got home at about 9:00 p.m., and they agreed he would come over to her house when he was feeling better.

Herb had been living by himself since his wife died of an illness three years before. He and Marie had shared their 13th Avenue North home near Centennial Park in St. Cloud since moving there from Rice in 1979. Herb developed arthritis and other ailments that typically accompany old age, but he still attended church nearly every day of the week. Although his health was deteriorating over time, he remained strong enough to live on his own with some assistance from his children and grandchildren who lived in the area. For example, the boyfriend of Mary Ann's daughter, Herb's granddaughter, took care of mowing the lawn. Other family members pitched in with household duties as well.

Another of Fromelt's daughters, Linda Wieber, was in St. Cloud along with her son who was attending his freshmen orientation at St. Cloud State University. The Wiebers lived about an hour away, in Crystal, Minnesota. It had been a typical hot and humid August day, with temperatures climbing well into the 80's. Linda stopped in to see her father at about 3:30 on Wednesday afternoon. As she approached the front door, she took note that the air conditioning unit was not running. She knew that probably meant it would be very warm inside her father's house, so she planned to make it a brief visit.

Linda and her son stepped into the house and she called out for her father. There was no reply. Herb Fromelt was hard-of-hearing, so she thought maybe he didn't have his hearing aids in, or perhaps he was taking a nap. She walked down the hall to check his bedroom and as she approached she could see him lying on the bedroom floor.

"Dad, wake up!" Linda shouted.[115] He didn't move.

Walking into his bedroom, Linda Wieber saw her father lying face down and in a pool of blood. He was still in his pajamas. She called 911 for help, and then called Bill Fromelt, her brother, to tell him what she had found. A few minutes later, Mary Ann called the Fromelt house. Linda told her sister how she had found their father. Soon after, Mary Ann's daughter and her boyfriend came to the house. Police and paramedics arrived minutes later, and family members were promptly ordered out of the house. Police sealed off the home and put crime scene tape up across the yard. They initially revealed few details about Herb Fromelt's death, referring to it only as "suspicious" in nature.

"We stood there on the front porch staring at each other not really knowing what happened," Linda Wieber said of what was going through the minds of Fromelt's children who had gathered outside his home. "When I saw the yellow tape going up across the yard, I went black. I knew it had to be something bad. I just thought of my daddy laying there by himself without any one of us being close to him. It was like an earthquake just swallowing you, and there's nothing you can do."[116]

Within a couple of days, autopsy results on Herb Fromelt's body confirmed his death was by homicide caused by multiple stab wounds to his chest. The St. Cloud Police Department then issued a warning to area residents to take appropriate safety measures. Evidence found at the scene indicated there had been a struggle between Fromelt and his attacker. It appeared Fromelt's killer might have interrupted a home burglary, but the motive remained a mystery after a thorough search of the home by family members failed to determine whether anything of value was missing. Fromelt was not wearing his hearing aids at the time of his murder.

An editorial by the *St. Cloud Times* lashed out at St. Cloud police for taking so long to warn the public about a killer on the loose. The editorial admonished the Police Department for initially terming Herbert Fromelt's murder only as "suspicious." The column acknowledged that withholding some information about such a serious crime was understandable, and good policy to protect an active investigation. However, the newspaper claimed that St. Cloud police had gone "overboard" in guarding the fact that an intruder had stabbed a man inside his home, and that they did so without a valid reason. The *Times* felt the circumstances of the crime dictated that the public deserved an immediate, frank warning that a murdering intruder was at large in the Centennial Park area of the city of St. Cloud.

Family, friends, and community members gathered at St. Paul's Catholic Church in St. Cloud on Monday, August 8, for funeral services for Fromelt. Herb had been born in Rice, Minnesota in 1912. He was married to Marie Springers at the age of 18, and became the mayor of Rice at the age of 21–a position he held for more than 20 years. During his tenure as mayor, he was able to get the town's roads paved and he oversaw the building of a new village hall, which was aided by Franklin Roosevelt's 1939 Work Projects Administration. Herb and Marie raised 11 children together and at the time of his death he had nearly 60 grandchildren and great grandchildren. He took over his father's business, which began as Herman Fromelt's General Store in Rice in 1880, the same year the town of Rice was born. Herb grew the business considerably, adding a farm implement dealership and renaming the enterprise Fromelt's Implement and Hardware. He retired in 1970, and within a few years moved from Rice to St. Cloud, where he became active in a host of community organizations including the Knights of Columbus, the Eagles Club and the Elks. Although he was retired from the retail business, he still owned commercial property in Rice.

After Marie died in 1991, Herb Fromelt and many of his children began taking summer vacations together. In fact, they had just returned home from a vacation in the wilderness of Ontario, Canada two weeks before his murder. Their first such trip together was in 1992, when Herb and six of his seven daughters hit the road for a 10 day trip to Glacier National Park in Montana and the Black Hills of South Dakota. Due to an illness, only Mary Ann May had been unable to join the family on their trip.

Following his death, neighbors recounted Herb Fromelt's friendly and generous nature. "He was a wonderful man—a kind, generous man who wouldn't hurt anyone," said Cathy Laubeck, a neighbor who lived directly across the street from Herb. "It's very sad for all of us. Knowing it was a violent act that killed him makes it hurt more." [117]

"They were very upbeat people, they saw life very positively," said another neighbor, Joe Friedrich. "He was a great neighbor."[118]

"The City (of Rice) will miss him," added current mayor David Happke. "He's part of the foundation of this community."[119]

The Centennial Park residential area was considered an upscale part of the city of St. Cloud. It was home to a large base of lawyers, college professors, and government workers. The stabbing death of Herb Fromelt scared many of them, including Bill Wade, who had lived in the neighborhood for more than 30 years. "It's woken up the neighborhood about what can happen," Wade said.[120] Just days after the killing he and other members of the neighborhood had already taken steps to form a neighborhood watch program.

"We've always felt safe here. Now we feel the need to look out for each other," added Cathy Laubeck.[121]

A large team of investigators went to work immediately on Herb Fromelt's murder case. In all there were 20 law enforcement officers investigating his death. The team included detectives from the St. Cloud Police Department, as well as several investigators from surrounding counties via the multi-jurisdictional Major Crime Investigation Unit. That team included officers from Stearns, Benton, and Sherburne Counties. Members of Fromelt's family were interviewed, as were many of his friends and neighbors. Pawnshops in St. Cloud were scouted for possible clues to the crime. Police report records of incidents in the neighborhood were reviewed for similarities between crimes. Forensic teams gathered fingerprint and hair sample evidence from Herb's home.

The owners of two neighborhood homes told investigators they had heard prowlers in their back yards late Tuesday night or early Wednesday morning. One man said he heard the sound of chain link fencing rattling, like someone had hit or bumped into it. He suggested perhaps someone grabbed the fence to stop it from rattling, and the commotion set off a motion light outside his home. The man further theorized there were two prowlers because he heard them making whistling sounds, as if they were communicating with one another. As alarming as the details of that incident seemed to be, apparently neither man reported it to authorities until police interviewed them after Fromelt's murder.

Investigators quickly focused on the likelihood that Herbert Fromelt had met his death after interrupting a robbery in progress. Witness accounts of prowlers in Fromelt's neighborhood coupled with autopsy reports which showed evidence of a struggle, led investigators to consider the likelihood that robbery had been the killer's or killers' motive.

The other key suggestion brought forward by investigators was that the murderer was likely a young person. They based their theory on evidence found at the crime scene, but declined to specify what that evidence was. St. Cloud Police Chief Dennis O'Keefe advised reporters such speculation were only theories at this point, not concrete conclusions. He added that investigators did not have any solid suspects within the first three days of the killing.

On Saturday August 6, 1994, a crew of City of St. Cloud employees searched the storm sewers in the neighborhood around Herb Fromelt's home. They removed storm drain catch basins and manhole covers, and crawled inside searching for possible clues to the killing. Their primary objective was to find the murder weapon—the knife that had been used to kill Fromelt. Initial reports from Chief O'Keefe indicated searchers were unable to locate any evidence. O'Keefe explained that the search of the storm drains was not prompted by any specific tip, but rather was simply part of a thorough investigative effort.

By Monday morning, however, O'Keefe revealed that the weekend's search actually did produce possible evidence related to Fromelt's murder. He initially declined to specify exactly what searchers had found on Saturday.

But the following day, investigators revealed that the item found in the storm sewer 150' from Herbert Fromelt's house was a 10" serrated bread knife believed to be the murder weapon. Unfortunately, it had rained heavily on the night of the murder and any blood or fingerprints had likely been washed away from the knife. Despite their misfortunes with recoverable forensic evidence from the knife, investigators were able to score undeniable proof that the knife was indeed the murder weapon. What's more, the knife turned out to be from Herb Fromelt's own kitchen.

Investigators executed a pair of search warrants related to the murder on Monday August 8th. One warrant was served at a residence near downtown St. Cloud, the other was for Fromelt's home. O'Keefe said the people who lived at the downtown residence were not considered suspects and the search revealed no new information. The warrants were later sealed to prevent them from being disclosed publicly, a legal maneuver by investigators to protect information contained in the warrant application, or to protect an innocent person.

During the first 10 days following the murder, investigators had identified and cleared as many as 70 potential suspects. They had interviewed 150 neighbors, family members, and other possible witnesses. The investigation generated a good influx of tips and leads, so much so that the St. Cloud Police Department requested authorization to continue utilizing agents from the Major Crime Investigation Unit.

Tri-County Crime Stoppers announced a $1,000 reward for information leading to an arrest and conviction in the case, which had seen its share of ups and downs throughout the three weeks since the killing.

"It's like a roller coaster—peaks and valleys," said St. Cloud police Sgt. Scott Knochenmus. "You have a real good suspect and then they are eliminated. You keep narrowing the investigation."[122]

While the extensive investigation into Herb Fromelt's murder had not led to an arrest or a top suspect in the case to that point, other open cases benefited from peripheral information gathered by investigators. A series of automobile break-ins near Fromelt's neighborhood was solved, but the individuals responsible were eliminated as suspects in the murder. Another city burglary case was solved, and a second arrest was made in an assault on a teenager during a recent gang fight.

Investigators collected DNA samples from a number of suspects to compare to samples of hair and blood found in Herb Fromelt's home. Many samples were collected at the crime scene, but officials did not have a great level of certainty about whether or not they had collected samples left behind by the killer. The first round of results was due by October. While the revolutionary technology was still a relatively new criminal investigative tool, and there was no general database available to compare results to, DNA comparisons between direct evidence and a known pool of suspects was commonplace by 1994.

One early suspect actually lived in California. Investigators indicated the man had been in St. Cloud at the time of the murders but offered little else in the way of details about the man, although speculation was he had been staying at the downtown residence that had been the location of a search warrant served early in the investigation. The man submitted a DNA sample to investigators.

Other suspects in the murder included workers at the Benton County Fair, which opened the same night Fromelt was last seen alive. The fairgrounds were two miles away from Fromelt's home. Investigators did not reveal details about how Fromelt and the workers might have crossed paths or whether there was evidence the workers had been in Fromelt's neighborhood.

By the last week of August, leads in the case had begun to dry up and St. Cloud police reduced the number of investigators working the case. They discontinued the use of officers from the Major Crime Investigation Unit, leaving just seven St. Cloud police officers to continue the investigation.

Just before Christmas 1994, St. Cloud Police Chief Dennis O'Keefe said investigators still lacked a motive for the murder. He said police had other details about Fromelt's death but they were withholding them on account of the ongoing investigation. Despite the lack of solid progress in the case, he expressed belief the case was solvable.

"I'm confident that it can be solved," O'Keefe said. "But it's a tough case. The motive, at this point, is difficult to determine."[123]

On the first anniversary of Fromelt's murder, in August 1995, Herb's daughter, Linda Wieber, contemplated the balance between finding answers to who killed her father and why, and the pain that comes along with finding those answers.

"It's going to mean more pain. It's going to be like living everything from Day One," she said. "If they don't solve it, I won't have to sit in court and hear it all over again. I don't know if it makes sense. But as it is now, you can try to take the pain and start putting it on the shelf and putting it away." [124]

Meanwhile, police reiterated they still did not have primary suspects in the case. They had collected 143 pieces of evidence and taken 156 crime scene photographs. Investigators had interviewed hundreds of people and logged more than 3,000 hours working on the Fromelt murder in the year that had passed since his stabbing death. Detectives had compared more than 69,000 fingerprints to those that were recovered from the crime scene, checking them against a national database of convicted felons.

"We have no idea who committed this crime, and at this point we don't have a suspect," admitted O'Keefe. "But somebody knows who committed this crime, and it's high time they came forward."[125]

New leads in the case stalled out. St. Cloud police detective Dale Marschel took over as the lead investigator in the case. He replaced Scott Knochenmus, who was placed on administrative leave after being investigated for forging a judge's signature on a search warrant in another criminal case.

"It's been a couple of months since we've had a new lead," said detective Marschel. "Most of the stuff that comes in, we've already checked on. When I took it over, the case was pretty cold by then. I was glad for the chance to do it. I wanted it solved in August 1994, and I still want it solved. It's my No. 1 priority to bring this case to conclusion."[126]

Although police maintained they had not been able to determine a motive for the slaying, Linda, the youngest daughter, speculated that robbery had been the motive. She said her father's den was disheveled to the point it appeared someone had been searching for something. She noted that some items in the basement were also out of place, and a window in her father's kitchen appeared to have been pried open. Police officials countered that they had conflicting information about how the den should have appeared.

"Maybe this will jog a memory about any strange incidents," Linda said. "They need to be aware that the perpetrator didn't just walk in and attack my father. Maybe someone remembers something now. Anything."[127]

In July 1997, as the third anniversary of Herb Fromelt's murder passed by, St. Cloud police announced they were offering a $20,000 reward in an effort to draw fresh leads in the case. The announcement, which was published in the *St. Cloud Times*, prompted a pair of phone calls with tips but nothing substantial was gained.

"It's not real promising," said lead investigator Dale Marschel. "It's about people we've already looked at."[128]

The reward expired without any significant developments coming from it. Two years later, in 1999, Tri-County Crime Stoppers announced a new $5,000 reward. Again, it produced no results.

In 2004, investigators released this photograph of a religious medallion they believed was worn by Herbert Fromelt's killer. Photo courtesy of *St. Cloud Times*

Without additional leads to follow up on, the Fromelt murder investigation ground to a halt and no progress was made in the case for several years. After essentially becoming a dormant case, it eventually fell into the hands of the Minnesota Bureau of Criminal Apprehension (BCA). Desperate to spur new leads at the 10-year anniversary in 2004, the BCA released previously unknown details of the crime, including a photograph and description of a religious medallion found near the crime scene at the beginning of the investigation.

"The thing is, there may be someone who knows something and says something," said Herb's eldest son, Herbert Fromelt, Jr., said of the investigation. "They (investigators) need a little more help, and this could point the finger in the right direction."[129]

The religious medallion was a significant clue because it was believed to have been a "pilgrimage" item, something that whoever it belonged to had to travel somewhere to get it. The medallion, which was determined by researchers to be relatively rare, had imprints of a woman and baby on the front, probably depicting Mary and Jesus. Investigators believed Fromelt's murderer was wearing it, and the fish line it was hanging from likely was broken during a struggle between Fromelt and his attacker.

BCA Special Agent Ken McDonald led the charge in releasing new information in the case. McDonald worked for the St. Cloud Police Department at the time of Fromelt's killing in 1994. He was assigned the Fromelt case in 2002, taking a fresh look at old leads contained in the file.

"In this case we do have physical evidence," McDonald said. "And it's a very solvable case."[130]

McDonald explained investigators typically retain certain details of crimes to keep the information from becoming public. Over time, however, releasing such information could help the case if it encourages people who have critical information to come forward and talk to authorities after years of not talking.

"We mainly do that because we want to preserve and protect some things that only the killer would know," McDonald said.[131] While he declined to offer specific theories regarding a motive, he did once again raise the possibility the killer was someone who was working at the Benton County Fair.

The BCA also released certain elements of the criminal profile of Fromelt's killer that had been put together by the FBI's Behavioral Science Unit.

- The crime was not sexually motivated
- The murderer was unlikely to be a stranger; they likely knew Herb Fromelt. The relationship may not have been close, such as casual friend or distant relative.
- The killer was not likely a very young person because the killer demonstrated a high degree of control over Fromelt. The killer was probably between 18 and 25 years old
- The killer was probably a Caucasian male
- Personal rage did not contribute to the crime
- Although there may have been more than one person involved in a related crime prior to the murder, there was probably only one offender inside the home at the time of the murder

Investigators have always maintained they have been unable to develop a specific motive for the murder of Herbert Fromelt, Sr. While that may be true, details of the crime and witness accounts would suggest his murder likely resulted from a robbery gone wrong and resulted in murder to cover up the original crime. A pair of Fromelt's neighbors reported hearing the sounds of prowlers in the neighborhood in the early morning hours on the night of the murder. A family member said publicly that a window in the home's kitchen appeared to have been pried open. A search by several family members failed to pinpoint anything significant missing from the home, although the disheveled state of basement and den areas seemed to indicate someone was going through Fromelt's belongings in search of something. Furthermore, the murder weapon, a 10" serrated bread knife, was from Fromelt's own kitchen. That indicates whoever killed Fromelt was in the house for some other reason and did not intend to kill him while in the house.

The August 2, 1994 stabbing murder of Herbert Fromelt, Jr. remains an unsolved crime. Although no one has ever been arrested in the case, and no suspects have been named or indicated publicly, it is a solvable case. The case is likely just one witness account or piece of critical physical evidence away from closure. Anyone with information about the death of Herbert Fromelt, Jr. is asked to call St. Cloud Police Department at 320-345-4444.

Bibliography – Centennial Park Mystery

Aeikens, D. (1997, July 30). $40,000 Offered for 2 Unsolved Crimes. *St. Cloud Times*, pp. 1A, 6A.

Aeikens, D. (1997, August 12). Tips Trickle in After Reward Offer. *St. Cloud Times*, p. 3A.

Ling, B. (1992, July 4). Dad, Daughters Hit the Trail on Unusual Summer Vacation. *St. Cloud Times*, p. 3A.

Nistler, M. (1994, August 7). North Side Search Yields no Weapons. *St. Cloud Times*, p. 1A.

Scott, K. (2004, August 4). Evidence Revealed in Former Rice Mayor's Killing - Officials Ask for Help Solving 10-Year-Old Case After Discovery of Medallion at Crime Scene. *St. Cloud Times*, pp. 1A, 4A.

St. Cloud Times Editorial Staff. (1994, August 6). Lack of Police Candor Didn't Serve Community. *St. Cloud Times*, p. 8A.

Unze, D. (1999, May 17). Reward Offered in Murder Cases - $5,000 to be Given for Information on 8 Unsolved Murders. *St. Cloud Times*, pp. 1A, 4A.

Walsh, J. (1994, August 5). Victim Was Former Mayor of Rice. *St. Cloud Times*, pp. 1A, 10A.

Welsh, J. (1994, August 12). Authorities Want to Keep 20 Officers Probing Slaying. *St. Cloud Times*, p. 1A.

Welsh, J. (1994, August 23). DNA Evidence Considered in Fromelt Death - Crime Stoppers Offers Reward for Information About August 3 Slaying. *St. Cloud Times*, p. 3A.

Welsh, J. (1994, December 18). Fromelt Family Still Trying to Make Sense of Father's Murder. *St. Cloud TImes*, pp. 1A, 7A.

Welsh, J. (1994, August 6). Investigation into Fromelt's Death Focuses on 2 Theories. *St. Cloud Times*, p. 1A.

Welsh, J. (1994, August 9). Knife Found in Sewer Belonged to Slaying Victim, Police Say. *St. Cloud Times*, p. 1A.

Welsh, J. (1994, August 5). Local Man Stabbed to Death in Home - 20 Police Investigators Probe Slaying of 81-Year-Old in Home. *St. Cloud Times*, pp. 1A, 10A.

Welsh, J. (1994, August 9). Police Find Possible Evidence in Sewer. *St. Cloud Times*, p. 1A.

Welsh, J. (1994, August 4). Police Investigating Death of 81-Year-Old. *St. Cloud Times*, p. 3A.

Welsh, J. (1995, August 3). St. Cloud's Only Unsolved Murder Haunts Family, Puzzles Police. *St. Cloud Times*, pp. 1A, 10A.

Welsh, J. (1994, September 9). State's Lone DNA Lab Increases Credibility - Local Officials Turn to Genetics for Clues in Solving Killings. *St. Cloud Times*, p. 3A.

Welsh, J. (1994, August 12). Tips, Investigation Help in Resolving Other Area Crimes. *St. Cloud Times*, p. 1A.

Chapter Ten

A Lost Sheep

Victim: Joshua Guimond

Date: November 9, 2002

Status: Unexplained Disappearance

Location: St. John's University in Collegeville, Minnesota

Luke 15:4

*What man of you, having a hundred sheep,
if he has lost one of them does not leave the
ninety-nine in the wilderness, and go after
the one which is lost, until he finds it?
And when he comes home, he calls together
his friends and his neighbors, saying to them,
'Rejoice with me, for I have found my sheep
which was lost.'*

Twenty-year-old Joshua Guimond, the only child of Brian Guimond and Lisa Cheney, was a year 2000 graduate of Maple Lake High School. He was very active in extracurricular activities there and served as class president and the student council representative on the school board. He played multiple instruments in various school bands, and played baseball and football as well. When a shoulder injury precluded him from participating in sports his senior season, he volunteered to voice the play-by-play from the press box rather than loiter around the field on the sidelines. Guimond was universally liked by students and faculty alike, and was selected by his classmates as the most likely to succeed. When a student-oriented activity in Maple Lake came into conflict with the city's curfew ordinance, Joshua was able to leverage his influence in the community to get the ordinance changed to allow the event to go on as scheduled.

By all accounts, Joshua's likeability and strong work ethic followed him from Maple Lake to the campus of St. John's University in Collegeville, Minnesota. The school is a men's liberal arts university, with a coordinated women's school in nearby St. Joseph–the College of

St. Benedict. The dedicated and hard-working student aspired to a career in politics, emulating his grandmother, Barb Vickerman. So impassioned was he about a future in the political arena, that he used the nickname 'SenatorJosh' in his email address. Joshua's short-term plans included earning a bachelor's degree in Collegeville and then moving on to law school. He had narrowed the field to a number of prestigious programs including Minnesota, Georgetown, and Yale. Friends said his decision would ultimately depend on earning a highly coveted Truman Scholarship.

Joshua balanced the afternoon of Saturday November 9, 2002 with studies and relaxation in the newly constructed St. Maur House apartment he shared with five other roommates. He took a break from his studies in mid-afternoon to smoke a cigar that was left over from some he purchased for his mock trial team. Guimond was co-captain of the team, along with one of his roommates and close friend, senior Nick Hydukovich. Josh chatted with his ex-girlfriend Katie Benson via AOL Instant Messenger for a while. The pair had dated for five years going back to their high school days in Maple Lake, Minnesota. Although they had broken off their romantic relationship about a month earlier, they still talked on a daily basis and remained good friends. By all outward appearances, both of them had been coping well with the breakup.

After a casual afternoon of studies, Joshua turned to an even more relaxing Saturday evening. He surfed websites about the Minnesota Timberwolves, the weather forecast, mock trials, employment opportunities, and the listings of movies scheduled to air on the St. John's-operated television station. Joshua was fond of the finer things in life, and he read through some online reviews for high quality cigars and the world's finest beers. One of his friends, Alex Jude, came over to the apartment and they enjoyed a few beers while Joshua sprinkled in some research for a history report about American statesman and Founding Father, Alexander Hamilton. After some time another friend, Greg Worden, joined Joshua and Alex at the apartment.

At about 11:00 p.m., Joshua, Alex, and Greg decided to go to a small party at Nate Slinkard's Metten Court apartment. Joshua, dressed in a St. John's logo hooded sweatshirt and blue jeans, left St. Maur with the others for the five-minute walk. They chatted as they made their way over the Watab causeway, which crossed the culvert at the northeastern tip of Stumpf Lake. There were ten students in all at the small party once Joshua's group arrived. Some played cards while others shared conversation, and all were enjoying a few beers.

Joshua's group had been at the apartment for about an hour when Nate Slinkard saw Guimond get up and walk out of the room. Joshua didn't appear to say anything to anyone. When his friends first noted his absence they figured he had gone to the bathroom. When he didn't return after some time they surmised that Joshua had walked home alone. One of the friends called Joshua's apartment but there was no answer, so they assumed he was already asleep. The party at Metten Court broke up at about 1:00 a.m. and everyone went home.

A political science major, Joshua was the treasurer of the 50 member pre-law society at St. John's. He had a meeting scheduled with student senate auditor Sarah Mathies at 2:30 p.m. on Sunday. Their meeting was to review the club's pending request to purchase $385 worth of practice exams for the Law School Admission Test. The club had recently reconsidered the purchase, deciding to forego spending the money on the exams. Instead, they wanted to utilize the funds for other club purchases. By early afternoon it occurred to Hydukovich that he hadn't seen Joshua at all that day. He was chatting online with Katie

Benson at about 1:00 p.m. and asked her if she had seen or heard from Joshua at all. She hadn't. Other friends made calls to classmates, but no one had seen him at all on Sunday.

Hydukovich was president of the pre-law club, and it struck him as completely out of character for Joshua to not show up at their apartment or contact him prior to the 2:30 p.m. meeting. Joshua was regarded as an organized, responsible, and reliable person. Nick attended the ten-minute meeting in Joshua's place. Afterward, he became increasingly concerned about Joshua's whereabouts—it just wasn't at all like his roommate to miss a scheduled activity like that.

This 2004 aerial photo of St. John's University shows the locations of the apartment buildings Joshua Guimond walked between. The most logical route of his six-minute walk would have taken him across the Watab Causeway.

Joshua's coat, wallet and eyeglasses were at the apartment. His car was still parked, undisturbed, in the student parking lot where it had been in the parking stall for the last two days.

Alex Jude, Greg Worden, and another of Joshua's friends, Dusty Schuett, began searching for Joshua all over campus. They reported him missing to St. John's Life Safety at 10:00 p.m., and later called the Stearns County Sheriff's Office (SCSO). The trio searched for Joshua all night with flashlights. Deputies from SCSO arrived on Sunday night for a brief search of the campus. Stearns County officials moved quickly to implement an organized search effort to begin Monday morning.

A total of 50 Stearns County deputies and reserve officers searched on foot and on horseback across the St. John's University campus beginning Monday morning. The marshy areas in the woods around the campus were difficult to get into.

"We searched every inch of campus," said Stearns County Lt. Dave Nohner. "We searched what we could in the dark. Our resources were activated by 7:00 a.m. on Monday and we conducted a search of the campus and its buildings, going basically room to room, including the power plant, the dorms, and all the wooded areas."[132]

At 10:00 a.m. a State Patrol helicopter joined the search by air. By Monday night all campus dormitories, classrooms, and buildings had been searched, including the monastery and the power plant. University officials allowed every building on campus to be searched. The all-inclusive, unrestricted search would ordinarily have required search warrants. Posters of the missing young man were displayed all across the campus. SCSO impounded Joshua's car to search it for evidence.

A bloodhound brought in Monday morning from Glenwood was able to follow Joshua's scent from Metten Court to the roadway that crossed over the culvert at the east end of Stumpf Lake. The dog then tracked Joshua's scent to the culvert. The dog's handler, Greg Meyers, said it was his belief that Joshua either went into Stumpf Lake, or he got into a car on the causeway. A Stearns County dive team was then brought in to search that end of the lake. They used underwater cameras but were unable to find any sign of Joshua. Deputies put up tape to secure the area of land between the road and culvert.

"If anybody out there knows anything call 911," Brian Guimond said, wasting no time in appealing to the public for their help in finding his son. He then added a plea to his own son with a simple message: "Josh, if you can hear this, get a hold of somebody and let us know what happened."[133]

Lisa Cheney joined in the public appeal for help as well. "We have no idea what happened," she said. "We thought something happened and he walked back to his house. All we want to know is that he's safe and he's back home."[134]

Officials from Maple Lake High School contacted St. John's University to offer assistance in the search for Joshua. Michael Hemmesch, St. John's director of communications, advised that at that time SCSO was not seeking help from outside sources.

"They have not asked for help from any local people at this point," Hemmesch said. "Other than prayers, there's really nothing else people can do."[135]

On Tuesday, November 12, Stearns County brought in 22 mounted reserves to help with the search. One horse sank in the muck up to its chest. Three rescue dogs joined the effort, including a bloodhound from Pope County. Deputy Sheriff John Sanner explained that the organized search effort was hitting all areas of the university property.

A bloodhound brought in by Stearns County tracked Joshua's scent to this sidewalk that divided Highway 159 from Stumpf Lake. Investigators believed that Joshua may have fallen over this 36" high concrete wall, through the brush, and into Stumpf Lake. Note that these photos were taken in 2017. Aerial photos from 2004 indicate the concrete wall and the brush alongside it were very much then as they are today.

"We're systematically searching through the university buildings and all surrounding wooded areas and waters," Sanner said.[136]

Stearns County Sheriff Jim Kostreba ordered deputies to get in contact with deer hunters who had participated in a controlled deer hunt around the campus on Sunday to see if anyone had seen any clothing or other signs of anyone in the woods.

About 250 volunteer searchers from the St. John's student body joined about 50 firefighters and rescue workers in searching some of the wooded and marshy areas on campus. At Sheriff Kostreba's request, Minnesota Governor Jesse Ventura ordered the National Guard to join the search for Joshua Guimond. The move marked the first time SCSO had requested assistance from the National Guard since the 1989 abduction of Jacob Wetterling. A total of 118 Guard soldiers from Rosemount and Brainerd arrived on campus the morning of Wednesday, November 13. They used all-terrain vehicles and a pair of helicopters to aid in the search. The soldiers broke up into groups of about a dozen each as they combed through the woods. By the time the Guard left at 5:00 p.m. they had scoured the 2,400-acre university property and 700 acres of other land, much of which was densely wooded. Some soldiers commented that the terrain was so dense they couldn't comprehend how anyone could get back there in the dark of night, as Joshua would have had to do if he had gone into the woods.

As Brian Guimond waited for news about Joshua's whereabouts, he stayed on campus in Joshua's St. Maur House apartment. He spoke of the agony he and Joshua's mother had endured the last few days since their son disappeared.

"Unless you've got a child missing, there's no way you can know how it feels," Guimond said. "You may think you can know, but you don't. It ain't easy. You don't get much sleep, but at least you're with his friends."[137]

After three full days of searching the campus failed to produce any sign of Joshua Guimond, except for his scent near Stumpf Lake, St. John's University officials sought permission from the Minnesota Department of Natural Resources to lower the level of the lake. With the weather starting to turn colder and the prospect of ice covering Stumpf Lake and the other lakes on campus, SCSO officials had to move quickly. They dragged the shallow, murky Stumpf Lake for any signs of Joshua. But again, nothing was found. Sheriff Jim Kostreba said that more than 20 square miles of property had been searched over the course of the three days since Joshua Guimond was reported missing. The campus areas, he said, had been searched three or four times.

St. John's students join the search effort for Joshua Guimond on Tuesday November 12, 2002. Photo courtesy of the St. Cloud Times, November 13, 2002.

SCSO ended the intense search effort for Joshua on campus but investigators went to Joshua's apartment on Thursday, November 14, to take his computer for review and analysis. Once the computer was returned, Brian Guimond turned it over to Fox 9 Television. Fox hired a computer forensics expert and ran a story saying that Adam McDonald, one of Joshua's roommates, had accessed Joshua's computer two days after Joshua disappeared. There were three accounts on the computer—Joshua's, Adam's, and an admin account. It appeared that a website called 'Internet Washer' had been accessed and that a large number of files had been deleted.

After the extensive multi-day search for Joshua failed to turn up any sign of the young man, Stearns County investigators began to interview Joshua's friends and roommates. None of them were sure how much alcohol Joshua consumed that evening. His friends knew that he had several beers, but all agreed that Joshua seemed fine when he was with them. After talking to his friends, investigators were still unable to find any evidence or reason to suspect foul play. Later, a report indicating that investigators had interviewed only eight of the nine people from the party who had last seen Joshua alive led to speculation about the whereabouts of that ninth person–a woman. Doubts about the investigative effort began to circulate.

"There are certain things that we thought should be done in a timely manner that have not been done," said Lisa Cheney, speaking of the apparent inability to locate and speak with that last witness. "We just don't know what to do right now."[138]

Interviews with campus students did yield some key information. One witness reported seeing Joshua walking along a paved path between Metten Court and County Road 159 at about midnight, a route consistent with Joshua's most logical path back to his apartment at St. Maur House. A group of witnesses who were walking toward a campus bus stop reported seeing someone fitting Joshua's description near the causeway over Stumpf Lake at about that same time. Again, if it were Joshua the group had seen, the timing and location fit with Joshua's route back to his apartment. But investigators know that Joshua did not make it back to his apartment, because entry into his building would have required a scan from his student ID. A check of usage revealed that Joshua had last entered his apartment at about 11:00 p.m. on the night he disappeared.

National Guard units arriving at St. John's. Photo courtesy of Maple Lake Messenger, November 20, 2002.

An Itasca County dive team came to Collegeville and used their sophisticated side scan technology to search Stumpf Lake again. That equipment was shared between 14 counties in northern Minnesota, and provided detailed images of the bottom of the lake. A growing layer of ice prevented the team from searching the entire lake, but nothing was found in the portions they were able to search.

In desperation, Joshua Guimond's family sought national media attention to publicize his case. Brian Guimond, Lisa Cheney, and other family members interviewed with several outlets including *Good Morning America*, Fox News, CNN, and others. They asked the public to come forward with any information about Joshua. Brian Guimond appealed specifically to local hunters who would be in the woods during the annual deer hunt. One hunter did locate a St. John's cap, but it was determined not to be Joshua's.

The Guimond family, along with help from Heavenly Grounds Coffee Shop, Madigan's, and Rev. Steven King in Maple Lake, organized a search party to look for Joshua on Saturday November 23. Volunteers gathered at Holy Cross Lutheran Church in Maple Lake and then drove together to St. John's. Despite the bitter cold weather more than 75 people searched for Joshua that day. They focused on sections of woods that were adjacent to walking paths on campus.

Nothing related to Joshua's disappearance was found that day, but the searchers did find a few unusual items. For example, a pair of brand new waders and a pair of army boots were found near a lake behind St. John's Abbey. National Guard troops most likely had left them behind when they searched the campus about ten days earlier. One searcher noticed the tip of a cardboard shoebox sticking out of soft ground. The box appeared to be some sort of time capsule containing letters, pictures, some cash, a necklace, a can of beer, and a bottle of mustard. The group searched until 3:30 p.m., then returned to Maple Lake where the volunteers were served a meal at Holy Cross Lutheran Church.

Joshua's disappearance was not the only case of college students from the area to go missing. A total of four college students from Minnesota and western Wisconsin disappeared during a ten-day stretch from October 30 to November 9, 2002. The first in the string of missing college students was Erika Marie Dalquist, 21, who disappeared after leaving a bar in Brainerd on October 30. She was last seen wearing blue jeans and a blue sweatshirt. Twenty-one-year-old Chris Jenkins, a senior at the University of Minnesota, went missing the next night, on Halloween. He had dressed up as a Native American Indian and was last seen leaving a party at the Lone Tree Bar & Grill in Minneapolis. On Wednesday November 6, 22-year-old Michael Noll disappeared from near the University of Wisconsin-Eau Claire campus after a night of celebrating his birthday.

Speculation about possible links between the missing students began to circulate after Noll disappeared, and were only amplified after Joshua Guimond disappeared three days later. The FBI began looking into the cases for any sign that they might be connected.

"The FBI is involved," explained Minneapolis-based FBI special agent Paul McCabe. "We're reviewing the cases, but I stress we're not the lead agency."[139] McCabe's remarks were a clear indication that the FBI had not found any reason to believe the cases were related, and their role at that point was strictly in terms of looking for possible links.

The only common link apparent between the missing individuals was they had all been last seen leaving a bar or a party where alcohol had been served. As the days passed, more information about the missing students started coming to light —except in Joshua's case. A report in the Eau Claire media suggested a man closely fitting the description of Michael Noll, a native of Rochester, MN, wondered into the home of an elderly woman near the area where Noll had last been seen. The man left behind a ball cap that was later confirmed to belong to Noll. Noll's family was encouraged by the information but their attention turned to speculation about what kind of foul play Michael might have been the subject of that night. In Brainerd, police chief John Bolduc assembled a team of 100 volunteers to search area woods for Erika Dalquist. Bolduc was mum about the reasons that led to the particular search area. In Chris Jenkins' case, the bar that he had last visited, the Lone Tree Bar & Grill, happened to be his girlfriend's place of employment. She was not working on the evening of his disappearance.

The four missing college students had one more thing in common, something that inhibited more significant law enforcement investigation in their disappearances. They were all adults—they had the "right" to be missing. When adults are reported missing the investigation of their cases must be balanced with their rights and freedoms as adults. Typically, there must be reason to suspect foul play or imminent danger before an investigative agency commits to investigating simple cases of missing adults. As of November 2002, FBI statistics showed there were 42,310 active missing adult cases in the United States. Of those, more than 25% were between the ages of 18 and 21.

Missing adults from Minnesota numbered 257, a disproportionately small number compared with the national figures. Melissa Kelly, a case manager from Missing Children Minnesota, explained that cases of missing adults are simply handled with less urgency than cases of missing children.

"Adults have every right to walk away, disappear, or do whatever they want to," Kelly said. "The same thing doesn't apply to children."[140]

Adult or not, the apparent backdrop of politics behind the perceived lack of interest in Joshua's case was difficult for Joshua's mother to accept. The process of initiating official investigative action into Joshua's disappearance frustrated her.

"He's not here to exercise those rights and he would want us to do everything we can to find him," Lisa Cheney reasoned. "I don't care how old he is. He's missing. It's like beating your head against a brick wall."[141]

Cheney's bitterness concerning the investigative effort put forth to find her son would not be the only point of contention between Joshua's parents and the SCSO. The tension between them was just beginning to show, and the wheels of speculation about conspiracies, cover-ups, and a questionable investigation were just beginning to turn.

While the divide between Stearns County and Joshua's parents began to grow, universal love and support for Joshua Guimond blossomed at the campus of St. John's and back in his hometown of Maple Lake. Posters of Joshua were seen everywhere on campus. A large sign with his picture was erected at the entrance to the campus.

A prayer service at Holy Cross Lutheran Church drew more than 250 of Joshua's family, friends, and neighbors. Rev. Steven King led the service, asking the congregation to pray for Joshua's safe return, and also asked for prayers for Jenkins, Dalquist, and Noll.

"The worst would be to let the questions, pain, and doubt of real experience defeat us," King told his audience.[142] He then quoted from the Bible, Luke 15:4, about searching for a single lost sheep. Those attending the service were offered yellow ribbons as they left the church, and they wore them as a display of hope for Joshua.

Rev. King's poignant sermon was well received, and his message was on target. Nick Hydukovich was moved by the service.

"The Bible verses were well chosen during the service, especially the ones about finding the lost sheep," Nick said. "That's exactly what we're going to do."[143]

Many of Joshua's close friends at St. John's and at home in Maple

Lake were deeply affected by his disappearance. Katie Benson experienced a high degree of agony over her missing friend. She and some of Joshua's other friends sought refuge in assisting with the search effort as much as they could. They had searched for him all over campus in the days immediately after he went missing, and later helped with distributing flyers at area universities stretching from the Twin Cities to Fargo, North Dakota.

"Hell would be an accurate way to describe it," Katie said of her anxiety. "We're hoping he just took a week vacation and he'll be back."[144]

Twenty-five of Joshua's classmates and friends gathered at St. Maur House the weekend after his disappearance. They made 1,700 yellow ribbons to be distributed at Mass on Sunday, and 900 buttons that were sold to raise reward money for information leading to Joshua's whereabouts. Michael Hemmesch from the St. John's staff, and a few of Joshua's friends created a display at the student center for classmates to leave tributes or write comments. A group of friends established the website Findjoshua.org, where users could download and print flyers and information about Joshua's disappearance.

Adam Streater, one of Joshua's classmates, lamented that his "life has kind of just fallen behind" since Joshua's disappearance. Streater went to group counseling sessions offered by St. John's. There, he hoped to find some form of answer or clarity.

Streater would later put Joshua's impact on him into a very personal perspective. "People come in and out of our lives all the time," he said. "There are certain people who come through your life, and they're shining stars. They're going to make a difference in their community. He was a shining star. Everything else aside, we lost someone who would have touched many lives."[145]

Back in Maple Lake, volunteers made 400 buttons for Joshua to be sold at the *Maple Lake Messenger* newspaper. The paper donated the $2 buttons and they sold out in just one day. Kathy and Alfred Wurm donated the materials for another 500 buttons, and Rick and Sheila Benson, Katie's parents, put them together. That batch sold out quickly, and another 500 buttons were ordered. A spaghetti supper fundraiser at Madigan's drew large crowds of people. More than $5,000 was raised for the Find Joshua Fund. A pork chop feed at the VFW in Maple Lake had similar success.

A raffle fundraiser organized by Joshua's uncle, Paul Guimond, quickly sold 500 tickets. But after an article about the raffle appeared in a Minneapolis newspaper, the state Gambling Control Board intervened because the appropriate permits had not been acquired beforehand. The Board understood the predicament and pledged to work with Guimond to get the raffle established in compliance with state gambling law.

After nearly a week passed since Joshua Guimond's disappearance from the campus at St. John's University, Joshua's family began to show their growing frustration over their perceived lack of investigative effort to find him. Brian Guimond, Lisa Cheney, and other close relatives met with the families of missing students Chris Jenkins, Erika Dalquist, and Michael Noll at a news conference in St. Paul. The news conference was scheduled to draw continued attention to the missing students and to encourage the Department of Public Safety to form a statewide missing persons task force.

Brian Guimond reiterated his strong belief that the disappearances were related. He pointed out again that all four had been last seen near water or that their routes home would take them near water. Furthermore, all were intelligent young adults, ambitious, and similar in appearance.

"On the way here, frustration was building," Guimond said. "I was like, 'Don't even look at me the wrong way.' But I feel better now."[146]

Lisa Cheney expressed the frustration that resulted from what she described as a lack of communication from the SCSO. "We feel there's just not enough communication," she said. We're saying to them that they need to call us every day."[147]

Joshua's parents lobbied to get the Minnesota Bureau of Criminal Apprehension (BCA) actively involved in the search for their son, but Stearns County held the position that was there was no evidence that a crime had been committed and therefore no reason to call in the BCA. Still, Cheney mentioned the family was considering hiring a private investigator and were exploring all options to coerce the involvement of the BCA.

"We're trying to find other avenues to go over their heads to see if we can get the BCA in there," Cheney said.[148]

The Guimond family soon took matters into their own hands by arranging a search of St. John's campus, utilizing bloodhound handler Penny Bell from Milwaukee, Wisconsin. The parents of Chris Jenkins had hired Bell for an earlier search for their son, and then joined forces with Joshua's parents to search for both young men together. Bell and her dog, Hoover Von Vacuum, arrived at St. John's on Sunday December 29, 2002. Steve Jenkins, Chris's father, had already utilized Penny Bell's help for several weekends in the Twin Cities. Hoover was said to have tracked Chris Jenkins' scent to a Minneapolis intersection along

Interstate 94. Bell said that she and Hoover had worked with 28 Wisconsin counties through an organization called Keeping Track.

Bell demonstrated a strong commitment to help the Jenkins and Guimond families find their missing loved ones. She declined an offer of payment, and would only accept reimbursement for her expenses.

"We do not care how long it takes," said Bell. "We do not care how much it interrupts our personal and social lives. We only stop when Josh is found. We will only stop when Chris is found."[149]

The families decided to bring Bell and Hoover to St. John's to test their theory that the disappearance of Joshua and Jenkins were related, even though there was no reason to believe Jenkins had ever been to the Collegeville campus. Bell trained Hoover to Jenkins' scent on Sunday morning, and the dog tracked him to a door at the back of the Abbey. Abbey officials refused to allow the search party to enter the monastery. Bell publicly acknowledged that the tracking of Jenkins' scent did not determine to any degree of certainty that Jenkins had ever been at St. John's, only that his scent was there on campus.

Bell and Hoover searched for Joshua in the afternoon. They started their search at the Metten Court apartment building where Joshua had been partying with friends when he was last seen. From there, they covered his likely route back to his own apartment building, as well as other areas of the campus. Bell said she was confident that Hoover had tracked Joshua's scent to the road across the culvert by Stumpf Lake, near the main entrance to the campus.

St. John's officials did not have advance notice of the private bloodhound search, and requested that in future the families coordinate their efforts through the SCSO. Sheriff Kostreba contacted Brian Guimond on Monday, assuring him his office remained open to new

Penny Bell and Hoover outside the Metten Court apartment building at St. John's. Photo courtesy of St. Cloud Times, December 30, 2002.

information uncovered by the family, but advised that there was nothing to link Joshua's case to any of the other missing students.

"If they're able to find information or discover something that hasn't been known before, and it's a benefit to the investigation, certainly we support that," Kostreba said.[150]

Bell, Hoover, and the families returned to St. John's for a second search on Saturday, January 4, 2003. This time, they coordinated their efforts with Stearns County. A representative from the BCA also monitored the search effort. Hoover again showed no interest in Stumpf Lake, Joshua's dorm, or his car. According to Brian Guimond, Bell also ruled out the possibility that Joshua was taken away by car.

"Penny is pretty confident that Josh is on campus somewhere," said Guimond.[151]

The private search party was allowed access to the St. John's Abbey complex, an area they were not allowed to search on their first visit to campus. Hoover indicated Joshua and Chris Jenkins' scent there, and along an outdoor route that led down to Lake Sagatagan, behind the Abbey.

"Josh was physically in the back part of the Abbey," Guimond claimed. "And Chris's scent was there in two different places."[152]

Stearns County detective Dave Hoeschen observed Bell's work with Hoover, and afterward expressed no confidence in her work. He noted that Bell actually pulled Hoover in a direction she seemed to want the dog to go in, rather than allowing the dog to lead, which would be protocol.

Brian Guimond defended the work of Bell and Hoover, saying there were examples of handlers and bloodhounds performing similar work, citing the case of a missing woman in California.

"They can say anything they want," Guimond said. "The head of that investigation said the time frame isn't that critical with a bloodhound. The police here from day one didn't want to hear anything about the dog and they were saying it was no good the minute it was brought here. They were saying it can't be done and we're saying it can't with the dogs they have."[153]

To enhance Hoover's credibility, Penny Bell requested assistance from members of the Maple Lake Fire Department. Todd Borell, Tom Neu, and Bart Lauer spent 12 hours with Bell and Hoover at St. John's that first weekend of January. Borell complimented Bell's work and described Stearns detective Hoeschen as uncooperative during the search.

"I was very impressed with the dog handler and the dog," Borell said. "And I was very unimpressed with the Stearns County Sheriff's Department."[154]

As a result of that weekend's search, Stearns County investigators agreed to have divers search that lake the following week. "We did seem to move forward," Guimond said. "But when you're in my shoes it's never fast enough."[155]

According to multiple experts, there was a big problem with the late December and early January searches, and that was the length of time that had elapsed since Joshua's disappearance. Experts in bloodhound tracking said that the seven or eight weeks that passed since Joshua's disappearance was too long a time to expect accurate results from a bloodhound.

"The longest fresh trail on a human scent that I would attempt realistically is seven days with a hound," said Ellen Ponall, president of the North American Search Dog Network. "I would realistically not give the family or the police any hope."[156]

Jerry Nichols, president of the Law Enforcement Bloodhound Association, echoed Ponall's remarks. "I don't know any dog, any credible dog, that can do that," he said regarding the seven-week period that had elapsed since Josh disappeared. "The best chance is within the first 48 hours. After that chances diminish greatly because of time and because of the elements."[157]

Penny Bell dismissed her critics, expressing confidence that her dog had the ability to track scents over long periods of time. She told reporters she had done it over and over again, adding that Hoover once tracked a scent more than two years old. She claimed great success in tracking scents for police in Wisconsin, saying she had often received praise from officials. Although Hoover was not accredited by any sanctioning organization, Bell pointed out that bloodhounds are natural at what they do. She added that she had trained Hoover herself after attending several days of seminars, and by watching television programs such as *CSI: Crime Scene Investigation*.

Officials familiar with Bell's work disputed her claims. "The dog does not have a clue," said Milwaukee Fire Department chief John Zautke. "She wants to get her picture in the paper. The more she sees her name in the paper or on the news, the bolder she gets."[158]

Zautke added that Bell once claimed to find a body in a river near Milwaukee, but in reality Bell and her dog had nothing to do with the find. "Not even close," he said. "This dog stopped every ten feet along there and drank some water. We have some real good search teams here, and they didn't want anything to do with her."[159]

John Ludwig, the fire chief in Muskego, Wisconsin, shared his experience working with Bell and Hoover. He said that Hoover once came within ten feet of finding a drowned boy's body, but that was only about four hours after the incident. He said Hoover once failed to track the scents of a pair of missing runaway boys. Ludwig said that under the circumstances, if Hoover was a credibly trained dog, he should have been able to track them with relative ease.

A Stearns County dive team reported to St. John's campus on Wednesday January 8, 2003. Based on Hoover's scent tracking Joshua to Lake Sagatagan, his family anticipated the dive team would be checking that lake. However, they focused their search on Gemini Lake for about three hours instead. They concentrated their efforts on parts of the lake they had not been able to search previously due to ice conditions. They used sonar and underwater cameras, but once again they found no sign of anything related to Josh.

Stearns County divers search East Gemini Lake on January 8, 2003. Photo courtesy of Maple Lake Messenger, January 15, 2003.

Despite pleas from Guimond's family, newly elected Stearns County Sheriff John Sanner said there were no plans to do an extensive search of Lake Sagatagan, where Hoover had indicated Joshua's and Jenkins' scents coming from the back side of the Abbey. Sheriff Sanner reiterated skepticism about Bell and Hoover's work record.

"They definitely questioned her credibility, and so far the jury is out," Sanner said of the bloodhound team's critics. "If she can help us, great. But the dog isn't trained and certified."[160] Despite that, the dive team did search one part of Lake Sagatagan where Hoover had detected a scent through the ice.

Brian Guimond blasted Stearns County officials for their decision to not search Lake Sagatagan. "If they can dive in that other lake, why can't they dive here where Hoover at least had an interest?" Guimond asked.[161]

Bell and Hoover returned to St. John's for a third search for Joshua on Saturday, January 18. Hoover picked up from the edge of Lake Sagatagan where he had previously tracked Joshua's scent from the Abbey. Hoover's path led out onto the lake where he indicated interest in several locations. Search volunteers drilled holes through the ice in to give Hoover a better opportunity to pick up a scent from the water below. After the search group advanced to the middle of the lake, members of St. John's Life Safety staff asked the group to leave.

"First, they said we were interfering with the investigation," Brian Guimond said. "And then they said you couldn't have pets on campus."[162]

Michael Hemmesch, St. John's Director of Communications, affirmed that the search group was asked to leave. "It's true, pets aren't allowed on campus," he said. "But they were asked to leave because the search was not coordinated through Stearns County and any search they do would impede on that investigation."[163] Hemmesch's comments were in reference to a stipulation agreed upon between St. John's and Guimond's family, that all search efforts at the school be coordinated through Stearns County.

With assistance from Rev. Steven King, pastor at Holy Cross Lutheran Church in Maple Lake, Brian Guimond reached an agreement about future searches with St. John's Abbot John Clausen. Pursuant to that agreement, a fourth private search of the St. John's campus was done on Saturday, February 22. Penny Bell brought Hoover to the middle of Sagatagan Lake to resume the search from where they had left off five weeks earlier. A gas ice auger was used to open up a series of holes about three feet apart, and then an underwater camera was lowered into the lake to search the bottom. The camera was purchased using money raised by the Find Joshua Fund. It was later donated to the Maple Lake Fire Department. The views from the new camera were very clear. Objects on the lake's bottom showed up in excellent detail, but no evidence of Joshua was found.

A private diving team paid for by the Find Joshua Fund followed up the efforts by Bell and Hoover with an exploration of Lake Sagatagan on Saturday, March 1. The divers focused their efforts on the edge of the lake by the Abbey, and also near the center of the lake where Hoover had showed the most interest. Six feet of silt on the bottom limited divers' visibility, and again, nothing was found. Bell and Hoover were on hand for the search as well, and had planned to search a building and two small boathouses near the lake. A Stearns County deputy wouldn't allow it, however, and advised that a search warrant would be required to search the boathouses.

Brian Guimond claimed that Stearns County had been notified about the group's intent to search the boathouses. However, Stearns County Captain Pam Jensen said the County was aware of plans for diving, but had not been told about the intent to search the building and the boathouses.

"It was a question of timing," Jensen said. "We didn't realize buildings would be searched. On this particular day, the Sheriff's Department didn't deem it necessary to go into those buildings. They've already gone through those buildings before."[164]

The popular theory that the fall 2002 disappearances of Joshua Guimond, Chris Jenkins, Erika Dalquist, and Michael Noll were all related to a sinister plot against college students began to unravel by mid-January 2003. First, a man was arrested and charged with Dalquist's murder on January 15, despite the fact her body had yet to be found. She had been last seen leaving a Brainerd bar with William Myears. Myears eventually admitted that he killed Erika and dumped her body. The body of Chris Jenkins was found in the Mississippi River in Minneapolis at the end of February. Jenkins' death was later determined to be a local homicide. Then in March, a passerby spotted the body of Michael Noll in Half Moon Lake in Eau Claire, Wisconsin. He had apparently drowned after stumbling into the water or attempting to swim. With those three missing persons cases resolved, any connection between Joshua Guimond's disappearance and the other cases was no longer a realistic possibility. Furthermore, with Chris Jenkins' death determined to be focused on the Minneapolis area, Jenkins' scent being found by Hoover at St. John's further undermined the legitimacy of Penny Bell and her bloodhound. Bell had never claimed that Jenkins was ever in Collegeville, but it was implied that Jenkins and Guimond would have had to be together at some point for Jenkins' scent to be found on the campus.

As the spring of 2003 approached, and the promise of warmer weather that would come with it, the focus of the search for Josh returned to the lakes at St. John's. The ice was beginning to melt and the water temperatures began to rise. If Joshua Guimond was indeed at the bottom of a lake, his body would probably surface once water temperatures rose above 45 degrees. At that temperature, gases build up in a body, causing it to be more buoyant. A couple of conditions could possibly prevent a body from floating, however. First, if Joshua's body was trapped under a limb or some other structure, his body might never rise to the surface. Second, if Joshua's internal organs had been punctured, any gases created by the rising water temperatures would be released under water.

Penny Bell, Hoover, and firefighters from Maple Lake search for Joshua on Saturday January 18, 2003. Photos courtesy of Maple Lake Messenger, January 22, 2003.

A private dive team searches for Joshua on March 1, 2003. Photo courtesy of Maple Lake Messenger, March 5, 2003.

When Brainerd officials searched for Erika Dalquist's body, Brian Guimond noted they used an organization called the Trident Foundation. Trident was a non-profit organization based in Colorado comprised of highly trained and qualified search divers. As far as underwater search teams go, Trident was as good as there was, unparalleled in their field of expertise. Guimond asked SCSO to bring the Trident group in to search the lakes at St. John's. Bob Guimond, Joshua's grandfather, explained that it was worth a try to bring the Trident professionals to Collegeville.

"Our utmost focus in all of this is to find Josh and bring him home," said Guimond. "We are not implying that the sheriff's department is inept, just that they don't have the tools to complete this difficult mission."[165]

Sheriff Sanner refused to request assistance from the Trident Foundation, expressing his belief that Joshua somehow fell into one of the lakes, and if he did, he would soon come to the surface. Sanner said he had spoken to Trident representatives and based on those discussions, it was Trident's position that anything they did would only duplicate what SCSO had already done.

"The absolute bottom line is that everyone wants to find Josh," the sheriff said. "The most logical thing is that he somehow got into the water. Now we're waiting for Mother Nature to help. I don't want to get into a guessing game (as to when Joshua would surface). We are being very careful not to put the family on a roller-coaster ride of false hope."[166]

Sanner added that his department was fully committed to finding answers for the Guimond family. He pointed out that his investigators had accumulated two three-ring binders full of statements and information about the case. He said investigators and searchers had spent thousands of hours on it, and that they were willing to spend thousands more.

"We routinely check the shorelines and we have scheduled additional examination from the air in the future," Sanner said.[167]

Not one to take 'no' for an answer, Brian Guimond brought his request to the Stearns County Board of Commissioners in early April 2003. Sanner and the Board declined to take action. Guimond came back two weeks later, on April 15, and repeated his request to the Board. This time, he brought Joshua's grandfather, Bob, and Nick Hydukovich along with him. Together, they made a strong case to bring the Trident Foundation into the search for Joshua. Guimond proposed that the Trident group's costs be paid from the Find Joshua

Fund. Sheriff Sanner then updated the Board on steps that had been taken to find Joshua. SCSO had executed four dive searches in two of the three lakes on campus. They had searched every building on campus, searched the underground tunnels, and interviewed 60 people to date. He told the Board that Trident's advice was to wait a while longer for water temperatures in the lakes to rise, increasing the likelihood that if Joshua had drowned in one of the lakes, his body would surface eventually.

Guimond remained skeptical that his son was in the water, and continued to believe as he always had, that Joshua was a victim of foul play. He referred to the dozen or so monks at St. John's who had been placed under restriction by the Abbot due to sexual misconduct. "I'm thinking like I did from day one," Guimond said. "Someone grabbed him. I've said that from day one, and nothing's come yet (from the lake searches)."[168]

A pair of cadaver dogs from North Star Search and Rescue and Canine Search Services was brought to St. John's on Sunday April 27. The dogs, which are trained to alert to human remains, both reacted on Stumpf Lake. Windy conditions precluded the dogs and their handlers from identifying a specific area to focus on. Sheriff's investigators then dragged Stumpf Lake for six hours on Tuesday April 29 but found nothing.

At the end of April 2003, SCSO received a phone call from a witness who said they saw someone dressed in bright yellow clothing jogging toward the St. John's campus on County Road 159 on the night of Josh's disappearance. Life Safety subsequently sent an email to all St. John's and St. Benedict's students, asking anyone with information about the jogger to come forward.

SCSO deputies returned to campus again on Thursday May 8, to drag Stumpf Lake once more, and again came away without finding any sign of Joshua. Divers focused on three specific areas of 35' deep water where the cadaver dogs had indicated the greatest interest.

Brian Guimond's persistence in asking SCSO to bring in the Trident Foundation finally paid off in May 2003. A team of four Trident volunteers brought their advanced underwater search equipment to Collegeville for thorough searches on May 13 and 14. All three lakes on campus were searched–Stumpf, Sagatagan, and Gemini. The underwater team sidescan sonar devices and employed a series of multi-directional passes to insure complete, overlapping coverage of the lakes.

At the conclusion of the two-day search, the Trident Foundation felt the lakes were cleared in Joshua's case. "There were no targets identified that will require any additional search efforts on these lakes," said Scott Romme, Executive Director of the Trident Foundation. "There is never a guarantee that human remains could have been hidden or dumped in a body of water and are now hidden from sidescan sonar technology. However, based on the reports from the field, I would recommend that the search for Josh head in another direction."[169]

Romme's comments were the strongest statement to date supporting what Brian Guimond had been saying since the day Joshua disappeared. Sheriff Sanner agreed that the Trident Foundation's clearing of the lakes reduced the likelihood that Joshua had fallen into one of them. However, he indicated there was no evidence leading anywhere else.

"I don't know that we can draw conclusions right now because

Joshua Guimond is a missing person," Sanner said. "And no one can say with any certainty that a crime has been committed. I can also tell you that in the past 20 years, and that's the amount of time I've been with the Sheriff's office, only the Wetterling investigation has exceeded the resources that we've used to try to find Joshua."[170]

Sanner said that his office would review all the reports and interview notes to look for clues that might have been missed previously. "We felt comfortable in looking at other possibilities after the Trident search," he said. "But that's not to say that Josh didn't walk into a heavily swampy area and sink into the mud."[171]

With the lakes at St. John's apparently cleared by investigators, Brian Guimond turned his attention to putting pressure on Sheriff Sanner and Stearns County. He organized a protest in front of the Stearns County Courthouse on June 18, 2003, Josh's 21st birthday. About ten other protesters participated, carrying signs with various handwritten messages. Guimond said the purpose was to push for a special prosecutor and grand jury investigation into his son's disappearance. Guimond never bought into SCSO's theory that his son had fallen into a lake.

"There was a bunch of brush between the path and the lake," Guimond pointed out. "If someone would have stumbled or fallen, he would have landed in the brush, not the lake."

Sheriff Sanner acknowledged the protest, and said he understood the family's frustration, but that such activity was not necessary, and his department was continuing to look at the case on a daily basis. He indicated there had been a new development that his office, the BCA, and St. John's were working on together.

"There are some things we're looking at that I can't share with the

Protesters march in front of the Stearns County Courthouse on June 18, 2003. Photo courtesy of Maple Lake Messenger, June 25, 2003.

media at this time," Sanner said. "But there are some things that have come to our attention that deserve a closer look."[172] Nothing further was ever revealed about the nature of that development.

Sheriff Sanner apparently wasn't the only official that Brian Guimond was putting pressure on, because St. John's Abbot John Klassen became increasingly concerned about Guimond's presence on campus. In a June 6, 2003 memo to Fr. Brennan Maiers, Klassen cautioned Maiers to avoid speaking with Guimond or getting into an argument with him. He referenced the thorough search of the lakes by the Trident Foundation, writing to Maiers "this avenue of the investigation has been closed off." Klassen's memo went on to suggest that with the clearing of the campus lakes, Guimond had been "following

213

up on the theory that has been operating in the back of his imagination since last fall, that one of our monks is responsible for Joshua's disappearance."

Lisa Cheney wrote a letter to Joshua on his birthday. It was displayed at the Sexton Commons at St. John's. The letter read, in part:

> *I remember the day you came into the world. I was so nervous and afraid. You were my first and only baby. Remember how I would tease you about taking care of me when I got old? How you would have a big mansion, and I would live in the west wing. Well, I'm still counting on you to take care of me. I want you to know how much I love you and miss you every day. I will always have hope that we will find you and bring you home.*[173]

A number of events were organized at St. John's campus on the one-year anniversary of Joshua's disappearance. An all-night vigil was held on November 6. Several of Joshua's friends distributed ribbons at bus stops at both St. John's and the College of St. Benedict. More ribbons were handed out at the Johnnies football game on Saturday. A banner with the phrases 'Keep Hope Alive' and 'Find Joshua' was unveiled at the game. Back in Maple Lake, an oak tree was dedicated to Joshua at Holy Cross Lutheran Church, and poinsettias were sold to raise money the for Find Joshua Fund.

The anniversary spurred further comment from Joshua's parents about the lack of investigative effort to find their son. Lisa Cheney reiterated her belief that the investigation was being kept as a low priority because Joshua was an adult. She, like her ex-husband, believed that someone kidnapped Joshua.

"I think somebody up there took him. I don't know if it was somebody on that campus or what," Cheney said. "But somebody on that campus knows and they aren't telling."[174]

Brian Guimond chastised the investigation as well. "They haven't done nothin' from day one and they aren't about to start now," he said. "They're still saying he's in the water. They say the turtles ate him."[175]

A television program on the FX channel, *P.I.*, aired an episode about Joshua's disappearance in the fall of 2003. Chuck Loesch, a private investigator hired by Chris Jenkins' father, appeared on the show and shared his belief that Jenkins' and Guimond's disappearances were related, and further speculated their cases were the work of a serial killer.

Sheriff Sanner downplayed the theory as speculation, and said his department had looked at a number of possibilities in Joshua's disappearance. He said there were a number of things done by investigators, such as giving polygraph tests to select people, which have never been made public.

"As far as looking at the possibility of Joshua's disappearance being connected to something much larger, that's something we did early on," Sanner said. "Speculation is one thing, and actual proof is quite another. Whenever there is new speculation, we need to support that with fact."[176]

Sanner said his department continued to review information in the case even though very little new information had come in since a few months after Joshua's disappearance. "We looked back at the information that we had done and we just started to look at it from a different angle, to see if there was something we might have missed when we initially took the statements and looked at the results of those statements," Sanner said.[177] He added that he was not at liberty to discuss parameters of the new angle.

Brian Guimond continued to search for answers to his son's disappearance, making frequent visits to the campus at St. John's over the next several months. In March 2004, the Order of St. Benedict asked a Stearns County court for a two-year restraining order prohibiting Guimond from being on St. John's campus without a campus escort. In their filing they alleged that Brian Guimond was harassing and intimidating students, as well as threatening school security staff. The university has been "tolerant because of their compassion for the father of a missing son," the court filing read. "But immediate and present danger of ongoing harassment by Brian Guimond warrants a court order."[178]

A Stearns County judge granted a temporary restraining order against Guimond and scheduled a hearing for March 24, 2004. The order banned Guimond from being on campus without an escort and further prevented him from talking to anyone who hadn't previously expressed a desire to speak with Guimond. Guimond was prohibited from yelling, using profanities, and name-calling. He would not be allowed to photograph or record anyone without permission. He was also barred from emailing or calling people who had requested Guimond not contact them.

Affidavits in support of the restraining order written by St. John's Life Safety Director Shawn Vierzba, and Dean of Campus Life Jason Laker, detailed Brian Guimond's behavior. The affidavits suggested that Guimond had evolved from a concerned parent into an abusive, derogatory, and degrading figure on campus.

Guimond responded by requesting a delay of the March 24 hearing so he could consult with an attorney. He criticized the SCSO for not investigating the possibility that Joshua's disappearance was related to monks living at St. John's Abbey who were under restrictions due to evidence of sexual misconduct.

"Why don't they want me up there asking questions?" Guimond asked. "I never once laid a finger on anybody. If I was grabbing students and throwing them around, well then, I could understand."[179]

St. John's and Brian Guimond reached a settlement in early December 2004. The agreement came just hours before a Stearns County hearing on the matter was scheduled to convene, and resolved the objections the university had with Guimond's visits to the campus. Terms of the agreement were not disclosed.

In December 2005, Brian Guimond again brought his concerns about the investigation into his son's disappearance to the Stearns County Board of Commissioners. He brought a packet of notes and information he had collected, and reminded the Board that it took two requests from him to convince Sheriff Sanner to bring in the Trident Foundation. He told them about Sanner's subsequent theory that Joshua had sunk into a swampy area on campus, and refuted that with information from a Minnesota Soil and Conservation employee, who said there was so such type of natural soil around the St. John's campus area. Guimond cited delays in conducting a search for Joshua, interviewing students, and searching Joshua's computer for clues. Commissioners briefly discussed Guimond's presentation and concluded they would not take any action on the issue. They sent a letter to Guimond stating they would not tell the sheriff how to run his department.

In the years that have passed since Joshua Guimond's disappearance in November 2002, there has been a great deal of public speculation about what happened to him. Very soon after he went missing, differing opinions and beliefs were held by law enforcement and the Guimond family and their supporters. SCSO has long maintained the theory that Joshua fell into the one of the lakes on campus, specifically Stumpf Lake. As a practical matter, SCSO's position on the case is difficult to argue against because the combination of Joshua's age, the fact that he had been drinking alcohol, and that he was near water all fit a pattern which had explained the disappearance of many young adults. Add in the absence of evidence of another explanation, and it all leads to a somewhat logical conclusion that Joshua might have drowned in Stumpf Lake.

But even after the Trident Foundation reported that all three lakes on campus were cleared, and suggested that investigators look elsewhere for the young man, SCSO left little room for foul play. Sanner only acknowledged that the Trident report opened the door to other possibilities. It seemed the next greatest possibility in the eyes of SCSO was that Joshua walked into a swampy area and sunk out of sight. Their resistance to more aggressively pursuing a foul play angle rests primarily on one simple fact—that there was no evidence or apparent reason to suspect foul play. Joshua was well liked, had no enemies, had never been in any kind of serious legal trouble, and had not been associated with unsavory company. Contrary to the popular opinion held in some circles, it appears that SCSO did, in fact, consider and actively investigate the possibility that Joshua Guimond was a victim of foul play. Unfortunately, those efforts are documented in files that are not public, and that lack of tangible information has led to speculation of cover-ups or shoddy investigative work. Opinions on whether SCSO pursued the possibility of foul play in a timely manner vary, and largely depend on individual perspective.

The Guimond family, along with many of Joshua's friends and others who have followed the case closely, have always maintained that Joshua was a victim of foul play. They supported, encouraged, and even pleaded for searches of the lakes at St. John's. They did so, not so much in the hopes or belief those efforts would find Joshua Guimond, but that clearing the lakes would close the door on that possibility and open another door to investigate other possibilities, specifically foul play.

The lakes on campus, Stumpf Lake in particular, were searched multiple times over several months. Those efforts yielded no sign of Joshua Guimond. No body, no items of clothing, nothing. While it's not entirely impossible that a body would go undetected after the multiple, thorough searches of those waters, each fruitless search made it seem more and more unlikely that Guimond had drowned on campus. With drowning seeming to be a diminutive likelihood, several alternate theories of Joshua's disappearance developed.

Some have suggested that Joshua may have wondered off campus on his own free will, perhaps catching a late night shuttle bus to the College of St. Benedict to visit his female friends there. Those who knew Joshua say that possibility is highly unlikely, however, because Joshua was simply too responsible to have planned something like that without telling anyone. Joshua had left his wallet at home and was wearing only a hooded sweatshirt in near-freezing temperatures. Investigators monitored his bank and credit card accounts. None of them revealed any unusual activity before or after Joshua disappeared. It's reasonable to assume that when he left his apartment on the night of November 9, 2002, that Josh planned to return home after the party at Metten Court. He seemed to have had no intentions of leaving the campus that night.

That leaves the possibility of an accident or foul play, of which there are several theories. One theory is that the files deleted from Joshua's computer by someone had something to do with his disappearance—that someone might have had a motive to kill Joshua. Speculation in online forums have for years rumored that Joshua and some roommates were involved in the production and distribution of fake identification cards to underage students, enabling them to get into bars or purchase alcohol from liquor stores. Joshua's computer did yield evidence of fake ID's made for several friends including Alex Jude, Greg Worden, and Nathan Slinkard, as well as a man named Quincy Jones (might have been a practical joke). It's highly likely that SCSO learned about the fake ID's and investigated any possible connection to Joshua's disappearance.

Another theory is that Joshua was the victim of a random abduction. Although that theory could explain why investigators were unable to find evidence that a crime had been committed, the possibility falls short in terms of motive. Why would someone want to abduct a 20-year-old-male?

The most prevailing theory about what happened to Joshua Guimond has bubbled under the radar of most media reporting, but has been quite prevalent in online forums for many years. That theory is that someone at St. John's Abbey was responsible for Joshua's disappearance. The basis of the theory is that Joshua was upset at the university and its role in covering up decades of sexual abuse committed by monks living at the Abbey. Television and newspaper headlines were filled with stories of the abuse, the cover-up, and the settlements with victims. St. John's Abbey was home to 196 monks at the time, and was the largest community of Benedictine monks in the world. Reports were that at least 13 of those monks had been credibly accused of sexual infractions ranging from pornography to sexual misconduct, including abuse of students at St. John's.

In October 2002, just weeks before Joshua Guimond's disappearance, St. John's Abbey settled cases with as many as 15 victims who had filed lawsuits related to same-sex abuse at the hands of monks living at the Abbey in Collegeville. The settlement involved financial compensation to victims, apologies from those who victimized them, and therapy. Eleven of the monks involved were placed on restriction at the Abbey, meaning they could not say mass, could not preach, teach, or mix with students at the school. Furthermore, the monks on restriction could not use many of the school's amenities, including the swimming pool, athletic facilities, or cafeteria. Two other monks left the Abbey to contemplate their commitment to the Benedictine life. None were charged criminally.

There has been speculation that Joshua had been working on a research paper about pedophile priests on campus. Some have suggested that Joshua was particularly upset about the two monks who chose to leave St. John's and take a sabbatical in the Bahamas. The stories about the files being deleted from Joshua's computer took speculation about Joshua's research paper to another level. Was Joshua close to uncovering even deeper secrets held at the Abbey? The paper in question was, in fact, written for a Political Science course taught by Phil Kronebusch. The paper was actually focused on the subject of plea-bargaining. It was not at all about pedophile priests, or even about the settlement between St. John's and the victims.

Speculation of a connection between his disappearance and the Abbey grew once again after a student filed a complaint against Fr. Bruce Wollmering on February 19, 2003. The complaint alleged human rights violations, including accusations that the priest engaged in sexually explicit and inappropriate conversations and other communications with the complainant. Wollmering, 61, attended high school and college at St. John's beginning in the late 1950s, and had been affiliated with the university for all but three years of his adult life. He frequently taught a human sexuality course between 1979 and 2003.

Fearful that news about Wollmering's harassment charge would become public, St. John's Abbot John Klassen wrote an internal memo on February 17, 2006, expressing his concern that scrutiny of Wollmering would make it difficult for Klassen to lead the Abbey.

Wollmering died unexpectedly on February 4, 2009. Shawn Veirzba from St. John's Life Services called SCSO shortly after 6:00 p.m. to report that Wollmering was found dead from an apparent fall in a locker room on campus. When details of Wollmering's autopsy report were leaked, the seemingly unusual circumstances surrounding his death began to fuel speculation that Wollmering's death was somehow related to Joshua Guimond's disappearance. Wollmering was found in a pool of blood around his head. Ramsey County Medical Examiner David Fredrickson's autopsy report indicated that the cause of Wollmering's death was traumatic head injuries sustained from a pair of falls, falls that were not witnessed. In addition, Wollmering sustained multiple cuts on his head, and suffered a rib fracture and liver laceration from the falls. Investigation at the scene of Wollmering's death indicated blood in the hallway between a dining area and the locker room, as well as blood on a sink and mirror inside the locker room. Wollmering's body was found near the sink.

Although the autopsy report did not provide any indication of foul play, many have speculated that the details of Wollmering's accident seemed suspicious. Wollmering had been in good health with no known medical issues, and there seemed to be no apparent reason for him to have fallen first in the hallway, let alone again in the locker room. Stearns County did investigate Wollmering's death. In fact, investigators taped off his room and took possession of his computer for nearly two months. The computer was returned to the university by SCSO after receiving a written request by Abbot John Klassen.

There are several possible explanations for Joshua's sudden disappearance, but there was no physical evidence to make any one possibility more likely than another. Although it seems as though he simply disappeared into thin air, obviously that did not happen. In November 2004, Aubrey Immelman, an associate professor of Psychology at the College of St. Benedict, wrote an analysis explaining that Joshua was likely abducted. Immelman laid out a few simple points to explain that position:

1. The premier underwater search team in the country, the Trident Foundation, had cleared the waters of the St. John's campus in May 2003. Up until that point, SCSO's position had been that Joshua had fallen into one of those lakes.

2. There were no facts or other evidence that Joshua had walked into a swamp or sunk in the mud in an area around the lakes.

3. There was no evidence that Joshua left campus by his own free will. He left his apartment without his wallet, a coat, eyeglasses, or his car keys. His credit cards and bank accounts had no activity since his disappearance.

For more information and updates about the disappearance of Joshua Guimond from the campus of St. John's University, visit www.findjoshua.com.

Photo from the November 9, 2009 'Justice for Josh' march.

The November 2002 disappearance of Joshua Guimond from St. John's University in Collegeville remains unsolved. Anyone with information or ideas about Joshua's disappearance is asked to call the Stearns County Sheriff's Office at 320-259-3700.

Bibliography – A Lost Sheep

Andrus, T. (2003, May 21). As Trident Goes, TV Crew Comes to St. John's. *Maple Lake Messenger* , pp. 1, 3.

Andrus, T. (2003, January 22). Bloodhound Returns to St. John's. *Maple Lake Messenger* , pp. 1, 3.

Andrus, T. (2003, January 3). Controversy Brews Over Dog as Search Continues at St. John's. *Maple Lake Messenger* , pp. 1, 4.

Andrus, T. (2003, May 14). Divers Come Up Empty in Search for Joshua. *Maple Lake Messenger* , pp. 1, 3.

Andrus, T. (2003, March 5). Divers Explore St. John's Lake in Search for Joshua Guimond. *Maple Lake Messenger* , pp. 1, 2.

Andrus, T. (2003, January 15). Divers Search Lake at St. John's. *Maple Lake Messenger* , pp. 1, 10.

Andrus, T. (2002, December 4). Friends and Family Work to Raise Funds in Search for Joshua. *Maple Lake Messenger* , pp. 1, 2.

Andrus, T. (2003, April 9). Guimond Family Asks Stearns County for Help. *Maple Lake Messenger* , pp. 1, 3.

Andrus, T. (2002, December 18). Joshua is Remembered at Christmastime in Maple Lake. *Maple Lake Messenger* , pp. 1, 12.

Andrus, T. (2002, November 20). Missing Without a Trace. *Maple Lake Messenger* , pp. 1, 3.

Andrus, T. (2003, November 5). One Year Later, Joshua is Gone but Not Forgotten. *Maple Lake Messenger* , pp. 1, 11.

Andrus, T. (2003, June 25). Protestors Urge Action in Search for Joshua Guimond. *Maple Lake Messenger* , pp. 1, 2.

Andrus, T. (2003, June 18). Search for Joshua Camera Donated to Fire Department. *Maple Lake Messenger* , p. 1.

Andrus, T. (2003, January 29). Search for Joshua Continues on Lake at St. John's. *Maple Lake Messenger* , pp. 1, 2.

Andrus, T. (2004, March 24). St. John's Seeks Restraining Order Against Guimond. *Maple Lake Messenger* , p. 1.

Andrus, T. (2003, April). Stearns County to Step Up Search for Joshua. *Maple Lake Messenger* .

Andrus, T. (2002, November 27). Weekend Search Yields No Clues. *Maple Lake Messenger*, pp. 1, 8.

Andrus, T., & Stegeman, a. A. (2005, December 15). Joshua's Dad Brings Search Concerns to Stearns County. *Maple Lake Messenger*, p. 1.

Associated Press. (2003, March 27). Eau Claire Student's Body Found in Lake. *St. Cloud Times*, pp. 1B, 4B.

Associated Press. (2002, November 26). Police: Missing Brainerd Woman is Probably Dead. *St. Cloud Times*, p. 1A.

Associated Press. (2012, November 12). String of Missing College Students Stretches to 4. *St. Cloud Times*, p. 4A.

Associated Press. (2003, January 16). Suspect Charged in Brainerd Mystery - Divers Search Mine Pit Lake for Body, Answers to Case of Missing 21-Year-Old. *St. Cloud Times*, p. 1A.

Furst, R. (2003, January 3). Searcher's Credentials Questioned, *Minneapolis Star Tribune*, p. B1.

Halena, S. (2002, December 30). Families Enlist Dog to Scour St. John's - Bloodhound Tries to Trace Scents of Guimond, Jenkins. *St. Cloud Times*, pp. 1A, 5A.

Halena, S. (2002, December 31). Hound Leaves Search Incomplete - Private Investigator Looking for Clues About 2 Missing College-age adults. *St. Cloud Times*, p.9.

Kompas, K. (2002, December 20). Maple Lake Teens Hang Ribbons for Missing Alum. *St. Cloud Times*, p. 1B.

Maple Lake Messenger Staff. (2002, November 13). Maple Lake Man Missing at St. John's. *Maple Lake Messenger*, pp. 1, 3.

Meryhew, R. (2003, November 8). A Year in Fruitless Search of Josh Guimond - No Explanation has Emerged for the Disappearance of the 20-Year-Old St. John's University Student, Who Left a Casual Card Game at Midnight Without Saying Goodbye. *Minneapolis Star Tribune*, pp. B1, B9.

Nowak, K. (2003, November 6). One Year Later, the Mystery Continues. *The Record - St. John's University/College of St. Benedict*, pp. 1, 2.

Scott, K. (2002, November 21). Guimond Family Asks Nation for Information. *St. Cloud Times*, p. 9A.

Scott, K. (2002, December 7). Guimond's Raffle Tangled in Red Tape. *St. Cloud Times*, pp. 1B, 3B.

Scott, K. (2002, November 23). Itasca Helps in Search for Guimond. *St. Cloud Times*, p. 9A.

Scott, K. (2002, November 16). Rights Can Complicate Efforts to Solve Missing-person Cases. *St. Cloud Times*, pp. 1A, 4A.

Scott, K. (2002, November 14). Town Prays for Guimond's Return. *St. Cloud Times*, p. 1A.

St. Cloud Times Staff. (2006, November 18). Jenkins' Death Ruled a Homicide - More Information Expected Monday in 4-Year-Old Case of U of M Student. *St. Cloud Times*, p. 1A.

St. Cloud Times Staff. (2004, March 18). Temporary Order Bars Guimond. *St. Cloud Times*, p. 9A.

Tan, M. (2002, November 13). Alcohol, Parties Link Stories of Missing Students. *St. Cloud Times*, pp. 1A, 7A.

Tan, M. (2003, August 27). Classes, Exams, no Josh Guimond. *St. Cloud Times*, p. 6A.

Tan, M. (2002, November 28). Dad Urges Prayers for Josh During Thanksgiving Meals. *St. Cloud Times*, pp. 1A, 6A.

Tan, M. (2002, November 17). Fear, Vigilance, Hope - Concern for Missing St. John's Student Hangs Over Local Universities. *St. Cloud Times*, pp. 1A, 6A.

Tan, M. (2003, March 5). Jenkins Discovery Increases Pain in Guimond Case. *St. Cloud Times*, p. 9A.

Tan, M. (2002, November 18). Officials to Review Guimond's Friends - Authorities Won't Search Campus, Lake for Missing St. John's University Junior. *St. Cloud Times*, p. 9A.

Unze, D. (2002, November 12). Authorities Search for SJU Student. *St. Cloud Times*, pp. 1A, 4A.

Unze, D. (2003, January 9). Divers Find no Clues of St. John's Student. *St. Cloud Times*.

Unze, D. (2002, November 15). Families Share Frustration, News - Relatives of Missing Young Adults Plead for Help in St. Paul. *St. Cloud Times*, pp. 1A, 5A.

Unze, D. (2003, April 13). For Guimond's Dad, Search is Grim, Lonely - Water in SJU's Lakes Almost Warm Enough for Body to Float. *St. Cloud Times*, pp. 1A, 5A.

Unze, D. (2003, November 9). Guimond, Closure Missing Year Later - SJU Junior's Disappearance Frustrates Family, Investigator. *St. Cloud Times*, pp. 1B, 3B.

Unze, D. (2003, April 2). Guimond's Ask That Divers Join in Search. *St. Cloud Times*, pp. 1B, 3B.

Unze, D. (2003, April 16). Guimonds Have Cash to Bring in Dive Team. *St. Cloud Times*, p. 11A.

Unze, D. (2002, November 13). National Guard to Join Search. *St. Cloud Times*, pp. 1A, 7A.

Unze, D. (2002, November 2002). Searches Yield No Clues in Man's Disappearance. *St. Cloud Times*, pp. 1A, 4A.

Unze, D. (2004, Marcy 17). St. John's Wants Escorted Visits for Guimond's Dad. *St. Cloud Times*, p. 1A.

Unze, D. (2004, December 4). St. John's, Father of Missing Student Reach Agreement. *St. Cloud Times*, p. 1B.

Unze, D. (2003, April 30). Stump Lake Search Lake Turns Up Nothing. *St. Cloud Times*, p. 11A.

Chapter Eleven

Intersection

Victim: *Officer Tom Decker, Cold Spring*
Date: *November 29, 2012*
Status: *Solved, Eventually Closed*
Location: *Winners Bar Parking Lot, Cold Spring*

Ryan Larson was frustrated. The 34-year-old man had been working hard toward a degree as a machinist at St. Cloud Technical and Community College. He had several projects in mind for his classes, but found the equipment available at the college was not adequate to complete them. It had been a tough year overall for Larson. On top of his career woes, he had a difficult break-up up with a long-term girlfriend a few months earlier.

Larson spent most of Thursday, November 29, 2012, working on his homework at a bar in Sartell, where he worked part-time. Later, he drove over to a friend's house to hang out for a couple of hours before going home to his apartment above the Winner's Sports Bar & Grill in Cold Spring at 5:30 p.m. Ryan was employed at that bar, too, working as an occasional fill-in bartender. He sat alone in his apartment the rest of the evening, and contemplated his future. Then he made a decision. He would take his life in a new direction, change schools, and start over. Larson was tired after a long day, and just before 8:00 p.m., he decided to go to bed. But just before he did, he texted his family, giving them a hint of his future plans.

"Tomorrow's going to be a big day," were the words he keyed into his phone.[180] Then he hit 'Send', turned off his phone, and crawled into bed. The message to his mother was vague by any measure, but for Ryan they hinted at the decisions he made that night to better himself.

As tough a day as it had been for Larson, little did he know that his life was about to get a whole lot more difficult than it already seemed.

Ryan Larson's mother read her son's text. She knew that Ryan had been struggling lately, and she interpreted his text as a warning–an ominous sign that he might intend to harm himself. She called the Cold

Spring Police Department at about 9:00 p.m., expressing her concerns about her son. She said she was unsure if Ryan had any weapons in his apartment. She then gave her son's address to the dispatcher and requested that someone go check on him to make sure he was all right.

Part-time Cold Spring police officer Greg Reiter took the dispatch call, and along with another officer arrived at Ryan Larson's apartment at about 9:00 p.m. Officer Reiter knocked on his apartment door, but after a few minutes of waiting there was no answer. Unknown to the officer, Larson was already sound asleep by that time. Reiter then contacted Larson's family, who informed him that Ryan had been making increasingly suicidal statements as of late. Reiter left Larson's apartment and made himself a note to check in on Larson again later in the evening.

Downstairs from Ryan's apartment, an unusually large crowd for a Thursday night had gathered at Winners Bar. All the regulars were there, but so was large contingency of newcomers. All were there vying for the progressive bingo jackpot that had swelled to $750 after weeks of no one winning the top prize. As many as 80 customers packed into the bar that night, reveling in the festive atmosphere.

Ryan Larson slept right on through all the commotion downstairs.

At 10:35 p.m., Officer Reiter returned to the parking lot shared by Winners Bar and the bowling alley next door to the west. This time, the officer took note of Larson's car parked in front of the stairway leading to his apartment. Reiter parked his squad car and called Officer Tom Decker for backup. Decker's shift had just begun a short while before. Reiter sat in his police cruiser and waited for him to arrive.

Decker was the logical choice to check on Larson. He had a knack for connecting with people who were in crisis mode, or those who were suffering from mental illness and in a highly stressful situation. Around Christmas of 2011, Officer Decker came to the aid of a Cold Spring woman who was threatening to kill herself. Her arm was already bleeding from a self-inflicted knife wound when Decker came in contact with her inside her apartment. As Decker engaged in conversation in an attempt to control the situation, she made a sudden, threatening move toward him with the knife. At just the precise moment, as the woman hesitated, Decker made his move and was able to restrain the woman, wrestling the knife away from her. Officer Decker received a commendation from the Cold Spring Police Department for his actions in that incident.

Officer Decker pulled into the lot and parked his patrol car directly behind Larson's vehicle. He was wearing his protective flap jacket when he stepped out of his car. Then, instead of walking toward Larson's apartment, Decker walked about 20 yards to the southwest. He had apparently seen something in that direction that piqued his interest. As he approached the walkway along the bowling alley, an unknown man suddenly stepped out from the shadows. Bang! Bang! Two shots rang out as bullets were fired into Officer Decker's face at close range. The officer immediately fell to the pavement.

Inside his patrol car, Officer Reiter was startled by the sound of the gunshots. According to an affidavit later written by Stearns County investigators, Reiter told them that he saw a man about six feet tall and wearing jeans, a dark-colored hooded sweatshirt, and a stocking cap, standing near the front of Decker's patrol car. The man was in a shooting stance, pointing a handgun at Decker. The assailant then walked away to the west. Rather than get out of his patrol car to assist his partner or pursue the shooter, Reiter put his car into reverse, turned around, and drove out of the parking lot to the east.

After leaving the scene, Officer Reiter used his radio to call dispatch. "Shots fired. Officer Down," he said. "I have no idea where the suspect went."[181]

Meanwhile, the crowd inside the Winners Bar had drawn down to about 30 patrons after a lucky winner finally claimed the big jackpot. Despite the thinned out crowed, apparently no one in the bar heard the pair of gun blasts that echoed outside just moments earlier.

At about 10:45 p.m., a woman left Winners Bar to retrieve a cell phone from her car in the parking lot. She saw a loud black van speed out of the lot and head north on 2nd Avenue, then west on Main Street. She saw a man lying on the ground next to a bus and simply assumed he was a drunk who had passed out. The customer returned to the bar and told the female bartender what she had seen outside. The bartender went out to the parking lot to investigate, and saw a police officer on the ground shining a flashlight under a bus. Upon further inspection, she realized that the officer had a serious head wound. The bartender rushed back inside and called the police department. It was 10:49 p.m.

The female bar patron who witnessed the van fleeing the scene also called 911 to report what she had seen. After describing the van, the caller then turned the phone over to another witness who added that the van headed west on Main Street, away from the Sauk River. Although that 911 call would seem to have been a logical starting point for the investigation, a few weeks would pass before law enforcement would publicly release the information about the van.

At 10:52 p.m., other police officers and Stearns County Sheriff Office (SCSO) deputies began to arrive at the scene. Officer Tom Decker was dead. An unidentified officer called dispatch on the police radio. "It appears a gunshot wound to the head," he said.[182]

Winners Bar & Grill as seen from the parking lot south of the bar. The bowling alley is on the left. Ryan Larson's apartment was at the top of the stairs, above Winners Bar.

A small circle of customers inside the Winners Bar took note of the bartender's emergency call. They walked outside, curious to see what was going on. But most inside the Winners Bar were completely oblivious to the murder that happened just a few steps away.

At 10:55 P.M, an officer advised dispatch of the situation at Winners Bar. "We're going to see if there's anyone else inside the bar. There's a bunch of people standing outside the bar. I told them to leave at this point."[183]

Some bar patrons figured the bartender was simply joking around when she turned off the blaring jukebox and told everyone to leave because an officer had just been shot. But a few seconds later, someone

234

from the police department called back. This time, the bartender was instructed to have customers exit the bar slowly through the east side door. Their orders were to walk single-file with their hands in the air.

As customers began to file out of the bar, they passed through a line of police officers armed with assault rifles. The flashing lights of police cars and emergency vehicles were scattered for several blocks. Spotlights were shining in everyone's faces, making it difficult for them to see as they slowly marched away from the bar. Everyone was frisked by police, had their identification checked, and names documented. They were then ordered to move further east toward the Sauk River, away from their vehicles. The lot where most customers' cars were parked had been sealed off as a crime scene.

"Everybody filed out through the door and once you got outside it seemed like there were a hundred cops," said Roger Binsfield, one of the bar's customers that night. "Realistically there was probably 20 of them. They all had their guns drawn. Assault rifles, pistols. All pointed at us. Because they didn't know if the guy who shot the cop went inside, or where he was."[184] I was running with my hands up down the middle of the street, and they wanted me on the sidewalk. But I couldn't see because of the lights shining on me."[185]

At 11:09 p.m., there was discussion by officers over police radio referring to Ryan Larson. "He lives above the bar, suicidal before," said an unidentified officer.[186]

At about 12:15 a.m., the Strategic Emergency Response Team (SERT) forcefully entered Larson's apartment. SERT was a special weapons and tactical team shared by Stearns and Benton Counties. Its team members were trained to respond to high risk building entries and arrests. Officers were yelling out to one another as they cleared doorways and rooms. Awakened and startled by all the commotion outside his bedroom, Larson saw flashlights coming through cracks in his door and he sat up in his bed.

"For your safety and mine," Larson warned, while having no idea why the officers were in his apartment. "I have a loaded handgun at the top of my bed."[187]

When officers entered Larson's room they saw a Smith & Wesson .40 caliber handgun lying next to his head. Larson was allowed to put on a pair of jeans, but no socks or shoes, and was then handcuffed and taken to the SCSO for questioning. On the way to the station, Larson repeatedly asked officers what was going on. He always got the same answer, that he would find out at the station.

Investigators Pam Jensen from the SCSO and Ken McDonald of the Bureau of Criminal Apprehension (BCA) grilled Larson all night long, quizzing him for six hours about the shotgun they believed was used in Officer Decker's shooting. Larson acknowledged being a gun enthusiast, but told the investigators the only shotgun he ever owned was a 12-guage, but he had sold it previously.

Investigators gathered a number of items from Larson's apartment, including a semi-automatic rifle, a surveillance system, a computer, his schoolbooks and a pair of muzzleloader rifles that belonged to a friend. They found a dark-colored, hooded sweatshirt that matched the one described by Officer Reiter. No shotgun was found. Although the surveillance system was in working order and the system's camera was pointing toward the parking lot where Decker was shot, there was no videotape in the recorder, so the system was of no use in helping piece together what happened.

Early Friday morning, investigators began canvassing the entire neighborhood around the crime scene. Several blocks were cordoned off with police tape. Officers were looking for guns—specifically for the sawed off shotgun they suspected was involved in Decker's shooting. They confiscated a new-in-the-box, 20-guage shotgun from the St. Joseph home of the owner of Winners bar, Jeff Scoles.

Ryan Larson quickly became the focus of investigators and the media alike. Media reports detailed his prior criminal record, including a disorderly conduct charge that stemmed from an incident in 2009. Newspapers, television news reports, radio stations, and the Internet–they all painted the picture that Larson was Decker's killer. The Decker murder was the top news story in Stearns County and the Twin Cities. Newspaper and television news accounts frequently referenced Larson as the suspect in the killing, and described the incident as an officer being ambushed while performing a welfare check on a man thought to be suicidal.

On Saturday afternoon, Stearns County Attorney Janelle Kendall filed an application for judicial determination for probable cause. The document, written by Stearns County investigators, detailed events leading up to Decker's shooting. It was used to hold Ryan Larson in custody while Stearns County detectives continued to investigate Decker's murder. According to the statement, Officer Decker was outside of Ryan Larson's apartment when Reiter saw a white male about six foot tall step in front of Decker. The man was wearing a hooded sweatshirt, jeans, and a dark stocking cap. As the investigation would go on, however, details in the written statement would ultimately contradict the facts of the Officer Tom Decker shooting case.

Jeff Scoles, who was both Larson's employer and landlord, co-owned both of the Winner's Sports Bar & Grill establishments. He considered Larson to be a good friend, and quickly came to Ryan's defense after his arrest. He told the media that Larson was a "normal person," and "not a monster." Scoles said he spent several hours with Larson at the Winner's bar in Sartell on the day of the shooting, and he thought Larson had been in a good mood.

"He liked guns, but he's very cautious with them," Scoles said of Larson. "He's not the type of person who would go out there like a monster. I don't see him as a murderer. I hoping they find out he didn't do it."[188]

Tom Decker was 31 years old and had been working for the Cold Spring Police Department for six years at the time of his death. He left behind four young children from his first marriage. They ranged in age from five to eight years old. He also widowed a new wife, who he had just married in the fall of 2011.

> Officer Reiter returned to this address at approximately 10:35 p.m. when he noticed that the vehicle registered to Ryan Larson was parked in the parking lot outside of the apartment. The vehicle was parked directly in front of the stairs leading up to Ryan Larson's apartment.
>
> Officer Reiter contacted Cold Spring Officer Tom Decker for back up and waited for Officer Decker to arrive. Officer Reiter was still in his squad car when Officer Decker arrived just prior to 10:45 p.m. Officer Decker immediately exited his squad car and walked toward Ryan Larson's apartment. Officer Reiter, still seated in his squad car, then heard two loud "bangs."
>
> A few seconds later, Officer Reiter observed a white male, approx 6 feet tall wearing a dark colored hooded sweatshirt and jeans, with a dark colored stocking cap standing near the front of Officer Deckers squad car pointing a handgun in a shooting position at him. Officer Reiter then put his squad car in reverse, exiting the parking lot to the east.

Excerpt from the application for judicial judgment filed by Stearns County Attorney Janelle Kendall for the purpose of detaining Ryan Larson.

Decker grew up with seven siblings on his parents' 200-acre farm just south of Cold Spring. He graduated from ROCORI Senior High School in 2000, and then went on to Alexandria Technical College, earning his degree in Law Enforcement. Upon graduation he worked as a police officer in several small towns in central Minnesota, including Watkins, Isle, and Kimball. Even as a young child, Tom had always wanted to be a law enforcement officer. His desire to be a cop was rooted in an experience he had at the age of five, when he wandered away from his older sister while she shopped at the Crossroads Mall in St. Cloud. The police were called, and an officer was able to locate the youngster. The officer then treated Tom to an ice cream cone as they waited to reunite him with his sister. That experience made a lasting impression on young Tom Decker.

The shocking murder of Officer Tom Decker hit the community of Cold Spring hard. Nowhere in town was the tragedy more felt than within walls of the police department, where Decker had served along with six other full-time officers and nine part-time officers. Police Chief Phil Jones recalled hiring Decker. When Decker applied for a position in the department, Jones already knew the young man as a hard worker, having grown up on a family farm.

"My expectations weren't that high. But he was a local boy and we wanted to give him a shot," Chief Jones remembered. "I was hoping to get a very stable work horse, but that analogy was a total underestimation of his talents. Tommy really surprised me. He didn't know it, but he was close to being promoted to sergeant."[189]

Cold Spring Mayor Doug Schmitz said his city was in shock over Decker's senseless killing. He noted that Decker led firearms training for the city's police department, and that he had a way of making learning fun.

"He kept everybody loose," Schmitz said. "Took his job serious but was kidding around to keep the people feeling like they're just loose, they're not stressed out."[190]

The town of Cold Spring practically shut down for Tom Decker's funeral on Wednesday, December 5, 2012. Signs that read "Closed for Funeral" were posted on several businesses throughout the community. City Hall closed its doors for the day. A large banner made by children at the elementary school hung inside City Hall. It was filled with tiny colored imprints of children's hands, and had a message written across it that read, "We thank all of you for your service to our community."

More than 3,000 people attended Decker's funeral at St. John's Abbey in Collegeville, including 2,300 law enforcement officers from across the United States and Canada. Following an emotional service, the funeral procession led from St. John's through Cold Spring and Richmond, to St. Nicholas Catholic Cemetery in the Township of Luxemburg.

Meanwhile, Ryan Larson had been sitting in jail since his arrest late Thursday night. When investigators weren't questioning him, he was being checked on every 10 minutes or so due to the belief that he was suicidal. Citing insufficient evidence to hold him at the jail any longer, SCSO released Ryan Larson from custody on Tuesday morning, December 4. A Stearns County jailer drove him to the St. Cloud Hospital and dropped him off there, telling Larson it would be his choice whether to check himself into the hospital for mental health treatment. Larson requested that his computer and schoolbooks be returned to him, but investigators retained them as possible evidence.

By law, Larson would have been required to be released on Monday if no charges in the Decker murder had been filed against him by then, but District Attorney Janelle Kendall had requested an additional 24 hours to put together a case. Upon his release, Larson continued to deny his involvement in the shooting, reiterating that he had been asleep at the time of the murder and was only awakened by the sound of officers storming his apartment.

"They have no evidence whatsoever that points in my direction. They have no gun. They have no fingerprints. They have nothing," Larson declared.[191] "I just want to be cleared as a suspect. That's the first step I can take in an attempt to get my life back, but I'll never get my life back. I'll never be the person that I was because there's people out there that will always judge me as the person that got away with killing a cop."[192]

"Our agencies have reviewed the investigative data collected thus far and must act within the time allotted by law, within the constraints of the law, and based upon the facts known at this time," Kendall said.[193]

At that point in their investigation, Stearns County investigators had produced no motive for Decker's murder, no murder weapon, and no substantive evidence of any kind. Without any of those, they had no probable cause to charge anyone in the killing. When she was asked specifically if the lack of a murder weapon was the primary reason Larson had been released, Kendall acknowledged that was part of the reason but was not the only factor in the decision.

Soon after Decker's shooting, rumors began circulating in Cold Spring about the motive for the killing. Some theorized that the officer had stumbled across a drug deal, while others suspected his murder had something do with the July 2012 discovery of 16 pounds of cocaine in a pallet at Cold Spring Brewery.

Larson was familiar with Tom Decker before the shooting. He had spoken with him a few times when Decker was in the Winners Bar while off-duty and while Larson was working. He was the bartender for Decker's engagement party and wedding celebration. He said Decker was a "great guy," and recounted an incident at the Winners Bar one night when Larson was in the process of kicking out an unruly customer. He said he was escorting the man out of the bar when one of the customer's friends made a move to jump Larson from behind. Decker saw what was happening and intercepted the second man, probably preventing Larson from being beaten that night. Larson bought Decker and his wife a round of drinks as thanks for his assistance.

"Thanks, Tom. I got your back now." Larson recalled saying to Decker at the time.[194]

Multiple agencies investigating the Decker murder remained tight-lipped about the case, releasing very few details of the incident. It was evident that investigators still viewed Larson a suspect, despite his release. BCA spokeswoman Jill Oliveira told the media on Tuesday, December 4, that despite Larson's release, he did remain a suspect in Officer Tom Decker's murder.

The frustration that Larson had been feeling in the hours before Decker's murder was only amplified by the focus on him as a suspect. He was frank in dealing with the media, telling them how he had been held and questioned by investigators, and that they had no evidence. He was tested for gunshot residue on his hands and clothing almost immediately after his arrest. He pointed out the unrealistic scenario that investigators seemed to have aligned themselves with, that Larson had gone outside and shot Decker, then was able to get rid of the gun, clean himself up, and then return to his apartment without detection—all while police began to swarm the area around the bar and parking lot. And yet Larson remained the focus of the investigation in the public's eye, even after his release. He was afraid to return to his apartment or even go to the town of Cold Spring due to the fear he felt at how others perceived him in light of his arrest in the Decker murder.

"I did not kill Tom Decker," Larson said emphatically following his release from custody. "As I've stated before, and my story is not gonna change, I was in bed sleeping when I found that all this happened. I did not hear anything, nor did anyone in the bar downstairs. I don't know why I've been put in this limelight, but I was forced into it."[195]

On Sunday, December 16, Larson finally returned to his Cold Spring apartment to gather his schoolwork, some clothing, and a few other belongings. What he found when he opened the door disgusted him even further. All his property had been scattered about his apartment. There were piles of stuff everywhere, much of it in different rooms than where it had been kept originally. The sheets and blanket from his bed were in the kitchen. The carpet in his bedroom had been pulled up and put into another room. Larson was clear in criticizing how investigators had ransacked his apartment, calling it "absolute vandalism." He promptly left Cold Spring and returned to the home of some friends with whom he had been staying since his release.

"I came back for half an hour and broke down, and then I left" Larson said. "I was irritated. I was confused before, now I'm mad. To turn it upside down like this. This isn't an investigation.[196] To have my reputation gone and then come back here and open this door. I got nothing left that they can take from me."[197]

243

Two weeks passed with little new information revealed about the Decker case. Then state authorities announced during a Monday, December 17th press conference that a $100,000 reward had been established for information leading to the arrest of Tom Decker's murderer. They also asked for the public's assistance in locating the black van with a loud exhaust that a witness reported driving away from the scene immediately after the shooting. Billboards advertising the reward were put up around the St. Cloud area. BCA Assistant Superintendent Drew Evans reiterated that Ryan Larson remained a suspect in the shooting.

"We fully believe that someone knows information that will help us solve this case and bring Officer Decker's killer to justice," said BCA Superintendent Wade Setter, in announcing the reward money. "Any piece of information that they have, no matter how menial it may seem to them, is critical as we work through the many, many leads that we have amassed over the past three-and-a-half weeks."[198]

Public revelation about the black van raised eyebrows, because it seemed unusual that investigators had not revealed the information earlier. It seemed to be an important clue that should have been keyed on from the beginning. When asked about the reward money and the lead about the van, Ryan Larson expressed support for the appeal and acknowledged that investigators had questioned him early on about the van.

"If this was a suspicious vehicle, boy, we should have had the public information on that immediately," added Joe Tamburino, a criminal defense attorney from the Twin Cities. "This way, everybody's looking for that car immediately. With all the time that's gone by, that car's gone."[199]

Increased scrutiny would come from the media and experts alike after the written statement drafted by Stearns County investigators that described what Officer Reiter saw that night became public. In that statement, Reiter admitted to investigators that he fled the scene after he heard the shots that killed Officer Decker, and that the killer had a handgun and was wearing a dark-colored hooded sweatshirt. Critics had problems with the statement on two counts. First, Reiter's reaction was unusual for a trained peace officer. Second, the descriptive details of the shooter were remarkably consistent with what Ryan Larson told interrogators he was wearing, as well as what SERT officers said they saw when they entered Ryan's apartment. But the statement sharply contradicted with the type of weapon that investiagators had been looking for since very soon after the shooting—a shotgun.

Ryan Larson's lawyer, Joe Friedberg, was quick to pounce on Reiter's statement. He argued that Reiter's appropriate reaction would have been to pursue the suspect, and if circumstances allowed, shoot him. Friedberg was perplexed about the gun details, knowing that all along investigators were searching for a shotgun connected to the murder—not a handgun like Reiter reference in his sworn statement.

"This is contrary to everything we know about this case," Friedberg said of Reiter's statement. "It just doesn't make any sense."[200]

"His actions are very suspicious in my opinion, and his explanation isn't very plausible," said local private investigator Michael Grostyan, weighing in on Officer Reiter's response to the situation. Grostyan also noted the lack of information released by investigators, which he characterized as unusual in cases of murdered police officers. "The silence tells me a lot, that they're struggling, and maybe they don't know what happened. But I think it's been awfully quiet."[201]

Law enforcement officials defended the delay in publicizing details about the van, saying there was no evidence the vehicle was involved in the murder. Stearns County Attorney Janelle Kendall said the van was not discussed earlier because it was part of an active investigation.

An FBI dive team from New York searched the Sauk River in Cold Spring on Monday, December 17. They used robotic equipment in an effort to find the shotgun that Decker's killer had used. Investigators speculated that if the suspect had fled east of the crime scene, that he might have tossed the weapon into the river one-tenth of a mile west of Winner's Bar. Investigators had previously searched the river in the days immediately following Decker's shooting.

The lack of progress in solving Officer Decker's murder was unusual because it was rare for the shooting of a police officer to go unsolved for more than a few days. A total of 38 peace officers had been killed by gunfire in the state of Minnesota from 1970 to 2012. Of all those cases, only the fatal shooting of St. Paul Police Officer James Sackett in 1970 went unsolved for more than four days. Although investigators in the Sackett killing knew the identity of the killer since early on, it took more than 35 years to develop the evidence needed to officially solve that case.

In most incidents involving the shooting of a police officer, there is a very large response and the area around the shooting is quickly secured. There are two reasons for this. First, most shootings of police officers occur during a response to some other active situation, and multiple law enforcement personnel are already at the scene or in route. Second, the shooting of a fellow officer in the line of duty tends to bring a rapid and massive response because the incident involves "one of their own" as a victim. According to media sources that reviewed dispatch recordings, the task of securing the area around the Decker crime scene took nearly 30 minutes.

At the time of Decker's shooting, the most recent murder of a police officer in Stearns County occurred in 1996, when St. Joseph Police Officer Brian Klinefelter was shot while attempting to arrest three individuals who were suspects in a liquor store robbery. The suspects were killed or caught within hours because multiple law enforcement officers had already been engaged in pursuing the robbery suspects prior to Klinefelter's murder.

While the mystery of who killed Cold Spring Police Officer Tom Decker went very cold during the month of December, the case heated up in dramatic fashion in January 2013. The reward offered in December and the publicity about the black van seen leaving the murder scene prompted a tipster to call in to suggest that 31-year-old rural Cold Spring resident Eric Thomes might have been involved in the murder.

Thomes had lost his job as a machinist at a local manufacturing company just before Decker's shooting. A warrant had been issued for his arrest following his failure to appear in court for a drunk driving citation. Investigators subsequently questioned Thomes on multiple occasions, beginning around Christmas time. They noted several inconsistencies in Thomes statements to them, particularly with regard to varying and untruthful accounts of his whereabouts at the time of Decker's shooting.

Thomes was said to have been drinking heavily on the night of the murder, going from bar to bar in Cold Spring. It was believed that Thomes had a 20-guage shotgun and was waiting in his van in the Winners Bar parking lot to confront his former boss. Thomes' boss was known to regularly visit Winners to take advantage of the bar's two-for-one drink special after bingo. Investigators alleged that as Officer Decker approached the van, that Thomes shot him twice with a shotgun.

BCA agents went to Eric Thomes' home at 2:00 p.m. on Wednesday, January 2 to interview him once again. As agents approached the house, Thomes fled to a metal outbuilding on the property. He remained holed up there for several hours while investigators tried to coax him to surrender. When his girlfriend arrived home from work late in the afternoon, agents asked her to try communicating with Thomes by megaphone. She tried, but there was no response. Agents finally stormed the shed, and after gaining entry at 7:00 p.m., discovered that Thomes had committed suicide by hanging himself.

Very soon after Thomes' suicide, investigators recovered his dark green van, and then a 20-guage shotgun at a neighbor's property—property they say Thomes had access to. Forensic testing determined that the shotgun was the weapon that had been used to shoot Tom Decker. Thomes had borrowed the gun from his neighbor for the recent deer-hunting season. Even though Thomes' suicide implied his guilt in the murder, BCA superintendent Wade Setter maintained that the man was merely a person of interest, and not necessarily a suspect in the case.

"That would be premature for us to even reach a conclusion that he is the presumptive suspect," Setter said. "Again, we're trying to figure out what his role is. We are a long ways from concluding it. We have many questions that remain unanswered. We can't stress enough the value that information people may have, even though it may seem insignificant to people in the community. We need to find out where he's been, who he's been talking to."[202]

Booking photo of Eric Thomes

Setter added that Ryan Larson still had not been excluded as a suspect in the Decker case.

Larson knew Thomes as a regular at Winners Bar, and was surprised when the man was named a person of interest in the murder. "There's a little sense of relief," Larson said, in acknowledging the news of Thomes' involvement. "But if you Google my name and Cold Spring, you get a million hits and my mug shot is on like the first 35 pages of the search results."[203]

Along with Sheriff Sanner, Setter appealed to the public once again, this time asking anyone with information about Thomes' activities since late November to come forward. Thomes' record indicated multiple convictions for driving while intoxicated, but he did not have a history of violent criminal behavior. Court records revealed that Decker was one of two officers who arrested Thomes for driving while intoxicated in 2011. Thomes had actually been picked up on a probation violation two weeks after Decker's shooting.

Thomes and his girlfriend had lived together for two-and-a-half years at the time of his suicide. She said he was a good father to his two children. They were his pride and joy, and he was always there for them. "To my boys, stay strong," was a message left for his sons in Thomes' suicide note. She said Thomes showed no signs of unusual behavior after Decker's shooting until after he was questioned for the first time by investigators. After that, he fell into a downward spiral, telling her he refused to go to prison for a crime he did not commit.

The next several months offered little in the way of news updates about Thomes' probable role in Officer Decker's shooting. Finally, in August 2013, the BCA and Stearns County acknowledged that Eric Thomes would have been arrested for Decker's murder had he not killed himself in January. Furthermore, BCA spokesperson Jill Oliveira finally acknowledged that Ryan Larson was no longer considered a suspect in the case.

"Although sufficient probable cause existed to arrest Ryan Michael Larson, continued investigation did not reveal sufficient evidence to charge Mr. Larson," Oliveira said. "At this time, the investigation has provided no information that Mr. Larson participated in Officer Decker's murder."[204]

Although the Decker investigation was no longer considered active, officials left the case open because there remained many unanswered questions. At the top of that list of questions was motive–why did Eric Thomes shoot Officer Decker? But there were other open questions as well, and officials appealed once again for the public's help in trying to answer them.

"The two big ones are: 'Did the shooter act alone, and what was the motive?" Sheriff Sanner explained. "Because we can't answer those definitively, we're going to leave the case open, at least for a period of time."[205]

In a September 2013 interview with the *St. Cloud Times*, Sheriff Sanner refused to disclose whether or not investigators believed another person was involved in Decker's death. He declined an opportunity to apologize to Ryan Larson, or to clear his name.

In letters written to Stearns County Attorney Janelle Kendall, The BCA recommended the case be closed, but for reasons that are unclear Kendall insisted the case remain open. In the spring of 2018, however, a review of the Decker case by Chief Deputy Jon Lentz led to his recommendation that the case be closed. Sheriff Don Gudmundson agreed, and the case was closed. Most of Larson's belongings have been returned to him, but despite several requests and even legal action, Stearns County has yet to return his firearms.

The November 29, 2012 shooting death of Cold Spring Police Officer Tom Decker remains an open case. If you have information concerning the possible involvement of other individuals who may be connected to the shooting, please contact the Stearns County Sheriff's Department at 320-259-3700.

Bibliography - Intersection

Baran, M. (2013, December 20). Analysis: Decker Case is a Rarity. *St. Cloud Times*, p. 1B.

Baran, M. (2012, December 7). *Dispatch Recording Reveals Some Detail of Police Response on Night of Decker's Shooting*. Retrieved from MPR.com.

Baran, M. (2012, December 17). *FBI Searching Sauk River in Cold Spring Case*. Retrieved from MPR.com.

Baran, M. (2012, December 20). *Unlike Decker Case, Most Officer Killings Solved Quickly*. Retrieved from MPR.com.

Brewer, J. (2012, December 6). An Officer Mourned. *St. Paul Pioneer Press*, p. A1.

Brewer, J. (2012, December 1). Death in a Dark Alley. *St. Paul Pioneer Press*.

Brown, C. L. (2012, December 6). A Week Later, Mystery Centers on Unnamed Parter, Missing Gun. *Minneapolis Star Tribune*, p. 1A.

Brown, C. (2012, December 1). 'We Lost a Brother Today,' Chief Says of His Fallen Officer. *Minneapolis Star Tribune*, pp. 1A, 4A.

Brown, C., & Oakes, L. (2012, December 7). Details of Slaying Emerge. *Minneapolis Star Tribune*, p. 1B.

Brown, C., & Smith, M. L. (2012, December 5). Suspect Freed in Cop Shooting. *Minneapolis Star Tribune*.

Dickrell, S. (2012, December 18). Larson Returns To Cold Spring Apartment. *St. Cloud Times*, pp. 1A, 6A.

Forliti, A. (2012, December 12). Report: Slain Minnesota Officer's Partner Backed Away. *Winona Daily News*.

Lindberg, J. (2012, December 5). Suspect in Cold Spring Cop Killing Released on Insufficient Evidence. *St. Paul Pioneer Press*, p. A1.

Minneapolis Star Tribune Staff. (2013, December 6). A Week Later, Mystery Centers on Unnamed Partner, Missing Gun. *Minneapolis Star Tribune*.

MRP Staff. (2013, August 7). *BCA: Dead Man Would've Been Arrested in Cop's Death*. Retrieved from MPR.com.

Nelson, T. (2012, November 30). *Police Call Cold Spring Officer's Shooting An Ambush*. Retrieved from MPR.com.

Oakes, L., & Brown, a. C. (2012, December 1). Suicide Call Sent Cop Into Ambush. *Minneapolis Star Tribune*, pp. A1, A4.

Shenoy, R. (2013, January 4). *'Person of Interest' in Cold Spring Officer's Killing is Found Dead*. Retrieved from MPR.com.

Simons, A. (2012, December 16). 'I Did Not Kill Tom Decker' - Ryan Larson, Angry After Five Days in Jail WIthout Charges, Hasn't Gone Back to Cold Spring. "Why Am I Being Accused?". *Minneapolis Star Tribune* , p. 1B.

Sommerhauser, M., & Dickrell, a. S. (2013, August 7). Officials Update Decker Case - Investigators Would Have Arrested Thomes had he not Killed Himself; Motive, Other Details Remain Unkown. *St. Cloud Times* , pp. 1A-2A.

St. Paul Pioneer Press Staff. (2012, December 19). 911 Transcripts in Officer's Slaying Released. *St. Paul Pioneer Press* , p. A3.

Unze, D. (2012, December 16). Document Provides Shooting Details. *St. Cloud Times* , pp. 1A, 4A.

Unze, D. (2012, December 8). Patron on Scene Also in the Dark - Decker Shooting Questions Linger. *St. Cloud Times* , pp. 1A, 4A.

Unze, D. (2013, September 8). Questions Linger - Almost 1 Year Later, Officer Decker's Shooting Death Still Open Case. *St. Cloud Times* , pp. 1A, 4A.

Unze, D. (2012, December 18). Reward Boosts Hunt for Clues in Decker Murder. *St. Cloud Times* , pp. 1A, 6A.

Unze, D. (2013, January 5). The Fatal Shooting of Police Officer Decker - 'Person of Interest' Dies - Officials Say Man Hanged Himself; Many Questions Remain. *St. Cloud Times* , pp. 1A, 5A.

Westphal, J., & Joseph Lindberg, a. M. (2013, January 5). Agents Say 'Person of Interest' Killed Himself Before They Could Question Him. *St. Paul Pioneer Press* , p. A1.

Wilson, C. (2013, July 12). 8 Months Later, Still no Closure on Decker Case. *St. Cloud TImes* , p. 2B.

Wilson, C., & Baran, a. M. (2012, December 12). *Cold Spring Police Chief Supports Investigation of Officer's Death*. Retrieved from MPR.com.

Wilson, C., & Baran, M. (2012, December 21). *Initial Response May Have Hurt Chances of Capturing Cold Spring Cop Killer*. Retrieved from MPR.com.

Works Cited

[1] (Torkelson, Week's Hunt, 'Inch-by-Inch,' for Paynesville Boy Fails - Whole Area Assists, Draws Only Blank, 1944)
[2] (Paynesville Press Editorial, 1944)
[3] (St. Cloud Daily Times Staff, 1944)
[4] (Torkelson, School Opening Recalls Lad's Disappearance, 1945)
[5] (Torkelson, School Opening Recalls Lad's Disappearance, 1945)
[6] (St. Cloud Daily Times Staff, 1957)
[7] (Dalman, 2011)
[8] (Anderson, Slain Girls' Final Hours Retraced, 1977)
[9] (St. Cloud Daily Times Staff, 9/30/74, 1974)
[10] (Anderson, Slain Girls' Final Hours Retraced, 1977)
[11] (St. Cloud Daily Times Staff, 10/01/74, 1974)
[12] (Peters, Dave, 1975)
[13] (Peters, Dave, 1975)
[14] (Peters, Dave, 1975)
[15] (Lewis, 1976)
[16] (Lewis, 1976)
[17] (St. Cloud Daily Times Staff, 10/08/76, 1976)
[18] (Pearson M., Sheriff Takes Control of Reker Killings Probe, 1977)
[19] (Anderson, Search Reopened For Sisters' Killer, 1977)
[20] (Anderson, Doubts Delayed Probe Of Slayings - Murder Clues Erased By Time, 1977)
[21] (Anderson, Discord Held Back Murder Probe, 1977)
[22] (Pearson M., Reker Slayings Unsolved But Not Forgotten, 1977)
[23] (St. Cloud Daily Times Staff 12/20/1977, 1977)
[24] (St. Cloud Daily Times, 2/13/79, 1979)
[25] (Daley, County Hasn't Written Off Reker Murders, 1979)
[26] (Daley, County Hasn't Written Off Reker Murders, 1979)
[27] (Haukebo, Investigators Hope Girls' Killer Will Slip Up, 1989)
[28] (Welsh, 1994)
[29] (Louwagie, 2002)
[30] (Unze, Rekers Hope For Clues In Killings, 2004)
[31] (Unze, Rekers Hope For Clues In Killings, 2004)
[32] (Unze, Rekers Hope For Clues In Killings, 2004)

33 (Kupchella, Seeking A Killer - A Cold Case Gets New Life Part 1, 2005)
34 (Petrie, Investigators, Rekers Maintain Fight For Answers, 2005)
35 (Petrie, Investigators, Rekers Maintain Fight For Answers, 2005)
36 (Unze, Sheriff: Beilke Isn't A Suspect, 2005)
37 (Petrie, Rekers' Clothes Provide No Clues, 2006)
38 (Petrie, Rekers' Clothes Provide No Clues, 2006)
39 (Kupchella, Seeking A Killer - A Cold Case Gets New Life Part 2, 2005)
40 (DeBaun, 2016)
41 (DeBaun, 2016)
42 (Baillon, 2016)
43 (Baillon, 2016)
44 (St. Cloud Daily Times Staff, 1976)
45 (St. Paul Pioneer Press Staff, 1976)
46 (Wilkins, Fears Still Linger in Kimball One Year After Fatal Bombing, 1977)
47 (Wilkins, Fears Still Linger in Kimball One Year After Fatal Bombing, 1977)
48 (Wangstad, Blast-Shocked Town Now Calm, 1976)
49 (Pearson M. , Expert Joins Hunt for Mail Blast Clue, 1976)
50 (St. Paul Dispatch Staff, 1976)
51 (Furst, 1976)
52 (Monn, Battery Sale Clues Sought, 1976)
53 (Monn, Battery Sale Clues Sought, 1976)
54 (Monn, 'Love Triangle' Blamed for Most Mail Bombings, 1976)
55 (St. Cloud Daily Times Staff, 1977)
56 (Wilkins, Fears Still Linger in Kimball One Year After Fatal Bombing, 1977)
57 (Pearson M. , Kimball Bombing Remains Unsolved, 1976)
58 (Wangstad, 20 Years Later, Kimball Parcel Blast Still Unsolved - Post Office Bomb That Killed One Destroyed a Vital Clue, 1996)
59 (Wangstad, 20 Years Later, Kimball Parcel Blast Still Unsolved - Post Office Bomb That Killed One Destroyed a Vital Clue, 1996)
60 (Wangstad, 20 Years Later, Kimball Parcel Blast Still Unsolved - Post Office Bomb That Killed One Destroyed a Vital Clue, 1996)
61 (Wangstad, 20 Years Later, Kimball Parcel Blast Still Unsolved - Post Office Bomb That Killed One Destroyed a Vital Clue, 1996)
62 (Kunkel, 2016)
63 (Haukebo, Evidence, Survivor Tell Horrific Story, 1988)
64 (Haukebo, Evidence, Survivor Tell Horrific Story, 1988)
65 (Haukebo, Evidence, Survivor Tell Horrific Story, 1988)
66 (Unze, Officer Briefly Suspected Deputy in Huling Killings, 1998)
67 (Daley, Billy Holding Key to Puzzle, 1978)
68 (Daley, Billy Holding Key to Puzzle, 1978)

69 (Daley, Mrs. Huling First Beaten, 1979)
70 (Daley, Motive for Huling Case Puzzling, 1979)
71 (Daley, New Sheriff Grafft to Take Reins on Murder Probe, 1979)
72 (Daley, Fear Haunts Neighbors Week after Huling Family Murders, 1978)
73 (Daley, Strong Clues Lacking in Huling Case, 1979)
74 (Daley, Lab Strike Crimps Huling Probe, 1979)
75 (Daley, Huling Probe Turns to Michigan Inmate, 1979)
76 (Daley, One Suspect Emerges in Year-long Huling Murders, 1979)
77 (Daley, One Suspect Emerges in Year-long Huling Murders, 1979)
78 (Daley, Two Years Later, Huling Murder Probe Drags On, 1980)
79 (Werder, Police Checking Ture Links, 1982)
80 (Werder, Police Checking Ture Links, 1982)
81 (Tri-County News Staff Report, 1994)
82 (CBS News, 2000)
83 (Unze, Toy Car Queries Angered Ture, 1998)
84 (Minnesota, 2001)
85 (Unze, Ture Sentence Please Huling Family, Doesn't Diminish Anger, 2000)
86 (St. Cloud Daily Times Staff, 1979)
87 (Darlin, 1979)
88 (Ruff, 1980)
89 (Werder, Ture Denials Won't Cancel Huling, Biersbach Probes, 1982)
90 (Werder, Divers Probe Quarry for Body of Woman Missing Since 1979, 1982)
91 (Minneapolis Star Tribune Staff, 1984)
92 (Adams, Inmate Testimony is Key to Tying Man to Several Unsolved Killings, 1998)
93 (Adams, Inmate Testimony is Key to Tying Man to Several Unsolved Killings, 1998)
94 (Unze, Investigator: Witness Saw Ture, Slaying Victim, 1998)
95 (Adams, Inmate Testimony is Key to Tying Man to Several Unsolved Killings, 1998)
96 (Unze, Attorney: Grand Jury Decision Will Come Soon in Huling Case, 1999)
97 (Unze, Ture Won't be Indicted for 1979 Killing - For Now, 2000)
98 (Unze, Ture Won't be Indicted for 1979 Killing - For Now, 2000)
99 (Werder, Murder - Authorities Awaiting Autopsy, 1981)
100 (Werder, Murder - Victim a Worrier, Say Friends, 1981)
101 (Coleman, 1981)
102 (Coleman, 1981)
103 (Werder, Report Reveals Little About Cole's Death, 2918)
104 (Werder, Report Reveals Little About Cole's Death, 2918)
105 (Werder, FBI Compiles Personality Profile of Cole Killer, 1981)
106 (Werder, FBI Compiles Personality Profile of Cole Killer, 1981)
107 (Brenden & Werder, 1981)

[108] (Werder, Sheriff Calls on Public to Help with Cole Killing, 1982)
[109] (Werder, Hand Print, Knife Clues to Unsolved Murder, 1982)
[110] (Werder, Hand Print, Knife Clues to Unsolved Murder, 1982)
[111] (Werder, Hand Print, Knife Clues to Unsolved Murder, 1982)
[112] (Kennedy, One Year Later, Cole Murder Still Unsolved, 1982)
[113] (Kennedy, Slaying Suspect No Killer, Says Friend, 1983)
[114] (Norton, 1986)
[115] (Welsh, Fromelt Family Still Trying to Make Sense of Father's Murder, 1994)
[116] (Welsh, Fromelt Family Still Trying to Make Sense of Father's Murder, 1994)
[117] (Welsh, Local Man Stabbed to Death in Home - 20 Police Investigators Probe Slaying of 81-Year-Old in Home, 1994)
[118] (Welsh, Local Man Stabbed to Death in Home - 20 Police Investigators Probe Slaying of 81-Year-Old in Home, 1994)
[119] (Welsh, Local Man Stabbed to Death in Home - 20 Police Investigators Probe Slaying of 81-Year-Old in Home, 1994)
[120] (Welsh, Local Man Stabbed to Death in Home - 20 Police Investigators Probe Slaying of 81-Year-Old in Home, 1994)
[121] (Welsh, Local Man Stabbed to Death in Home - 20 Police Investigators Probe Slaying of 81-Year-Old in Home, 1994)
[122] (Welsh, Authorities Want to Keep 20 Officers Probing Slaying, 1994)
[123] (Welsh, Fromelt Family Still Trying to Make Sense of Father's Murder, 1994)
[124] (Welsh, St. Cloud's Only Unsolved Murder Haunts Family, Puzzles Police, 1995)
[125] (Welsh, St. Cloud's Only Unsolved Murder Haunts Family, Puzzles Police, 1995)
[126] (Welsh, St. Cloud's Only Unsolved Murder Haunts Family, Puzzles Police, 1995)
[127] (Welsh, St. Cloud's Only Unsolved Murder Haunts Family, Puzzles Police, 1995)
[128] (Aeikens, Tips Trickle in After Reward Offer, 1997)
[129] (Scott, 2004)
[130] (Scott, 2004)
[131] (Scott, 2004)
[132] (Andrus, Missing Without a Trace, 2002)
[133] (Unze, Authorities Search for SJU Student, 2002)
[134] (Unze, Authorities Search for SJU Student, 2002)
[135] (Maple Lake Messenger Staff, 2002)
[136] (Unze, National Guard to Join Search, 2002)
[137] (Unze, Searches Yield No Clues in Man's Disappearance, 2002)
[138] (Andrus, Friends and Family Work to Raise Funds in Search for Joshua, 2002)
[139] (Unze, National Guard to Join Search, 2002)
[140] (Scott, Rights Can Complicate Efforts to Solve Missing-person Cases, 2002)

[141] (Andrus, Friends and Family Work to Raise Funds in Search for Joshua, 2002)
[142] (Scott, Town Prays for Guimond's Return, 2002)
[143] (Scott, Town Prays for Guimond's Return, 2002)
[144] (Tan, Fear, Vigilance, Hope - Concern for Missing St. John's Student Hangs Over Local Universities, 2002)
[145] (Unze, For Guimond's Dad, Search is Grim, Lonely - Water in SJU's Lakes Almost Warm Enough for Body to Float, 2003)
[146] (Unze, Families Share Frustration, News - Relatives of Missing Young Adults Plead for Help in St. Paul, 2002)
[147] (Unze, Families Share Frustration, News - Relatives of Missing Young Adults Plead for Help in St. Paul, 2002)
[148] (Andrus, Weekend Search Yields No Clues, 2002)
[149] (Halena, Hound Leaves Search Incomplete - Priviate Investigator Looking for Clues About 2 Missing College-age Adults, 2002)
[150] (Halena, Hound Leaves Search Incomplete - Priviate Investigator Looking for Clues About 2 Missing College-age Adults, 2002)
[151] (Andrus, Controversy Brews Over Dog as Search Continues at St. John's, 2003)
[152] (Andrus, Controversy Brews Over Dog as Search Continues at St. John's, 2003)
[153] (Andrus, Controversy Brews Over Dog as Search Continues at St. John's, 2003)
[154] (Andrus, Controversy Brews Over Dog as Search Continues at St. John's, 2003)
[155] (Andrus, Controversy Brews Over Dog as Search Continues at St. John's, 2003)
[156] (Furst, 2003)
[157] (Furst, 2003)
[158] (Furst, 2003)
[159] (Furst, 2003)
[160] (Unze, Divers Find no Clues of St. John's Student, 2003)
[161] (Andrus, Divers Search Lake at St. John's, 2003)
[162] (Andrus, Divers Search Lake at St. John's, 2003)
[163] (Andrus, Bloodhound Returns to St. John's, 2003)
[164] (Andrus, Divers Explore St. John's Lake in Search for Joshua Guimond, 2003)
[165] (Unze, Guimond's Ask That Divers Join in Search, 2003)
[166] (Unze, Guimond's Ask That Divers Join in Search, 2003)
[167] (Unze, Guimond's Ask That Divers Join in Search, 2003)
[168] (Unze, For Guimond's Dad, Search is Grim, Lonely - Water in SJU's Lakes Almost Warm Enough for Body to Float, 2003)
[169] (Andrus, As Trident Goes, TV Crew Comes to St. John's, 2003)
[170] (Andrus, As Trident Goes, TV Crew Comes to St. John's, 2003)
[171] (Andrus, As Trident Goes, TV Crew Comes to St. John's, 2003)
[172] (Andrus, Protestors Urge Action in Search for Joshua Guimond, 2003)
[173] (Tan, Classes, Exams, no Josh Guimond, 2003)
[174] (Meryhew, 2003)
[175] (Andrus, One Year Later, Joshua is Gone but Not Forgotten, 2003)

[176] (Andrus, One Year Later, Joshua is Gone but Not Forgotten, 2003)
[177] (Nowak, 2003)
[178] (Unze, St. John's Wants Escorted Visits for Guimond's Dad, 2004)
[179] (Andrus, St. John's Seeks Restraining Order Against Guimond, 2004)
[180] (Simons, 2012)
[181] (Baran, Dispatch Recording Reveals Some Detail of Police Response on Night of Decker's Shooting, 2012)
[182] (Baran, Dispatch Recording Reveals Some Detail of Police Response on Night of Decker's Shooting, 2012)
[183] (Baran, Dispatch Recording Reveals Some Detail of Police Response on Night of Decker's Shooting, 2012)
[184] (Baran, Dispatch Recording Reveals Some Detail of Police Response on Night of Decker's Shooting, 2012)
[185] (Unze, Patron on Scene Also in the Dark - Decker Shooting Questions Linger, 2012)
[186] (Baran, Dispatch Recording Reveals Some Detail of Police Response on Night of Decker's Shooting, 2012)
[187] (Simons, 2012)
[188] (Oakes & Brown, 2012)
[189] (Brown C. , 'We Lost a Brother Today,' Chief Says of His Fallen Officer, 2012)
[190] (Nelson, 2012)
[191] (Lindberg, 2012)
[192] (Simons, 2012)
[193] (Lindberg, 2012)
[194] (Simons, 2012)
[195] (Simons, 2012)
[196] (Dickrell, 2012)
[197] (Dickrell, 2012)
[198] (Unze, Reward Boosts Hunt for Clues in Decker Murder, 2012)
[199] (Simons, 2012)
[200] (Unze, Document Provides Shooting Details, 2012)
[201] (Baran, Unlike Decker Case, Most Officer Killings Solved Quickly, 2012)
[202] (Shenoy, 2013)
[203] (Unze, The Fatal Shooting of Police Officer Decker - 'Person of Interest' Dies - Officials Say Man Hanged Himself; Many Questions Remain, 2013)
[204] (MRP Staff, 2013)
[205] (Sommerhauser & Dickrell, 2013)

CPSIA information can be obtained
at www.ICGtesting.com
Printed in the USA
LVHW082039260123
738009LV00009B/842